Major Truths On the End of Our World & the World to Come

Dr. Keith Sherlin
PhD; ThD; PhD
President of Christicommunity

Foreword
Dr. Paige Patterson

Christicommunity®

1

Copyright, Publisher, Permissions & Cover Design

Dedications

To some of our earliest leaders in Christicommunity: Dr. Dan Kitinoja; Rev. Luke Morrison; Brandon Garcia; G. Prasad Rao; Joseph Agba; Michael Anania; Maston Davite; Luvanga Reuben Omusula; & Hannah Peterman. I am so thankful for your wisdom, love, and passion for the Great Commission around the world. I pray God gives to Christicommunity many more leaders over the years with hearts and minds as you all have. I am blessed by you.

To some of the men at my local church and the Christicommunity ordination class: Matt Padula; Dan McFerrin; Justin Horton; Dakota Hester; John Robert Gimler, Craig Moore; Doug Hester; Robert Farmer; & Dustin Drake. I pray the seeds sown with you are still being used by you. I still use 1.317.443.1212 in my own ministry and pray that you will continue to build from it. I praise the Lord for you men and that I am on this journey to heaven with you as we do the work of the Lord locally and beyond. You men have shown resilience, resolve, and righteousness through your studies and service to the people in a vicissitude of ways. I pray more like you arise to carry the flaming torch of faith.

To some of our local pastors and prayer warriors for mission Christicommunity: Caleb Bruce; Mark Bishop; Kenny McDowell; & Jeff Valentine. You men are a blessing to this region. I praise the Lord for your devotion to Scripture, passion for serving people, and your friendship. Kenny I hope this book helps you as you seek to counter the full preterism movement that you see developing. You are a blessing to me and our region with your courage and convictions in Christ. Caleb I am so thankful for you, your family, friendship and ministry. Mark your easy-going personality, friendship, and love for people and doctrine is a great model for aspiring ministers and a blessing to this community. I praise the Lord for you. Jeff I will always be grateful for our years together at the Sheriff's Office and how you blessed us younger officers there. You were then and remain now a great role model for us all who love and follow Christ. I praise the Lord for your ministry and friendship.

To Dr. Sheila Breitweiser for your dedication to service for those with special needs and your mentorship to me early in my professional career. The great news about the resurrection, which this book covers, is that the children and families you and I served at SCSDB and other places in your career will through Christ experience new bodies in the resurrection. Your love and dedication to those with special needs this side of heaven remains a testimony of grace from heaven for all who reflect upon your legacy. Furthermore, thank you for taking the time to give me books to read to help me in my own professional growth through the years. I still miss those late afternoon conversations in the President's Office about various matters we collectively faced at SCSDB. I learned much from you.

To Jennifer Lauer for your many years of service to our state and for your time at SCSDB with me. You placed a lot of trust in me to lead the way with me becoming a Public Safety Director at such a young age. I am thankful for your leadership and as the years passed for the friendship we have in the Lord. You are a treasure and blessing to your family and all of us who know you. I will forever cherish the great times we had serving together at SCSDB (even the challenges we collectively handled). So many of my blessings in my career and ministry began because of your leadership for which I am grateful.

To Scott Ramsey for the many years your supervision. We survived some unique moments there together, especially 2008. And on a few occasions your grace, kindness, and wisdom helped me remain in my role during some challenging moments, such as 2012. I appreciate also the reasonable handling of several issues that from time-to-time surfaced. And during my dad's decline of health and departure for glory you made sure I had all the time I needed to care of him. You blessed me greatly in those ways. I am thankful for the 14 or so years we served together and for how good you were to me and our team overall.

Lastly, to mom, as I see your final season of life approaching due to age and physical struggles. I look forward to you receiving your heavenly body and the rejuvenation you will soon experience in heaven as you, dad, and many other family members rejoice there until the final resurrection. Though life on earth for awhile with both parents in heaven will be very different, the joy I have knowing you and dad will walk, laugh, worship, and live in heaven together will remain an inspiration until I too join you all there. As far as I have memory, being with Christ in eternity has always been the ultimate goal taught to me by you and dad. From my earliest of memories you and dad taught me to know the reality of heaven and hell that this book discusses. Such a foundational truth cannot be underestimated. I praise the Lord you and dad made sure that understanding existed in our family. I'll pass it on to others until we join together again in eternity.

8

Endorsements

Dr. Keith Sherlin's Major Truths on the End of Our World & the World to Come is a deeply engaging and academically solid exploration of the major eschatological questions Christians have pondered for centuries: What happens when the world ends? What awaits us after death? And how should we understand the prophetic texts of Scripture?

Sherlin—holding multiple doctorates and decades of experience as a teacher and leader—writes with a passion and personal depth rarely seen in theological works. The book opens with an honest testimony of the author's own journey from doubt and confusion to firm conviction—a journey shaped by mentorship, theological inquiry, and a deep commitment to Scripture.

What stands out most is the book's combination of scholarly weight and pastoral warmth. Sherlin shows how a consistent historical-grammatical approach to the Bible not only yields theological clarity but also provides genuine hope and comfort. This is particularly evident in his insistence that eschatology is meant not to incite fear, but to offer encouragement and joyful anticipation.

The structure is well-designed and accessible. The book presents seven major "truths" about the end of the world and the world to come—including the soul's conscious state after death, Christ's physical return, the millennial reign, and the new heaven and earth. It also addresses important philosophical foundations, practical questions about heaven, and timely theological debates (e.g., preterism and premillennialism).

Though Sherlin's eschatological position is clearly premillennial and dispensational, he demonstrates admirable respect for other orthodox perspectives. His polemic is directed not against fellow Christians with different views, but against what he sees as theological errors that undermine biblical authority.

Conclusion: Major Truths on the End of Our World & the World to Come is well-argued, spiritually enriching, and intellectually stimulating. It speaks to committed students of theology, curious lay readers, and ministry leaders who want to teach faithfully about the end times. Sherlin's confidence in the authority and clarity of Scripture is contagious—and his careful method offers a compelling model for how to think about biblical prophecy today. Highly recommended.

Pastor Jan Áki Andreasen
Give Baptistkirke, Denmark
Christicommunity Minister

In a generation that is engrossed by instant gratification in the "here and now," this book prompts the reader to lift their eyes to what is coming in our very real future. Dr. Sherlin treats prophetic questions with biblical accuracy and thoughtful research, nailing each question squarely on the head. This book is a genuine gift to those who worship the God who inhabits eternity.

Hannah Peterman
Apologist & Christicommunity Minister

Dr. Keith Sherlin's book explores biblical prophecy and end-times theology to provide clarity and encouragement for believers. In doing this, he describes his journey in forming convictions about prophecy and navigating theological debates. The book emphasizes a historical-grammatical approach to scripture, critiquing allegorical and multi-meaning interpretations of Scripture. Keith's main focus throughout the book is for the interpreter of Scripture to believe what Scripture says and not add to it or take away from it. He addresses many topics, such as the millennium, life after death, and Christ's return, while pointing out several heretical movements to avoid. The final chapters tackle questions about heaven and the believer's eternal hope, aiming to inspire faith, edification, and cultural engagement. Keith utilizes insights from respected theologians and focuses on scriptural authority. This book is a resource for those seeking a biblically grounded understanding of the future, proper hermeneutics, and hope for "the blessed hope and glorious appearing of our great God and Savior Jesus Christ" (Titus 2:13).

Pastor Luke Morrison
Western Trail Cowboy Church in Vernon, Texas
International Christicommunity Leader

Dr. Keith Sherlin has written one of the most vital works on Eschatology, the study of End Times, in the 21st Century, and I highly recommend every Christian, both clergy and laity alike, to both buy and read this pithy tome. Dr. Sherlin teaches that Jesus Christ, the Jewish Messiah, God-man, Lord, Savior, Prophet, Priest, and King, will come back again a second time literally, physically, and really in both the flesh/body and soul/spirit. Maranatha (1 Thessalonians 4:13-18; 1 Corinthians 15:1-58).

Kyle Rushnell
B.A. & MTS @ Southwestern Baptist Seminary
B.A. in Christian & Great Commission
Studies @ Truett McConnell University

Have you ever wondered if you will remember people you knew when you get to heaven? Or maybe you have wondered what happens to your soul the moment that we die, or about the events and timing of the end of the world as we know it? If you have ever thought about things like these you

13

are thinking about what in theology is known as eschatology, the doctrine of last things. The doctrine of the last things is an area of study that is both theological and pastoral, academic and practical. Yet for so many it remains confusing and perhaps scary. Dr. Sherlin approaches this topic from a personal, practical, and academic point of view. He encourages Christians to take the study of eschatology seriously because it is a part of the hope we have in Christ. Indeed, as Dr. Sherlin says, "Eschatology, like all doctrine, is designed to promote faith, hope, and love in us." The Last Things is written to build your faith, hope, and love, and I encourage you to read it.

Dr. Dan Kitinoja
Pastor, Calvary Baptist Church
Tilton, Illinois
International Christicommunity Leader

Dr. Keith Sherlin's Bible prophecy book entitled "Major Truths On the End of Our World & the World to Come" clearly lays out why taking a grammatical-historical hermeneutic approach to understanding the entire Bible, including books of Prophecy, is the most consistent approach to interpreting the text. With that basis, he defines seven major truths about the end of our world that GOD and the apostles have made known to us. Because of these truths, we, as believers, can be assured of our great hope in salvation and be assured we will live with Christ eternally. Dr. Sherlin presents this in a clear, easy to follow approach that many readers should find as refreshing as I did. I recommend his book to any Christian that is trying to determine their viewpoint on prophecy and the end-times.

Karry Elson
Assistant Professor
Anderson University

Foreword by Dr. Paige Patterson

When was the last time you listened with rapt attention to a Sunday exposition on the book of Zechariah or on the last eight chapters of Ezekiel or of Daniel or the Apocalypse? You are an unusual evangelical if your pastor has attempted to float his boat in those waters! The sorrow of this dilemma is that the majority of our congregants have a plethora of queries they want to ask biblical exegetes to explain! And they would welcome the opportunity just to be informed of the possibilities by an interpreter who had done his homework. But few pastors consider eschatology to be a biblical doctrine that merits the effort. Busy pastors seldom provide time and effort for such careful endeavor.

That is precisely why thousands will welcome Dr. Keith Sherlin's courageous embarkation into these waters entitled appropriately, *Major Truths on the End of Our World & the World to Come*. Sherlin answers seven frequently posed questions with the comprehension of a learned theologian, the insight of a prophet, and the skill of a preacher. Should you differ with his conclusions, you will expand your grasp of the biblical perspective on the end-times. You will delight in the fresh hope discovered from the pages of Holy Scripture.

After providing a survey of eschatological considerations and a philosophical introduction, Sherlin devotes himself to biblical responses to seven prevalent questions about which the average church member is more than just passingly interested. For example, at the moment of physical death is their immediate consciousness in heaven or hell? Or will Christ physically return to the Earth? Or will Christ rescue His Bride before the time of His wrath?

As an adroit hermeneutician, Sherlin teaches his readers the various possibilities that have been advocated by interpreters. He proceeds to explain the salient texts in such a lucid way that possible misunderstandings are rendered unlikely. The book concludes with three appendices addressing contemporary mistakes often made.

In the study of eschatology, Sherlin's own perspective would be called premillennialism, which is a confidence that the return of Christ ushers in the promised reign of the Savior for one thousand years at the end of the age. That is preceded by the appearance of Christ to take His church out of the world before the awesome judgment events described in chapters six through nineteen of the book of Revelation. What makes Sherlin's approach so unique is that his own views are ardently held and powerfully presented in a kind and gracious way, which leaves harshness of judgment to others.

If you are a follower of Christ sensing that we may be living in the beginning of the final era and if you harbor a hunger for eschatological truth, this is the book you want. Read and rejoice in what God has planned for you. Learn herein how to digest the whole of Scripture in the light of Christ's consummation of all things. Read and graduate from pessimism to prophetic confidence in the mighty hand of God.

Paige Patterson, President
Sandy Creek Foundation
Dallas, Texas

Chapter 1.
End Times: An Enigma or Enlightenment for our Encouragement?

Introduction: My Journey to Proper Prophecy Convictions

Confused and concerned, puzzled but persistent, and somewhat zealous, there I stood in my local Christian bookstore examining massive shelves of books that all pertained to the doctrine of Christ's return. On this divine, providentially gracious, and certainly preordained day (see Psalm 139:16), my life, which had been remarkably prepared by the many years of guidance of many others, intersected with the writings of a man known as Pastor Mal Couch. On that divine day my journey towards a healthy eschatological position took a giant leap, a leap that carried me for fifteen years with a precious and beloved overseer-pastor, scholar, and friend in the body of Christ.

The sacred seeds from my parents on the truthfulness of Scripture, the many teachings from my childhood Sunday School teachers and/or Vacation Bible leaders (Olvie Campbell, Betty and Wanda Littlefield, Marie Fuentes, and Mary Pace), and my youth Pastors and Pastors of my teenage years (Jeff King and Joe White, and Elaine Roark who sparked in a new level of Christlike dedication in my teen years) were finally sprouting and consequently those convictions led me to profoundly respect and admire those who took the word of God seriously. Through my teen years I like most children had those in the entertainment field that I admired and expressed as much about through anecdotal accolades. As I matured over time the solemn seeds of the Savior led me to savor and settle upon as my ultimate heroes of the faith those who sacrificed their lives, time, and energy in learning and obeying Scripture and the Savior.

As it seemed to me then, and ever more so now, the men and women of God who made the most beneficent and commendable impact upon time and history have always been those who truly from their inner souls cherished and adored the Word of God. The words of Scripture come to my mind: "The fear of the LORD is the beginning of knowledge; fools despise wisdom and instruction" (Prov. 1:7 ESV).

On that day in the bookstore, as a second year theology student, I found it troubling that I could not harmonize the truths about the end times. Having been in various local church assemblies from the time of my birth, I could not recall hardly any extended teaching and training in this area from the pastors I sat under. If they did teach much on it I may not have been paying good attention.

Of course, sadly, in my particular context at that time in the Southern Baptist denomination we sometimes did not receive much in depth discipleship in biblical doctrine as a whole. Many of us received bits and pieces in topical sermons, but beyond that many in the denomination at that time suffered from our good, godly, and gifted ministers receiving weak doctrinal training in the seminaries they attended. Many professors in that era prior to the conservative resurgence did not have high doctrinal standards. That in and of itself was disturbing as I could see God had devoted large segments of Scripture to this topic in both the OC as well as the NC. Yet doctrinal conversations and teaching on prophecy were not common.

The biblical foundation I had received was from a devoted youth pastor early on in my life. My questions to Elaine must have been from some curiosity or fear I had because her responses to my questions about what would happen to us in the future comforted me. She helped me tremendously not to worry about the future. She taught me enough to know that our LORD would for sure return because he promised he would (an epistemological base), that his return would be in the future (a paradigm for

18

futurism that protected me from the heresy of full preterism), and that the doctrine was to help us have hope and courage (a missiological base).

Pastors I had sat under, great men like Reverend Robert Johnson, Reverend Harold Thompson, and then Reverend Joe White all affirmed the essentials of Christian orthodoxy on the future return of Christ. Though they may all have had some differences in timelines and minor particulars related to the rapture or the millennium, all stood firm on the major truths that Christ Jesus would return to rule and reign over his universe.

Additionally, Elaine's guidance gave me enough to know I could trust God with my future. She gave me the broad essentials as well as the motive behind the biblical instructions which were to help us not worry about the future as we labored for God today. Though I am not sure she would have exactly said it in this way then, what she communicated to me reminded me of the need to major on the majors (that he would return for us in the future to judge the world) and not to get so caught up in the minor timeline details that it caused me to worry.

Yet it seems that even she, albeit with an Albert Einstein like I.Q., suffered from the same dilemma most of us within the Southern Baptist culture did within those years. By and large we were untaught in these areas and left to ourselves in navigating the turbulent eschatological waters. Sadly, in the era in which we matured in the SBC circles, doctrine was not a strong point to life in the SBC. Many areas of doctrine, including eschatology, were taught with little substance and sometimes not even taught at all. Shallowness in doctrine reigned in SBC life during those years largely because the seminaries at that time were not very strong. What many of us learned we had to learn through our own personal study or from doctrinal works outside of the SBC mainstream.

Diverse Views Among the College Faculty & Student Body

Additionally, within my university of choice, I realized that the students as well as theology faculty had a variety of theories as to how and when Christ would return. It revealed in me that I too lacked clear convictions in my own faith in this area. Even some of the foundations I had received from my childhood pastors were challenged (not a bad situation for an educational context), even though later confirmed.

Swirling around the North Greenville University campus where I studied theology for the first time in an in depth way were the following ideas: (1) that we would certainly suffer the wrath of God in the times of a future tribulation mentioned in Revelation 6-19 (post-tribulation premillennialism); (2) there was no future millennium to come and that we were right now in the Kingdom of God (amillennialism); (3) that Christ had already returned in and through the coming of the Holy Spirit and/or through his judgments on the nation of Israel in AD 70 (full preterism; no professor who taught there affirmed this heresy); and (4) that we would be spared from the awful time of God's wrath to come (a type of dispensational premillennialism).

My hermeneutics professor Dr. Charlie Draper seems to have stood alone among the faculty in that he affirmed God still had a plan for ethnic Israel, which was not the same as the body of Christ, and that the body of Christ would be removed prior to the great judgments of God at the end of time. Others were either some form of historic premillennialism or some form of amillennialism. Some were hybrids of various models. Usually these teachers embraced the idea that the body of Christ and Israel were now the same with the promises to Israel finding some type of fulfillment that negated the land promises to Israel.

However, Dr. Draper's hermeneutic class made very clear the need for a consistent hermeneutic. His class made a huge impact on my life in how to apply the same scientific rules of interpretation to the whole Bible. His stances on God's promises to ethnic Israel were ideas born from the hermeneutic he used. His hermeneutics class had a major impact on my growth in learning how to read and apply the Bible to life.[1]

Furthermore, then (5), because there was a strong dose of Calvinism among the faculty, some students had ventured back to the bright-eyed, optimist, and Colonial faith of men like Dr. Jonathan Edwards where they espoused a post-millennial view of Christ's return. I do not recall any professor affirming this view, but it did emerge among the student body. This post-millennial group was for sure an attractive breed of brothers as they championed the power of the cross and God's sovereignty to convert the world to his truths in order to usher in the Kingdom of Christ.

Examining my First Prophecy Books While Retaining a Communal Heart

As I stood in that Christian book store, contemplating those five ideas which were swirling around my college campus, I had a desire to learn all I could on these matters. And the two salesmen at this store laid out on a table numerous books that represented several of the major prophecy views. They shared their views and explained the positions taught in these books. Additionally, they shared where those views agreed or differed to their positions. I was perplexed on where to start.

---

[1] I took so many notes in that class that I earned an A+ on my notebook. It was so thorough Dr. Draper asked me if he could use my notes to help him reproduce a class he was preparing for students at Boyce College and Southern Seminary in Kentucky.

But I was eager and with a serious and sincere heart to know the truth of Scripture while also struggling to discern where to even begin in my personal studies. Honestly, I believe I had probably flirted with every view before coming to the realization that I needed to do some serious study before subscribing and committing to any of the views.

These various schools of thought arose not from any liberal or weak minded professors. And the books set forth before me were from credible Bible believing teachers of the word. Just as within history various godly, gifted, and grace focused teachers adopted one or more of these ideas on eschatology so too today great men and women of God embrace these various views.

Sadly, too often secondary, third, or even fourth order issues related to the doctrine of end times causes good brethren to lose peace, harmony, and collective cooperation from one another. This grieves the Lord. Thankfully, my teachers taught me not to let that happen. These friends of mine in this bookstore, who differed with each other on the timeline of Christ's future return, also modeled before me great unity of the faith with their own distinct end time perspectives.

We must remember here, that as long as a teacher avoids heresy (on eschatology or any other major doctrinal area), we must allow for some diversity of thought in some areas of eschatology. Disciples today, especially those affiliated with Christicommunity or other conservative missions movements or churches, would do well to heed the wisdom of our forefathers on this matter.

Proper Parameters: The Faith versus Doctrines Related to our Faith

Though I became premillennial after moving through all the conservative options on the table, and I arrived at this after being heavily influenced by non-premillennial teachers for a season, I stand in this stream with a hand of fellowship to my other brothers who hold different views. I agree with my older teachers of the faith who rightly taught us that if we are premillennial, even pre-tribulational premillennial, that we ought not to make this a cardinal doctrine of the faith. We can and should cooperate with those who share other views so long as conservative and within historic orthodoxy on the fundamentals of the faith. As Drs. LaHaye, Mayhue, and Brindle have wisely said:

> The timing of the rapture is not a cardinal doctrine that should divide God's people, but those who interpret the Bible literally find many strong reasons to believe that the rapture will be pre-tribulational.[2]

The same should exist too from those in the other perspectives to us who are premillennial. If you are reading this from a conservative amillennial view, or as a conservative post-millennial view, or as a conservative mid-trib, pre-wrath, or post-trib premillennial view, there ought to be a deep abiding respect from your heart towards your godly premillennial brethren in the faith. As long as we embrace the fundamentals of prophetic truth, and vehemently denounce full preterism, and all forms of liberalism from all other perspectives, and all of the heresies with liberalism and full preterism, good Bible believing men

---

[2] Tim LaHaye, Richard Mayhue, & Wayne Brindle, "Pretribulationism," in *The Popular Encyclopedia of Bible Prophecy*, eds. Tim LaHaye & Ed Hindson (Eugene, OR: Harvest House Publishers, 2004), 289.

filled with the Spirit can wrangle and wrestle with one another on other finer matters of prophecy. Dr. O Palmer Robertson, an amillennial teacher, spoke with praise of his premillennial family. He stated:

> Covenant theologians and dispensationalists {premillennialists} stand side by side in affirming the essentials of the Christian faith. Very often these two groups within Christendom stand alone in opposition to the inroads of modernism, neo-evangelicalism, and emotionalism. Covenant theologians and dispensationalists should hold in highest regard the . . . evangelical productivity of one another.[3]

Beware of those from either side or from any conservative prophecy view that elevate this subject into the ring of the essentials. Sadly, I see younger premillennial teachers who have shunned the wisdom of their forefathers on this. I also see it among those outside the premillennial family who sometimes mock and look down on their premillennial brethren, as if they lack a credible faith. Dr. Robert Lightner warned us about these sinful attitudes and attitudes. He rightly said of this matter that "all the positions evangelicals hold on unfulfilled prophecy have strengths and weaknesses. No one view is all right and all the others wrong."[4]

Dr. Lightner wisely taught us to remove this doctrine from the central ring of the faith. We do not need to fight each other as enemies over this matter as if the issue rises to

---

[3] O. Palmer Robertson, *The Christ of the Covenants* (Phillipsburg, NJ: Presbyterian and Reformed Publishing, 1980), 201-202.

[4] Robert P. Lightner, *Prophecy in the Ring* (Denver, CO: Accent Books, 1976), 119.

the same level of importance as say the doctrine of who is Christ Jesus, or what must we do to be saved from sin, or the full inerrancy of the Bible. As Lightner reminded us, "Evangelicals believe the whole Bible. They believe everything it teaches to be true. And yet having said that in all honesty, we must add . . . there are some things in Scripture which we hold with more certainty than other things."[5]

Some truths in Scripture on prophecy are crystal clear and to deny those moves one outside of the historic faith and into apostasy. Those like Gary Demar who deny Christ's future physical future return to earth to establish an eternal New Heaven and New Earth would be one example. Consistent physicalist annihilationists like Chris Date and Glenn Peoples, who believe Christ experienced annihilation in death as will sinners in hell, would be another example of apostate teachers. Numerous examples exist and godly Bible believers must rebuke and reject these apostates with a resilient resolve.

Yet fighting for "the faith" (Jude 3) does not mean all particular issues constitute "the faith." Some truths relate to the faith, but do not equal the essence of the faith. The fundamentals of the faith call us to a defense with no exceptions. Yet doctrines of our faith or related to our faith do not require that level of defense without exceptions. Dr. Lightner reminded us of this too.

> Scripture does tell us to fight, but not over prophecy. Paul told Timothy to fight the good fight of faith (1 Tim. 6:12). And that is the responsibility which every believer has. Specifics of unfulfilled prophecy though can hardly be called essentials of the faith once delivered to the saints. We, like Timothy, are all

---

[5] Ibid., 116.

to keep the faith (2 Tim. 4:7). "The faith" surely cannot be construed to mean every particular order of future events . . . . Evangelicals have so much in common. It is such a shame that we so often fight each other instead of our real enemies. Some seem more willing to oppose and attack a brother who has slightly different view of things to come than they are those who deny the faith (2 Peter 2:1; 2 Cor. 11:13-15). They are more willing to join hands for some Christian cause with those who deny the faith than they are with other evangelicals who are not aligned with their view of future things . . . . We need to exert ourselves against the real enemy of our souls and of the faith once delivered to the saints.[6]

Agnostic Approaches & Buffet Bar Beliefs Dishonor God

To understand eschatology properly we must address several issues prior to a thorough examination of prophetic texts. I have split this eschatological doctrinal presentation into four major chapters. The first two chapters explore some fundamental root issues that form the proper presuppositions when approaching the prophetic truths of Scripture.

Often mistakes happen in eschatological conclusions because people begin with the wrong underlying presuppositions about language, especially prophetic language. People seem to suffer from eclectic or agnostic presuppositions when approaching prophecy. It is as if they are eating ice cream with various flavors all mixed together or selecting food from a buffet bar (eclecticism), or in the opposite direction they simply avoid the material all together and claim prophetic language or texts cannot be understood

---

[6] Ibid., 117-118.

(agnosticism). Sadly too many Bible teachers today are feeding the sheep with shallow, substantively short, and substandard sessions when dealing with prophecy or major doctrinal meat of scripture.

Of course as we know, at least for those of us who had mature parents who did not cater to everything we wanted (a sad but all too common phenomenon today), a diet made of fudge ripple ice-cream, or any other mixture of ice-cream for that matter, cannot replace our main diet of substantive food that gives to us the necessary minerals and vitamins for overall energy. Due examination of all eschatological options is healthy as some helpful principles may be found in all major orthodox views, but blending and blurring all doctrines together (as Philo and others did in mixing Greek philosophy with Christianity) does not produce the purity God so desires. Instead it produces an irrational system that loses credibility before both God and man.

Examination and experimentation is healthy. I for sure did much of that in my initial stages of growth. But I also knew that if I desired to have the full energy and support of Christ Jesus I had to tackle this subject with honesty and let the Bible conform me to it. Eclectic (buffet bar methods) or agnostic approaches (we cannot know or really defend any prophetic view) dishonor God. He wrote these portions of Scripture for us to understand his heart and mind.

Sadly though, too many today remain stuck in the examination, experimentation, and eclectic circles of eschatological agnosticism. They remind me of the people that Paul spoke about when he said that some were "always learning and never able to arrive at a knowledge of the truth" (2 Tim. 3:7). Dr. Charles Ryrie has rightly said of this issue:

> I used to tell students that I would rather they come to some conclusion concerning what the Bible teaches about the future, even if it were not

27

premillennialism, rather than to be eschatological agnostics. An eschatological agnostic is one who says the biblical teaching about the future is unknown and unknowable and therefore a subject to be avoided.[7]

It reminds me of Dr. Paige Patterson's words to us in class when he told us to remember this slogan: "Often wrong but never in doubt." In a postmodern age where tolerance has morphed into doctrinal relativism we would do well to remember that in all fields of theology, especially in regard to eschatology, which seems to be one doctrine where agnosticism reigns as a norm among otherwise respectable bible believers, conviction remains healthy and profitable. "God's people ought to have convictions regarding future things. . . . What one believes about unfulfilled prophecy is very important. . . . A good number of unfulfilled prophecies of future events are very clear in Scripture. {However}, what is wrong, and seems to be rather prevalent, is the affirmation of our views in ways which are not Christlike."[8]

Therefore, thinking back again to the time I stood there in that bookstore gazing at all of the various prophecy books, I recall the intense struggle of my heart as to what to buy. Two of my friends, and longtime employees of the book store, Herschel and Angie, came to my rescue. They laid out on the table for me several good books that could help me in my zealous new quest. Ironically, as we all stood there talking about each book, I noticed that even these two

---

[7] Charles. C. Ryrie, "*Foreword*," in *When the Trumpet Sounds*, eds. Thomas Ice and Timothy Demy (Eugene, OR: Harvest House Publishers, 1995), 7.

[8] Robert P. Lightner, *Prophecy in the Ring* (Denver, CO: Accent Books, 1976), 114, 116.

believers differed in their understanding of the specific time of Christ's return.

Yet even so, as I examined the various books I eventually made my choice. As it seems to me, there was a great providential chain in this where God's hand supernaturally, at least as I see it now in hindsight, guided this event (as he does every single event in the universe; see Eph. 1:11). I chose for my base book to begin my studies a theological dictionary on eschatology, one authored and edited by a man who would shortly thereafter become my primary mentor and leader for over 15 years. At this time standing in that bookstore I had no idea I would ever meet this author, much less one day become a disciple under his guidance and teaching for so many years.

The Dictionary by a Devout Doctor that Defined for Me a Doctrine

We shall arrive at the theological meat shortly. However, I want to share just a little more on how I arrived by way of providence to these positions. This groundwork is important in the overall understanding of eschatological convictions. The method we use to interpret and understand language is fundamental to this subject in Christianity. So much confusion exists in this doctrine of eschatology because people do not examine prior presuppositions such as interpretive methodology. In fact, the decline of a thoroughgoing premillennial view of eschatology, the view held by the "earliest post apostolic Christians,"[9] and the

---

[9] Paige Patterson, *The New American Commentary: Revelation*, Vol. 39 (Nashville, TN: B&H Publishing, 20012), 36. Patterson following George Eldon Ladd mentions the following as premillennial advocates in the early church: Didache; Epistle of Barnabas; the Shepherd of Hermas; Justin Martyr; Irenaeus; Tertullian; Lactantius; and Hippolytus. Patterson also says, "If this were the hope of the church in the earliest

subsequent switch to other views has much to do with hermeneutics. "The virtual triumph of Augustinian theology suppressed the literal understanding of the Apocalypse" and that lasted "for more than a thousand years."[10]

Back to this dictionary, I figured what better type of book to buy than a dictionary that covered everything dealing with eschatology from the letter "A" to the letter "Z". I love dictionaries, regular and theological. I find them very fun to read and explore! The book I therefore chose was: *Dictionary of Premillennial Theology: A Practical Guide to the People, Viewpoints, and History of Prophetic Studies.*

It covered an enormous amount of history on all of the viewpoints and key issues of eschatology. It was a book composed of fifty-six Bible scholars who Dr. Mal Couch had brought together for this massive project. Some who have articles in this book tell me stories today about how this vision and project came together under Mal's leadership. As the editor he brought together these teachers of the Word to set forth a comprehensive view within a readable monograph. The dictionary covered all of the various viewpoints while also staying true as possible to a plain method of biblical interpretation in the positions it accepted and advocated.

This book was the first book that introduced me to Mal Couch. After purchasing this book I later wrote a letter to Mal with many questions to which he so graciously replied with detailed biblical responses. It was this book that set in motion what later became a 15 year long discipleship journey that I had with Mal. He, along with others he introduced me to, became my spiritual heroes, spiritual

---

era and a hope endorsed by those closest to the apostle John, there appears little rationale for embracing another perspective."

[10] Ibid, 29.

fathers, teachers, pastors, and elders [11] in whom I could safely rest as I matured in the faith.

Why did I choose this book? There were several reasons. As noted earlier, I had been taught by my youth minister Elaine Roark early on in my faith journey (14-15

---

[11] A bishop or overseer (Thayer's Lexicon uses the term superintendent) is a male, most likely a married elder (see 1st Tim. 3:2) who fits the qualifications of 1st Timothy 3:2-7 and Titus 1:5-9, and he will have one or more of the spiritual gifts listed in Ephesians 4:11 and 1 Corinthians 12:8-10, *but not all elders, pastors, or teachers are bishops* (overseers or superintendents). The term episcopas is a distinct ruling position within a geographical segment for the body of Christ. Historically the term comes to us from the civil life ruling positions. The episcopas is the one charged with the final executive disciplinary authority (authenteo means master, autocrat, independent and domineering authority; see 1 Timothy 2:11-12; it would be the type of authority exercised in Matthew 18:15-20 and 1 Corinthians 5) over a geographical segment of Christ's body (like a father in the home familial environment). The married man (or for some interpreters, a faithful man) in this role is to exercise discipline and guidance over the other leaders and disciples in the body of Christ within his sphere of ministerial authority just as a modern superintendent would today in a city or school type setting. Understanding this distinction within Scripture can be an aid to the patriarchal or complementarian and egalitarian debate within the body of Christ. In fact, it leads us to a third position, a *familial position.* The family of Christ is to run like that of a physical family where a man leads like Adam was to do along with an Eve at his side helping to extend the dominion / ministry further. Just as in the original creation God called Adam and Eve to take dominion over the earth so too in the new creation of humanity (i.e. redeemed) God uses a male overseer and his female mate (who is equally as valuable and also a complement unto him) to take dominion over the body of Christ (as we see with Aquilla and Priscilla and others). For those of us who knew Mal we witnessed this firsthand with him and Lacy who led as a ministry team like Aquilla and Priscilla. We see the ultimate example of this in Christ Jesus who is called the "Shepherd [poiomon] and Bishop [episcopas] of your souls" (1 Peter 2:25). Christ Jesus is a male who is joined to his bride through the baptism of the Spirit and he is the ultimate and final authority over the entire body of Christ as well as even over humanity in general. He is both the ministerial authority but also the civil authority too as King.

years of age) that Christ's return would be in the future. It was under her ministry that my passion for the Word of God came alive as never before, a passion that still burns hot today. Furthermore, she used the doctrine not in some esoteric way. Whatever she believed about the details (if she even knew herself at that time) she made sure to tell me about the essentials, i.e. she gave to me the big picture.

I was taught Christ was *coming in the future*. I was taught that I was to take *comfort* in that and not *fear it*. And I was taught that the Bible would give me these answers if I were to *read it* and *trust it*. Thankfully, she did not give me some fancy humanistic answer. Nothing in her guidance ever led me to doubt, distrust, or discard any verse of Scripture, unlike some who will trivialize Scripture for the sake of human reasoning. She just set forth the obvious texts of Scripture as she did on so many other subjects.

Her reliance on Scripture as the authority may have shaped me as much as did any of her particulars in any specific teaching. From her I knew I could trust this divine book we call the Bible with not just my present moment of salvation but for my future salvation too, which would culminate when our King returned. She loved the Bible and because she loved me I too grew to love the Bible. My passion for it has not stopped even to this very hour of writing, which is of course the natural fruit of the elect believers who are born again. [12] From those seeds I developed the attitude that I wanted to know "the Word more than I want[ed] anything else."[13] To know the Word is to know God.

Of course, on the other end of the spectrum she did not give me a detailed chart with elaborate, meticulous, and

---

[12] John MacArthur, *Moments of Truth*, (Nashville, TN: Thomas Nelson Publishing, 2012), 101.

[13] Ibid.

precise timelines on when each and every event would occur. I was neither inundated with inferences and ingenious insights as if such were inspired nor left in insipid ignorance either. As Dr. Charles Ryrie has said, "Eschatology seems to suffer at the hands of both its friends and foes. Those who play it down usually avoid assigning specific meaning to prophetic texts. Those who play it up often assign too much."[14]

In Elaine's ministry to me whenever I had questions on basically any subject she simply pointed me to certain Scriptures that she knew of or discovered through research that spoke to the issues whether it was dealing with his future return and his judgments to come (1 Thess. 4:13-18; Rev. 21-22) or to peer pressure and the dangers of it (Matt. 14:1-12). In regard to eschatology, if my memory serves me right, I read per her instructions 1 Thessalonians 4:13-18 (and/or Revelation 21-22) and she used the text of Scripture as Apostle Paul so instructed, "to encourage one another with these words" (vs. 18). Prophecy gave me hope and peace. It brought me joy and comfort.

Additionally, in a parting ministry gift she gave to me a Bible promise book. I do not suppose any other gift could have been any more marvelous than that gift. I never let that book depart from me and to this very hour, even to this very minute that I type, that beloved precious gift rests beside me in my library. The small promise book contained hundreds upon hundreds verses of Scriptures that spoke to a wide array of subjects listed from A-Z. I read the entire book from A-Z and in it was the teaching of 1 Thessalonians 4:16-17 that spoke of Christ literally descending into the air to translate his saints home to glory. Though she left the particular ministry post geographically the gift she gave to

---

[14] Charles C. Ryrie, "*Foreword*," in "*The Footsteps of the Messiah: A Study of the Sequence of Prophetic Events*" by Arnold G. Fruchtenbaum (Tustin, CA: Ariel Ministries, 2004), xxvii.

me inspired me year after year to love the very words of Scripture. Though unknown to me at the time, I was traveling the road of a good Evangelical Reformed Protestant believer (Scripture Alone) before I even knew anything about such terms.

Elaine's simple, yet sacred, teaching to us was not overly complex or confusing. Texts, passages, and books of Scripture were taught in a simple, straight forward manner, and I was led to accept the Words of Scripture as my ultimate authority to which my spirit and will needed to submit unto for true happiness in life and for the life to come. She nurtured me in the graces of Christ as would a mother to her son and in that divine process led me to a solid foundation, i.e. an erudite epistemological base that was none other than Christ Jesus in Word form (see John 1:1).

What Elaine sowed into me at such a young age I would later see and gravitate towards in my journey of grace with other leaders. Men and women who truly loved, adored, cherished, hungered, and appreciated each and every Word of the Bible (not those who gave it lip service) were those whom I would submit myself unto, or covenant with organizationally, to learn from as I received discipleship from them in either formal or non-formal ways. What Elaine taught me as far as my epistemological base I would later find in other heroes of the faith that I met through divine providence. Her seeds sown in love led me to those whom I consider to be some of the great men and women of God, one of which was Mal Couch.

What Elaine planted in me gave me a love for the very words of God. In fact, her note she left me as she left the ministry she pointed me to a verse I had learned and memorized under her guidance. She wrote out 2 Timothy 3:16 in the book of Bible verses she left me and through that note urged me to find my answers in life by Scriptures. Her note was a visible reminder of what she had last made me promise her before she left the ministry. She admonished me not to stop following Christ Jesus with all of my heart.

In essence it was like what we see in Paul telling a young Timothy to guard the good deposit entrusted unto him (2 Tim. 1:13-14). She did not want to per se leave the ministry but she knew the time had come for her to leave that particular area of ministry. Consequently on that last night together she instructed me one last time not to forsake the deposit of grace that had been given to me. I think she was worried that I would dwindle away and lose my passion for Christ that she saw the Spirit ignite during her time of ministry.

And that basic, yet absolutely essential of all essentials for cognitive maturity, truth she instilled in me would later lead me to other great men and women of God who possessed a great fervency for divine Scripture. From her tutelage in grace I was trained to respond to those who accepted the Word of God for what it was: a real, true, and authoritative message from YHWH, our God and LORD.

What I would later read from a staunch gospel warrior of the faith like Dr. W.A. Criswell, who said "if I impugn or dishonor the Word, I disgrace and dishonor my Lord,"[15] I first learned in seminal form from Elaine. Like Timothy who had received so much from his grandmother Lois and from his mother Eunice (2 Timothy 1:5), I had received a solid basis to my faith from Elaine who had been a spiritual mother to me at a crucial time in God's providence over my life.

Though in a seminal form, I learned that a saint who truly loves the LORD will neither establish intellectual ideas nor sensual experiences as our highest authority. Rather our highest authority is Christ Jesus our LORD who has spoken in Scripture to us because he loves us and wants us to know

---

[15] W.A. Criswell, *Great Doctrines of the Bible, Vol. 1. Bibliology*, ed. Paige Patterson (Grand Rapids, MI: Zondervan Publishing, 1982), 36.

how to live for his glory and our eternal benefit.[16] Elaine spoke words of life to me through her biblical instruction. What she admonished me to do in word throughout her ministry and especially her last night with me, and what she left me in print to see while gone, taught me the great and most important truth for my vertical relationship from a finite world to an infinite world. She set me and left me on an epistemological rock, the rock of Christ Jesus as revealed in his holy Word!

I received the basic and, so help me God, irreversible conviction that by Scripture I could chart my entire life. As Dr. Couch would say, "Only the Bible, which gives instructions from the Lord who created us and fully understands our makeup, is sufficient for our life and practice. It is God's manual for Christian living and is adequate in itself." [17] Or as another Evangelical Dispensationalist, Dr. W.A. Criswell, masterfully articulated concerning this epistemological issue:

> There is a branch of philosophy called epistemology, which is the study of how we know what we know. Epistemology searches out the origin, the validity, the limits, and the methods of knowledge. What are the processes of learning? What are the origins and the limits of our knowledge?
>
> The ancient philosophers discussed and studied epistemology at great length. Plato said the ultimate source of knowledge lies in the mind (the nous in Greek), in the processes of reasoning, in ideas. . . . All idealists trace their origins back to

---

[16] Mal Couch, *God Has Spoken: Inspiration and Inerrancy* (Chattanooga, TN: AMG Publishers, 2003), 279-283.

[17] Ibid, 283.

Plato. On the contrary, Aristotle taught that true knowledge is gained by the senses and by factual observation. All secular humanists, empiricists, pragmatists, secularists trace their origins back to Aristotle. But the faith avows that neither one of these theories leads to the true and full knowledge of all that God means and does. In contrast to Plato, the Christian faith maintains that a man cannot know God by mere human reasoning [as Job 11:7-9 teaches]. . . .The mind cannot answer these questions: Where did I come from? Why am I here? What is the meaning of my existence? What is my destiny? What lies in the future?

In contrast to Aristotle, the Christian system of theology avows that we cannot know ultimate truth by our human senses or by factual observation. The senses are limited. All we can do is to see what we see or feel what we feel or observe what we observe. But the truth, the real and actual purpose or meaning, lies beyond what the senses are able to realize and above what factual observation is ever able to know. Therefore, the Christian system of truth binds itself to the self-revelation of God. It is *only* as God reveals and discloses Himself that we finally come to the knowledge of *ultimate and final truth*, which we call *didaskalia*, the doctrine of the faith.[18]

From that honorable, holy, faithful, and firm foundation, to which I am still utterly grateful for and irreversibly sealed unto as heat is to a fiery flame, my life matured in the mercies and graces of the author of that divine love book we call the Bible. Those early days prepared me for my future providential meetings with others (like Mal

---

[18] Ibid, 15-16 (emphasis mine).

and his colleagues and associates) whom took the seminal flame of fire within me and fanned into a stronger flame for Christ.

So to ask again, why did I choose Mal's theological eschatology dictionary standing there on that particular fall day in 1996? Why did I later choose to study under him for so many years (approximately 15)? I did so because I saw in that book a coterie of leaders dedicated to the *Word of God rightly interpreted* and that stirred my soul and connected to my very core! I could see from the various articles I scanned that the theologians in that book were dedicated to a solid epistemological base while also being equally as zealous for the science of proper interpretation of that resource from Genesis to Revelation. Logically for me they, and especially Mal, were the leaders God had set before me so I could continue to guard the "good deposit" that I promised Elaine I would guard after her departure.

The Importance of a Proper Interpretive Methodology for All of Scripture

I want to back up once again to speak to another concurrent event in 1996. Another key reason as to why I gravitated towards the discipleship of Mal Couch, which subsequently led me to a consistent premillennial view of Scripture, had to do with my fall semester hermeneutics class at North Greenville University. The seminal truths I gained as a 14 year old on the truth of Scripture were later fanned into a brighter flame under the tutelage of Dr. Charlie Draper in his class on hermeneutics, which I took in the fall of 1996. That key step in his class gave me the right understanding of how to properly, scientifically, and with precision unpack the words of Scripture so as to arrive at the proper meaning of it.

Therefore, because of this class when I examined the *"Dictionary of Premillennial Theology"* I realized the contributors to that book were all in agreement on the plain, normal, literal, and single sense to Scripture texts. What I had learned in that class under Dr. Draper was highly praised and emphasized in this book edited by Dr. Couch.

During that fall semester, at which time I also purchased the eschatological dictionary, I embraced the idea that we must let the Bible speak for itself if we truly desire to know God and his will. If we want to really know God (and not play mystical games), and if we truly want to understand his message to us (instead of substituting his message with our own humanistic reasoning) then we must let Scripture guide us as our *highest authority in all things*. I learned in that class that we ought to interpret scripture like we do any other language used for communication.

For sure, we certainly interpret most all other forms of communication in our lives in a normal or plain manner. When it comes to serious matters of life how often do we substitute the normal process of interpreting language or verbal communication with some allegorical or heavily mystified method? How often do you see someone who receives a prescription from the doctor, which instructs a person to take in the future some particular dose of medicine, apply some allegorical method to the instruction?

I wonder how many pharmacists across the globe receive phone calls where the patient asks "*what is the real or the hidden meaning behind the prescription instructions?*" Or, I wonder how many people would want their surgeon reading his or her biology books with the goal of finding some hidden meaning behind the words rather than the plain, literal, singular meaning of the text?

When it comes to real physical life or death issues we desire for people to reveal the information in a plain, clear, and normal way without any attempt to cleverly conceal the meaning behind the words used. We normally do not mind if some metaphors or symbols are used, or if a figure of speech is used here or there in order to highlight some literal reality. But we for sure do not expect any type of literature given to us that deals with important life or death issues to be written in such a way we must try and find some hidden meaning. To think something as important as life or death issues would be written that way is an asinine thought.

If such is so for the physical realm issues, then how much more so is it for eternal life and death issues? In light of the fact that our maturity of faith will affect our eternal rewards why would God choose to conceal his heart and mind instead of making it plainly revealed to us? He for sure spoke in parables to those who refused to believe, which he said was because his Father had not chosen (elected) to give the truth to them (Matt. 13:11-15), but when it came to his believers he spoke clearly to them (even explaining the illustrations to them privately) and they had then (and do now) the heart for right understanding of his messages, even when at times given through parabolic formulas.

My class with Charlie Draper helped me to grow in this area. I came to realize that God's purpose was to reveal his heart and mind to us through the revelation of Scripture that we ought to interpret in a normal way as we do any other written communication to us in the world outside of Scripture. God gave us a language so he could communicate with us. As Dr. Charles Ryrie said of this point:

> Certainly an essential part of God's revelation is a provision of means for communicating that revelation. . . . For this purpose God gave language . . . . We can certainly believe that the omniscient God made provision for languages that were sufficient to communicate his self-revelation to man. . . .[19]

---

[19] Charles C. Ryrie, *Basic Theology* (Chicago, IL: Moody Press, 1999), 29, 128.

Dr. Draper strongly emphasized in the fall of 1996 semester that God wrote a Bible for us to understand him and his ways. He taught us that God's book was given to us as a revelation to be *understood*. I recall him shocking us in class on the importance of how to read and understand Scripture. He used a shocking method to grab out attention. After people shared their opinions on what a text meant without paying close attention to the actual words of Scripture ("this text means to me this type of answers), Dr. Draper stated: "*I do not give a damn what you think the Bible says, nor does it matter what I think the Bible says. What matters is what God actually says. And for us to know what He says we must learn to properly interpret language, and thus the purpose for us in this course.*"

Of course some who read this will be more upset that he used that terminology than you will about the poor interpretations of Scripture passed off as a true Word from God (if so please read Matt. 23:23-24). Many of the evils and errors we have today surfacing or flourishing within the body of Christ occur because saints today butcher the sacred text of Scripture. They either do not read Scripture to submit to it, or when they do read it they wrongly interpret it and submit to erroneous ideas adopted as accurate reflections of God's mind. How can we Evangelicals ever forget the black eye and horror, not to mention the grotesque damage done to many people, when some of our own leading Evangelical forefathers of the faith in the 20th century accepted convenience abortions as a biblical ethical option?

Such a tragedy as that ought to remind us how serious it is to properly interpret Scripture. A person's life (physical and possibly even eternal life) may be on the line by how we interpret Scripture.

Major Doctrinal Error Due to Bad Hermeneutic Methods

Today we find professing believers in Christ asserting that Scripture supports chauvinism/misogyny (and its degradation of women's value), gender feminism/misandrism (and its rejection of unique abilities by each gender for feminine superiority), [20] materialism, physicalism, abortion for reasons other than to save the physical life of the mother, the "health and wealth" prosperity gospel, open theism, universalism, Arianism, false world religions, works based gospel presentations, Pelagianism, humanism, full preterism, fascism, communism, Marxism, existentialism, Darwinism (macro-evolutionary theories in contrast to micro-evolution),[21] anti-Semitism, [22] and a myriad of other corrupt perversions

---

[20] I make a distinction between a basic historic or classic feminist and those who embrace gender feminism. A basic or historic feminist is classically one who believes women "are to be allowed to live as freely as men" through "fair treatment, without discrimination" (*Who Stole Feminism: How Women Have Betrayed Women* by Christina Hoff Sommers, p. 24 and p. 22). In contrast, a Gender Feminist is one who believes "that all our institutions, from the state to the family to the grade schools, perpetuate male dominance. Believing that women are virtually under siege, gender feminists naturally seek recruits to their side of the gender war. They seek support. They seek vindication. They seek ammunition" (p. 16).

[21] Scientists Dr. Henry Morris and John Morris affirm micro-evolution but they prefer not to use that term. They prefer to use the terms "horizontal variation" or "recombination" for alterations "at the same level of complexity (e.g. change in color)." They additionally assert with great evidence in their favor that "no one has ever observed macro-evolution taking place in the present, there are no transitional forms in the fossils to show it taking place in the past, and the basic laws of observed change in nature clearly indicate it could never have happened at all" (*The Modern Creation Trilogy: Science and Creation*, Vol. 2, Green Forest, AR: 1996, p. 30 and 313.).

because of poor interpretive skill. Like an untrained person who uses a scalpel and calls himself a surgeon we have many untrained persons today who use the Bible and call themselves teachers, pastors, or bishops/superintendents (see James 3:1) and yet their skill in interpreting Scripture reveals some serious problems.

And to be very clear, I do not think to be trained one must have a *formal education*. In fact, when possible and without sacrifice of pedagogical quality, I am inclined more towards personal discipleship in both the spiritual as well as physical spheres of academic disciplines. Certainly we see this principle taught in Scripture (Deuteronomy 6:6-7 and Ephesians 6:4).[23] In fact some educators think the informal model has more advantages to it when the goal is to develop the entire person.[24] In past years, for example, lawyers could be trained without any formal educational university setting. Instead of that model some would receive education under actual practitioners of their respective field. Strom Thurmond, the long-time United States Senator from S.C., was a self-trained lawyer who learned the practice of law from his father.

But the key to such a process is discipleship. To learn the art or skill of some field does require discipleship by a more mature person or set of persons! Therefore, I can identify with my early hermeneutics professor's (Charlie Draper) emphatic point. I concur with him and find myself

---

[22] See Mal Couch's Book, *Issues 2000: Evangelical Faith and Cultural Trends in the New Millennium*. Many of these issues are addressed in that work.

[23] Wesley Black, "*Informal Education*," In *Evangelical Dictionary of Christian Education*, ed. Michael J. Anthony (Grand Rapids, MI: Baker Book House Company, 2001), 362.

[24] Lawrence O. Richards, *A Theology of Christian Education* (Grand Rapids, MI: Zondervan, 1975), 64.

much more broken over the failure of others to properly use the Bible than I do over the vernacular he used to communicate this truth to us.

We Can Trust Every Word of Scripture & Apply it Rightly When Understood

Consequently, from his marvelous instruction, and from the base I had from prior discipleship, I realized that Mal's book would be the right choice for me. His book from the beginning was based off of the premise that the Bible was fully inspired and inerrant.[25] He noted that if we are to trust in the written promise of Christ's future return then we had to also believe in a fully inspired Bible. *If not how else can we trust God's promise if the message he sent the promise to us in is corrupted in the slightest?*

If one verse is corrupt, in error, or false in any way at any point maybe the verses about his future coming, our home in heaven, or life after death are in error too and the entire hope is fanciful and wishful thinking established to appease the emotional whim of humanity's desire for more than this short life. I am just utterly perplexed as to how anyone can call themselves a believer in Christ and yet call into question the method by which the Almighty chose to communicate his love and heart to us.

And despite some within so-called Evangelicalism who want to extend the olive branch to some who reject biblical inspiration, I find that I would be more comfortable sleeping next to a poisonous cobra than partnering with someone for the cause of the gospel who denies the inerrancy and full verbal plenary inspiration of Scripture (see 2 Cor. 6:14-18). A recent example of that has been with those

---

[25] Mal Couch, "*Foreword,*" in *Dictionary of Premillennial Theology*, ed. Mal Couch (Grand Rapids, MI: Kregel Publications, 1996), 9.

accepting ministers like Dr. Michael Licona and others like him who through false critical methodologies deny the full inerrancy of the Scripture.

At least if I am sleeping next to the cobra I know the snake will act in accordance to its nature. In such a case I have some predictability as to how the serpent will respond. No such blessing of predictability is available when partnering with someone who denies the inspiration, inerrancy, sufficiency, and applicability of Scripture.

When the pressure and weight of the Word bears down on one's life such a person may either repent and adjust to the authority of Scripture or alternatively just dismiss it as an error or relegate it to some form of cultural relativity while responding practically in a myriad of unpredictable ways. As to when and where and how often such happens a person is left only to guess.

Consistent Application of Rules to All Portions of Scripture

Additionally, beyond the essential issue of inspiration, inerrancy, and its sufficiency in application Mal emphasized in this book that the scholars in this Dictionary affirmed the "historical-grammatical methodology or literal hermeneutic. From Genesis to Revelation, the Bible is [to be] interpreted by the same rules of grammar that govern the interpretation of literature in general."[26]

The first way someone undermines the authority of God is by an outright denial of inspiration and inerrancy and/or its sufficiency in application. At least these people, however, are honest enough to openly confess their sin. The second group of people often hides their sin and guilt through the sophistries of allegorical hermeneutic

---

[26] Ibid, 9-10. Brackets mine, added for literary clarity.

45

methodologies and they baptize their sin of unbelief in scripture with religious language that sounds intellectual.

My hermeneutics course had taught me the absurdity of establishing different rules for different books of the Bible. God wrote his Word to us in language. His purpose was to reveal to us his will, not to hide it and conceal it. Though Jesus sometimes used parables when he wanted to conceal something from others (Matt. 13:11), those are declared to be such in Scripture (see Matt. 13:3). It is not hard to discern what is parabolic in nature, especially when we are almost invariably told by the divine word itself what is a parable.

I could not then, nor even now, fathom how anyone could justify in one sentence of Scripture a literal or historical meaning from the text (such as with the predictions of our salvation in Christ) and then in the very next sentence (sometimes even in the same sentence) shift to some allegorical, mystical, or hidden symbolic meaning that required some erudite scholar to unlock the meaning with his or her advanced scrupulous studies of some piece of archaic literature that supposedly sheds more light on the text than the Scriptures themselves. Dr. Couch affirmed rightfully so the idea that the passage of Scripture has one meaning.[27]

We learned from him that we discover the meaning or sense of a text through the application of a grammatical-historical hermeneutic which leads to the discovery of truth from the inspired and inerrant meaning of texts read through a proper scientific interpretation method.[28] Dr. Ryrie's words on this are helpful:

---

[27] Robert L. Thomas, *"The Principle of Single Meaning,"* in *Dispensationalism Tomorrow & Beyond: A Theological Collection in Honor of Charles C. Ryrie,* ed. Christopher Cone (Fort Worth, TX: Tyndale Seminary Press, 2008), 97.

[28] Ibid, 108-109.

The purpose of language itself seems to require literal interpretation. That is, God gave man language for the purpose of being able to communicate with him. God created man in His image, which included the power of speech, in order that God might reveal His truth to man and that man might in turn offer worship and prayer to God. Two ramifications flow from this idea. First, if God originated language for the purpose of communication, and if God is all-wise, then we may believe that He saw to it that the means (language) was sufficient to sustain the purpose (communication). Second, it follows that God would Himself use and expect man to use language in its normal sense. The Scriptures do not call for some special use of language, implying that they communicate on some deeper or special level unknown to other avenues of communication.[29]

Ancient Methods for the Modern Science of Proper Biblical Interpretation

Furthermore, I also find today the guidance of Dr. Robert Thomas, Dr. Walter C. Kaiser, and Dr. Mal Couch greatly helpful in this area of emphases on the *single meaning* of each text to be *absolutely vital* to a proper methodological approach to Scripture, especially eschatology. What good is it to claim to believe in the inspiration and inerrancy of Scripture if we butcher the meaning of the text by the way in which we interpret it? God help us if we do such an atrocious and asinine act as that! In such cases we would be guilty of giving lip service to the

---

[29] Charles C. Ryrie, *Basic Theology* (Chicago, IL: Moody Press, 1999), 128.

authority of the Bible while at the same time undermining it in our interpretive approach. I think I hear the words of Christ, *"they honor me with their lips but their hearts are far from me,"* (Matt. 7:6) or the words of his half-brother James who said *"he is a double-minded person, unstable in all his ways"* (James 1:8).

Yet it is common among many to hear them say: "The verse of Scripture means this to me" while others say the exact opposite. I do not fault people for trying to arrive at an understanding of Scripture. I wish to God more were trying to read and understand Scripture. At least at that point we would all be in one field, better yet in light of some theories I see today better stated as within the same universe of thought.

The problem, however, arises when we claim or believe that various contradictory meanings are all equal and simultaneously possible options. In fact, we have very popular books on the Bible today that openly promote the idea of each text of Scripture having multiple meanings or senses to it.

For example, the popular book *30-Second Bible* by the University of Aberdeen Professor Russell Re Manning promotes the idea of a single text of Scripture having four senses that really comprise that text's real meaning. Those senses he lists are the "historical, allegorical, moral, and anagogical (or spiritual)" senses.[30] The "historical, textual, and archeological tools and techniques of research" are not enough for someone to discover the true meaning of a text of Scripture.[31] In other words, a historical and grammatical study of the text is not enough. We must resort to "literary

---

[30] Russell Re Manning, *30-Second Bible* (New York, NY: Metro Books, 2013), 11.

[31] Ibid.

and religious interpretations to unlock the full meaning of these rich texts."[32]

The Chicago Statement of Inerrancy & Hermeneutics: A Gold Standard

One of the greatest evangelical confessions of church history has spoken to this issue of retaining the functional sense of inerrancy through an affirmation that each text has one sense or meaning to it. Confessing an affirmation of inerrancy is great, but such a confession can be undermined when the methods used to interpret the Bible violate the confession. The Chicago Statement of Inerrancy and Hermeneutics has rightly captured this ideology of both inerrancy and the method to discover the truth from the inerrant text.

The Importance of Affirming a Historical Grammatical Hermeneutic

In Article XVIII the Chicago Confession on Inerrancy affirms the right way to interpret the inspired and inerrant words of scripture. It stated, "that the text of Scripture is to be interpreted by grammatico-historical exegesis, taking account of its literary forms and devices, and that Scripture is to interpret Scripture."[33] This historical grammatical hermeneutic confession received more intense focus and explanation in the Chicago Confession on Hermeneutics.

The authors of these great confessions realized that while believing in inerrancy and confessing it with precision

---

[32] Ibid.

[33] R.C. Sproul & Norman Geisler, *Explaining Biblical Inerrancy: The Chicago Statements on Biblical Inerrancy, Hermeneutics, and Application with Official ICBI Commentary* (Arlington, TX: Bastion Books, 2013), 10.

remains vitally important for the life of the church, they also realized another aspect of the confession could further strengthen that confession. As they said, a "belief in the inerrancy of Scripture is basic to maintaining its authority, the values of that commitment are only as real as one's understanding of the meaning of Scripture."[34] The wrong rules applied to interpreting scripture can easily ruin one's confession and commitment to inerrancy.

The Importance of Affirming a Single Sense to Each Text

The evangelical believers behind these Chicago Statements realized that to maintain the confession of inerrancy called also for them to rightly confess the proper methods to understand the inspired inerrant text. One of the major key ways in a proper method relates to a rejection of sensus plenior models of hermeneutics. Sensus plenior views of the text break the foundational link of the original author's words to the ideas from those words. It allows the interpreter freedom to go beyond, behind, and around the words of the text to construct a meaning that may not have a root in the actual words of the text.

The Chicago authors confessed that the "meaning expressed in each biblical text is single, definite, and fixed."[35] This rule and principle remains important not only in prophetic portions of scripture, but it applies to all of Scripture. Allusions, typology, and correlations may exist between a text and other texts, but if we move away from this gospel centered, Christ honoring, and time tested linguistic truth we will remove the rudder from the gospel ship and lose many truths, maybe even the gospel itself. Each text in its context interpreted through the historical

---

[34] Ibid., 23.

[35] Ibid., 27.

grammatical hermeneutic leads to objectivity, stability, and accurate meanings that correspond to reality.

Sadly, many godly believers use that rule when examining major doctrines related to creation, the Trinity, salvation, Christology, and other fundamental truths, but they inconsistently shift gears so to speak into some other interpretive method when dealing with prophetic truths. They sometimes begin to adopt some type of sensus plenior models, i.e. the text may have multiple meanings in it.

Conservative Bible Believers Oppose Multiple Meaning Ideology (Sensus Plenior)

God fearing, Christ honoring, Spirit walking exegetes desire to let God speak through Scripture. They do not desire to add to or take away from his word. The best avenue towards honoring that goal remains within the model that accepts each text has one single sense to it. Though other texts from progressive revelation may build on top of it additional revelation, all texts have objective meaning in itself.

It could be viewed as one building a house. The concrete foundation has a purpose and meaning to it. The floors, walls, and roof of the house can add to the concrete foundation additional purpose (a finished house one may live in), but none of that voids, cancels, or undermines the concrete foundation. Scripture functions this way too.

For example, prophetic portions of Scripture in Revelation (the completion of the biblical house so to speak) do not alter the prophetic OT concrete foundations. Each text in its own historical setting has meaning, purpose, and comprises a real portion of reality for those who received it. Meaning did exist and occur to those who received it. Meaning did not only occur when the NT revelation came into reality. NT revelation builds on top of OT revelation.

To highlight this point I will share some quotes from various Bible teachers on this matter. It cannot be stated strongly enough that the interpreter must seek to discover a fixed and objective meaning from the words of the text. Sensus plenior models undermine the consistent confession of inerrancy by diluting objectivity into subjectivity where the reader creates meaning, and very often meanings with no validation from God.

Dr. Robert L. Thomas: Demonic Doctrine Emerges when Abandoning the Single Sense of Scripture

Doctrinal deviation and demonic ideology surfaces when one moves away from the objective standard of seeking to discover the single sense of Scripture. He noted that one reason so many Bible interpreters arrive at wild, contradictory, and devilish doctrines relates to their hermeneutic and belief one can find multiple meanings in a text. He rightly asked if one embraces the multiple meaning model then how does one "propose to place a limit on these additional meanings."[36] He added that the

> believing community currently uses the Bible to support all sorts of teachings . . . . from homosexuality to heterosexuality, from openness of God to the complete sovereignty of God, from conditional immortality to unconditional eternal punishment for the lost. Ultimately, all these differences stem from someone allowing a given passage to have more than its grammatical-historical sense. The believing Christian community has no consensus that limits meaning beyond the grammatical historical one. The absence of a consensus leaves the interpreter free to follow his or her own personal whims.[37]

---

[36] Robert L. Thomas, *Evangelical Hermeneutics: The New Versus the Old* (Grand Rapids, MI: Kregel Publications, 2002), 150.

[37] Ibid.

In contrast to the corrupt Roman Catholic Church that has wrongly argued only Popes and the bishops (magisterium) can declare the true infallible meaning or sense of Scripture,[38] the Bible believing believers of all ages till present day stand upon the truth that believers who submit to the authority of Christ can read and understand the Lord's love book he gave to us by taking it and reading it in a normal or plain sense.[39] As Dr. Sproul noted, it is a myth that the "Bible is so difficult to understand" and that "only highly skilled theologians" can rightly "deal with the Scriptures."[40]

Such ideas as this lack merit. If we understand the rules of language, use the historic-grammatical hermeneutic, and seek the objective single sense of each text we can understand a vast amount of truths in Scripture. As Dr. Sproul noted, if we use these principles we can "read the newspaper" or we can read and understand the "Bible."[41]

For us to read a newspaper, a legal document, a contract, or the Bible, we can find and discover the author's intent by seeking to find the stable and fixed meaning in the words used by the author. We do not need to seek some other meaning beyond the words of the text. As Sproul rightly said, "what we are doing is seeking to understand what the word says in its context . . . . A particular statement may have

---

[38] Thomas P. Rausch, *Systematic Theology: A Roman Catholic Approach* (Collegeville, MN: Liturgical Press, 2016), 115-116.

[39] R.C. Sproul, *Knowing Scripture* (Downers Grove, IL: IVP Press, 1977), 34-35.

[40] Ibid., 13.

[41] Ibid., 14.

numerous possible personal applications, but it can only have one correct meaning."[42]

To arrive at this objective meaning Sproul urges Bible readers to apply the literal hermeneutic to the text. He stated, "to interpret the Bible literally is to interpret it as literature. That is, the natural meaning of a passage is to be interpreted according to the normal rules of grammar, speech, syntax, and context." This is how we discover the real meaning God wanted us to have from him. Though the Bible is a "very special book, being uniquely inspired by the Holy Ghost," this does not mean "inspiration" alters or transforms "the letters of the words or the sentences of the passages into magical phrases."[43]

If we fail to apply these rules we will miss the meaning of the biblical text. If readers go "beneath the surface of the plain sense of Scriptures" then the interpreters have came up "with all sorts of odd things" and "abuses."[44] The remedy of these errors remains the gold standard as confessed in the Chicago Statements. We confess inerrancy and discover the inerrant meaning by applying the plain hermeneutic with a goal to discover the single sense of the text. We must stand by the golden rule here: "a scriptural passage has one meaning" though it may have "applications to the wide variety of nuances to our lives. . . . {these} are necessary safeguards against unbridled speculation and subjective interpretation."[45]

---

[42] Ibid., 39.

[43] Ibid., 48-49.

[44] Ibid., 55.

[45] Ibid.

If one adopts the idea that God gives readers today new insights into a text beyond the inspired author's words then the reader becomes king over the text and the actual biblical writer becomes a problem to the discovery of real meaning. Dr. Kaiser wisely notes how destructive this method is for discovery of the objective meaning of Scripture.

He stated, "this theory of sensus plenior would make the inspired writer a secondary element in the process and even a nuisance at times, while God, the principal author, is viewed as supplying directly to interpreters many additional meanings that exceed those originally intended by the human authors."[46]

The solution is to remain within the historic model of the ancient faith. We must retain the "Antiochian school" of thought with its "advocacy of a single meaning to the text (the author's meaning)" because this is for sure a "far and away much better position methodologically, historically, and theologically than is the Alexandrian school of allegorizing."[47] Conservatives agree here with Kaiser in that we "are most confident that the meaning of any given word . . . will be discretely contained in a single intention of the author."[48]

All other methods lack the ability to verify meaning and no one to date can lay out how such a new "process works or how we may authenticate the additional

---

[46] Walter C. Kaiser, *Toward an Exegetical Theology* (Grand Rapids, MI: Baker Books, 1981), 109-110.

[47] Ibid., 112.

[48] Ibid., 113.

meanings."[49] Proverbs 30:6 reminds us God's view on this matter. "Do not add to his words, lest he reprove you, and prove you to be a liar" (NET).

Dr. Mal Couch & Josh McDowell: Affirming Multiple Meaning Sows Disastrous Seeds of Pluralism

I recall how Mal used to speak about some of these ideas. I know what I am about to say is not polished academic language, but I can hear Mal's voice in my head on such subjects. He would say in a jovial and comical manner this: *"I have a giant theological term for you in this matter. It is called garbage!"* Now do not think Mal was being mean spirited when he said such. He was not. It was his way of setting us up to think we were about to hear some profound term or truth when in reality he would say this to show us in simple terms that some ideas just make no logical sense.

To this idea above about language he noted that it is really nothing more than a sophisticated way of saying the text has multiple layers of meaning to it that can only be unlocked by something or someone beyond the text itself. To that tune the church could just march in dance and song right back to the dark ages where knowledge was controlled and held captive by the Roman Catholic Magisterium. This concept spells a disaster for the body of Christ. It sows the seeds that produce the fruit of pluralism (the text means whatever we want it to mean) or authoritarianism (the text means whatever the Roman Catholic Church says it means).

It makes me think too many Protestants in religion are like too many American citizens in regard to political history. Many American citizens have long forgotten what we revolted from in order to be here today. Likewise, too many Protestants have long forgotten what saints of all

---

[49] Ibid.

stripes protested against centuries ago to get us to this point in religious history.

Sadly, though I admit this is an empirical observation, it seems to me that my culture and society has become so nurturing, so soft, or so ideologically driven by the spirit of pluralism that many are too afraid to tell people "no," or that one or more views are incorrect. Dr. Josh McDowell and Bob Hostetler have said before that tolerance has been altered to another definition. The "New Tolerance" means we must accept all ideas as equally valid. Of that perverted demonic ideology Dr. McDowell and Mr. Hostetler say specifically:

> The new tolerance is defined as the view that all values, beliefs, lifestyles, and truth claims are equal. . . . In contrast to traditional tolerance, which asserts that everyone has an equal right to believe or say what he thinks is right, the new tolerance—the way our children are being taught to believe—says that what every individual believes or says is equally right, equally valid. So not only does everyone have an equal right to his beliefs, but all beliefs are equal. All values are equal. All lifestyles are equal. All truth claims are equal . . . . [but] the Bible makes it clear that all values, beliefs, lifestyles, and truth claims are not equal. It teaches that the God of the Bible is the true God (Jeremiah 10:10), that all his words are true (Psalm 119:160), and that if something is not right in God's sight, it is wrong (Deuteronomy 6:18).[50]

Such acts or ideas of relativity are at times fundamentally rooted in the godless humanistic psychology we know as behaviorism popularized by the materialist B.F.

---

[50] Josh McDowell and Bob Hostetler, *The New Tolerance* (Wheaton, IL: Tyndale House Publishers, 1998), 19-20.

Skinner. Author and theologian Francis Schaeffer noted that Skinner's pedagogical instruction stressed that educators ought to use only positive reinforcers instead of anything negative or punishment based.[51] To use the word *no* has become less than vogue in this postmodern culture. It violates the ideological root that has produced the "New Tolerance" symptom of this age.

We see that theory at times when in some competitions no child or person loses. All are declared winners. That ideology carries over into the realm of biblical interpretation as well. All proposed ideas are sometimes seen as equally valid truths even though different and at times contradictory. The *"no answer is wrong"* pluralism ideology has even shown up in basic mathematical and spelling sphere of grammar schools. Some texts used in some schools embrace ideas known as *"new math"* and *"inventive spelling."* The idea is that a teacher or parent should not tell the child the mathematical computation or particular spelling of a word is wrong for the fear that it will discourage the child.[52]

Whether these wishy-washy, weak, and warped pedagogical models occur are due to leaders drinking deep from the wells of a materialistic ideology like that of a B.F. Skinner, or because of an out of balance and overly soft and nurturing environment, or even because of some new educational theory that the academy has embraced due to some of the most novel ideas being proposed in doctoral dissertations by the youngest intelligentsia I do not know. But what I do know is that whenever we embrace an ideology that asserts there are no rights and wrongs in math,

---

[51] Charlotte Thomson Oserbyt, *The Deliberate Dumbing Down of America* (Ravenna, OH: Conscience Press, 1999), 185-186.

[52] John A. Stormer, *None Dare Call it Education* (Florissant, MO: Liberty Bell Press, 1998), 1-13.

in spelling, or in how we define and interpret language (which includes Scripture), at that point we have turned away from YHWH, the God of the Bible, and have turned to a false god who has cleverly disguised his deceptive ploy of pluralism as that of an angel of light (2 Cor. 11:14).

Unorthodox Full Preterist Heresy

This warning applies to the entire Bible of course, but especially such a reminder is applicable in the field of eschatology where so many otherwise competent Bible interpreters go, as Mal called it, *"brain dead"* when interpreting portions of prophetic Scripture. What did he mean by brain dead? Take for example someone who embraces full preterism (the view Christ has already returned in AD 70) yet otherwise affirms biblical truth in other doctrines. In the other doctrines that person will interpret the Bible in a normal, plain, historical manner and by doing so he or she arrives at the proper meaning of the text. It may be the doctrine of salvation by grace through faith in Christ. Or it may be the affirmation that Christ Jesus physically arose from the grave.

Such truths like this are discovered when a person applies the plain interpretive methodology to the text of Scripture. But then when an allegorical method is embraced the person's brain goes dead to the normal rules for how to interpret language. Then strange and very contradictory ideas arise from the interpretations of the text.

For the full preterist, the return of the Lord has happened in some past moment of history. Usually they point to some time around AD 70. In "full preterism" the people believe "all the prophecies regarding the coming of Christ—including the millennium and the last judgment—were fulfilled in the first century."[53]

---

[53] R.C. Sproul, *Everyone's A Theologian* (Sanford, FL: Reformation Trust Publishing, 2014), 314.

This ideology undermines the gospel. The gospel encapsulates the birth, life, death, resurrection, and future second coming of Christ to consummate redemptive history. As Dr. Sproul rightly said of this ideology, "full preterism is regarded as heretical, as it denies an essential truth of Scripture: the return of the King."[54]

So impose some symbolic coming of Christ into the text violates the plain teachings of Scripture. Language means what it means in the original context to the original audience to which it was originally penned. Language does not become mystical, allegorical, or with some hidden spiritual meaning just because that portion of literature under study is prophetic in nature. The text has a fixed and stable meaning. Symbols, metaphors, similes, and other like communicative devices in scripture can be faithfully and adequately handled through a normal, plain, historical-grammatical hermeneutic that seeks to find the single sense of each text.[55]

---

[54] Ibid.

[55] One modern approach is to speak of a canonical hermeneutic. For example, Dr. Chad Brand and Tom Pratt Jr. say this on a canonical approach: "Richard Lints has pointed out that Scripture has three horizons: the textual, and epochal, and the canonical" (*Perspectives on Israel and the Church*, ed. Chad Brand, p. 153). This does not seem to be the same as the analogy of faith where we let Scripture interpret Scripture. In this work Robert Saucy discussed too his view of a canonical hermeneutic. He asserts that "Because Scripture is God's Word conveyed through a human author (2 Peter 1:21), a text may have a more limited meaning to the human author in his historical context than it does to the divine author. . . . The truth that later revelation can enrich the meaning of an earlier revelation, however, does not mean that later revelation changes or reinterprets the earlier revelation. The meaning of the early revelation may be developed by elaboration" (p. 157,158). Saucy's canonical approach is much more tight and restrictive than is Brand and Pratt's view that allows for the NT revelation to be "transformed" to such a degree those OT revelations no longer remain as originally specified. It seems to me Elliot Johnson's single sense with multiple referents and Robert L. Thomas' inspired sensus plenior

Think of it this way in a physical world illustration. It would be like us claiming to believe the prescription of the medical doctor is essential and necessary and yet when we read it we assign multiple meanings to it. Doing so in the physical realm would lead to catastrophic and deadly results. Is that not also so in the spiritual realm? What damage are we doing to ourselves (and others whom we teach) now and for the eternal state by claiming in one sentence we believe in the full inspiration and authority of Scripture while at the same time skirting out from underneath its authoritative weight by our dancing with double or more meanings from one text? As Professor Thomas from Master's Seminary said:

> Single meaning is a principle that safeguards against deconstructionism and postmodernism. In the words of Bernard Ramm, "but here we must remember the old adage: interpretation is one, application is many. This means there is only one meaning to a passage of Scripture which is determined by careful study." Deconstructionism and postmodernism allow for multiple interpretations of a single passage . . . . Violation of the single-meaning principle leads to . . . the sensus plenior (fuller sense) principle. To find a sense fuller than the grammatical-historical meaning of a passage clearly enters the realm of allegorical interpretation. Traditional grammatical-historical interpretation does not import new ideas into the text of Scripture, or new dogma to any words or passages. . . . Such a practice is in total disharmony with traditional literal interpretation . . . The only remedy for this sickness [the postmodernist and deconstructionist methodologies] is a return to

application (ISPA) approach handles the progress of revelation from the OT to the NT better than does other options.

61

traditional grammatical-historical principles of interpretation as our only sure guideline to understanding the true meaning of the biblical text.[56]

In the case of preterism, these teachers fail to read the Bible in a straightforward and natural way. The idea that all prophecy has been fulfilled cannot stand when examined by the clear, plain, and direct assertions about the literal, physical, tangible, and climatic event of Christ's future second coming.

Multiple Meaning Models Requires Something Like the Roman Catholic Magisterium to Understand the Bible

Dr. Walter C. Kaiser of Gordon Conwell Theological Seminary, and one who participated in the great Chicago Statements of Inerrancy and Hermeneutics, has been a champion of the single sense of Scripture for many years. He has noted that when people embrace the Roman Catholic view of sensus plenior that such a position logically necessitates a system like they have, i.e. the magisterium, church tradition, and the Church itself.[57] As he rightfully asks, "what shall Protestants use in place of these?"[58] He even highlights the soul wrenching pain people face when they shift from the single sense of Scripture to the plural sense. The move leaves people with a never ending search that yields a life of uncertainty.

---

[56] Robert Thomas, "*Hermeneutics*," in The *Popular Encyclopedia of Bible Prophecy*, eds. Tim LaHaye and Ed Hindson (Eugene, OR: Harvest House Publishers, 2004), 140-141.

[57] Walter C. Kaiser, *Toward an Exegetical Theology* (Grand Rapids, MI: Baker Books, 1981), 109.

[58] Ibid.

Practically it can even make people lose courage, confidence, and conviction and then that yields the fruit of inward frustrations, anger, dismay, despondency, discontentment, depression, and a spirit of ambivalence in life to those souls. In short many of them lose purpose for life as they have no rudder to their ship. Such a life of relativity will eventually lead to the agony of the soul. God created us to know him and his will. But when we adopt an interpretive approach that robs us of that ability we yearn with agony to know but we find ourselves trapped emotionally, mentally, and psychologically in a system where we cannot truly know. We lose at that point vision, mission, and purpose for life.

Why is that so? Of all the possible meanings proposed by various people to a text of Scripture how can anyone ever be sure of the right meaning? How can anyone really, truly, and with integrity of heart know God's will when we cannot be sure of the meaning to his words he used to convey his will to us? It leaves people lacking in so many ways it can utterly shipwreck them in their life journey. As Dr. Kaiser noted of one Jesuit scholar, "Norbert Lohfink illustrates the agony of this search for authority and normativeness once one declares a text is free and autonomous from its author."[59] As Kaiser adds even further,

> this theory of sensus plenior would make the inspired writer a secondary element in the process and even a nuisance at times, while God the principal author, is viewed as supplying directly to interpreters many additional meanings that exceed those originally intended by the human authors. According to this view, though the same words are being investigated, normal rules of exegesis fail to yield as high a

---

[59] Ibid.

payload as when the exegete digs into the "fuller sense" . . . . what is all this [the multiple meaning methodology and what does it mean to me ideology] but . . . a return to some type of fourfold (or more) sense of Scripture as practiced by some in the patristic and medieval Church? The Antiochian school with its advocacy of a single meaning to the text (the author's meaning) is far and away a much better position methodologically, historically, and theologically than is the Alexandrian school of allegorizing. It does not matter whether one adopts the method of linguistic analysis—with its stress on the fact language has a force and meaning of its own even apart from man as its user—or a Whiteheadian process-form of understanding language—where language is important more for the number of lures for feeling that it can elicit from a reader than for its presentation of certain facts in some kind of logical relationship. The bottom line will still be: Which meaning? Which use of language? Which lure and personally interesting feature of the text is the valid one and therefore normative and divinely authoritative for our generation? These questions spoil everything for some exegetes who have uncritically drunk deep gulps of modernity.[60]

Postmodernism & Subjective Language

Too many today still drink from the postmodernism wells of thought. Language means whatever they so desire for it to mean. In such approaches "knowledge is uncertain"

---

[60] Ibid, 109-112.

and "the objectivity of knowledge is denied." [61] Many haphazardly approach the sacred text as if the text can mean today what it never meant to the original author or audience. The safeguard guard against such an error and the sacred way unto a proper understanding of God is through the historical-grammatical methodology with *all of Scripture.* As Dr. Mal Couch has taught:

> The literal method of interpretation is the usual practice in the interpretation of literature. Whenever we read a book, an essay, or a poem we presume the literal sense in the document until the nature of the literature forces us to another level. This is the only conceivable method of understanding literature of all kinds. Allegorical interpretation must be rejected as an overall interpretive system. No specific doctrinal area, such as eschatology, is to be interpreted by the allegorical system. The whole of the Bible, and all specific doctrines, are to be studied with the normal and historic sense in mind. Of course it is understood that within the framework of literal interpretation, there is room for illustration, symbols, figures of speech, and poetry. But to recognize these literary devices does not mean that literal interpretation is being abandoned. Luther rejected allegory. He calls allegorical interpretation "dirt," "scum," and "obsolete loose rags." Calvin also rejected allegorical interpretation, saying it led men away from the truth of Scripture . . . . interpreters can assume that all literary devices depend on the literal, normal stratum of language. Parables, types, allegories, symbols, and figures of speech presume a

---

[61] Millard J. Erickson, *Postmodernizing the Faith: Evangelical Responses to the Challenge of Postmodernism* (Grand Rapids, MI: Baker Books, 1998), 18.

level of understanding audience. For example, the parable of the sower is understood only within the context of a literal "farm" language. The symbolism of a lion is based upon what is asserted about lions in literal speech.[62]

I love how Kaiser turns the tables on multiple meaning advocates. He highlights the erroneous thinking of the multiple meanings ideology and methodology by showing that they hypocritically or ignorantly expect us to read their papers in a historical and grammatical (literal) manner so as to accept their view that the single sense of Scripture is incorrect. For those who try and argue against the single sense position they use words with only one meaning assigned to them to make their case. They are defeated by their own effort to use words to describe their position.

As Kaiser said of them, "It never ceases to amaze me how those interpreters who wish to fight the theory that meaning is singlefold . . . demand that all who read their papers and books do so with the understanding that their meaning is singlefold and must be understood literally. But though we have granted this privilege to them, they wish us to resume interpreting all other texts as they advocate—with this new polyvalence theory of meanings!"[63] It appears the issue is one of hypocrisy or ignorance (I hope the latter). But in either case it is a serious issue when the art of interpreting language is lost or undermined.

---

[62] Mal Couch, *An Introduction to Classical Evangelical Hermeneutics: A Guide to the History and Practice of Biblical Interpretation,* ed. Mal Couch (Grand Rapids, MI: Kregel Publications, 2000), 60-61.

[63] Walter C. Kaiser, *Toward an Exegetical Theology* (Grand Rapids, MI: Baker Books, 1981), 113.

All of this reminds me of Dr. Millard J. Erickson's discussion of the dangers of postmodernism, especially in regard to language. Much of the deconstruction of the sacred text of Scripture today, especially in the field of eschatology where so many approach it allegorically and with a multiple meaning/sense ideology, comes from those who have consciously or unconsciously been trained or influenced in postmodern ideology.

Dr. R. Albert Mohler mentions this issue as well. He mentions that the French philosopher Jacques Derrida fathered the deconstructionism ideology that asserts "texts mean nothing in themselves."[64] When this philosophy is applied "it is the reader who comes to the text with meaning and determines what will be found within the text."[65] In many cases this has occurred from the secular/common discipline universities or from cultural entertainment. Dr. Erickson's marvelous exposé of this issue in his work, *The Postmodern World: Discerning the Time and the Spirit of our Age*, highlights this crisis in an applicable scenario for us:

> There was a time when the opinion of an expert, who had devoted much time to studying a given subject, was highly valued. Now, however, such expert opinion, which claims special knowledge of the subject, is often considered irrelevant. Truth is not something objective, to be understood more and

---

[64] R. Albert Mohler, *The Disappearance of God: Dangerous Beliefs in the New Spiritual Openness* (Colorado, CO: Multnomah Publishing, 2009), 166.

[65] Ibid.

more completely. Truth is what is truth for me, and that may be different than it is for you or others. A friend of mine who is a New Testament professor says that he comes to class and offers an interpretation of a passage, on which he has spent much time and labor, building upon the years of study that he spent acquiring a doctorate in the field. When he gives his interpretation, however, a student may object, suggesting that the passage says something different to him, even though he may not have invested any time studying the passage. If the professor does not grant equal validity to the student's interpretation, he is regarded as close-minded and authoritarian.[66]

Erickson's point illustrates for us that once we concede that language has no fixed meaning and that it can be multilayered (or whatever it means to me may not be what it means to you) in meaning within a specific sentence and context we have sold out to postmodernism and substituted the teaching and witness of Christ for that of idolatry. That none of us can do if we want to claim Christ as LORD of our lives.

Thus, we must be diligent and even downright dogmatic on this foundational point: God's word is just that, a written revelation to us that has a fixed, single, stable, and certain meaning to it that we can discern when properly interpreted through linguistic analysis.[67] If we give an inch

---

[66] Millard J. Erickson, *The Postmodern World: Discerning The Times and the Spirit of Our Age* (Wheaton, IL: Crossway Books, 2002), 13-14.

[67] Elliot Johnson, *Expository Hermeneutics: An Introduction* (Grand Rapids, MI: Zondervan Publishing, 1990), 10-11, 36, 185. Johnson does take a qualified stance where he affirms single sense with sometimes multiple referents which he argues differs from multiple meaning or senses. But the referent is rooted in the actual range of meaning within the word. So it seems to me he maintains the proper stance of single sense

on this we might as well relinquish the faith as a whole. Do you think that is too strong of a statement? Hardly, that statement may not even be strong enough! Why not? Think about it in this light. *What good does it do to claim Christ is God in the flesh, that he came to die for our sins, he arose, has offered us redemption, and that he will come again to judge the world if the very words we interpret to arrive at those conclusions can <u>legitimately</u> mean something different?* As Dr. Elliot Johnson says,

> If the meaning of the biblical text were truly equivocal, then the communication of meaning would be indeterminate and a truthful statement would consequently be impossible. An interpreter would never know if A or B is meant if A and B can claim equal support. *Thus, if the textual meaning were equivocal, the Bible's claim to revelation would be deceptive and false.* So any claim to see multiple, textually unrelated senses in the biblical text *must be rejected outright.* The Bible communicates a single, textually determined meaning.[68]

---

meaning. The referents could easily be how other inspired writers of Scripture apply the meaning to new contexts in the flow of progressive revelation. It would be like saying the wood walls added to the concrete foundation form a new structure to the house. The walls are rooted to the concrete foundation. The walls and roof (multiple referents) within the term house encompasses the various referents, concrete foundation, walls screwed to the concrete foundation, and roof nailed to the walls that rest on the concrete. All of these referents exist in the term house. Scripture terms can have a single sense with multiple application referents to the meaning.

[68] Ibid, 34 (emphasis mine).

Therefore, to build upon any *sensus plenior* doctrine (texts can have multiple, even contradictory, meanings) is to build not on the rock of Christ Jesus but rather on the sinking sand (see Matt. 7:24-27). I say we had better heed the warning of Christ on this lest we lose not only the faith we want to communicate to others but even the entire ability to communicate altogether with reason and objectivity in normal discourse and discussion!

If we lose objectivity within the science of interpreting language not only is the biblical text diluted due to deconstruction methodologies but also ordinary, common, day-to-day speech collapses when we accept the theory that words may have contradictory multi-layered senses to them. Communication in such cases, both biblical as well as common, crumbles and we are in such times marching in unison with the same type of spirit that produced the dark ages where people could not truly know the will of God. Therefore, let us who are Evangelical (gospel centered believers) see to it that as a part of the redemptive motif of Scripture we apply the redemptive graces of Christ to the realm of scientific interpretation of both biblical and common communication.

An Anomalism in Interpretation Illustrated through Acts 1:11

Examples can greatly help us see the application of what we are saying here in this book on the proper method for honest biblical interpretation. To illustrate the point of how people "shift horses" in the interpretive process from the literal to the allegorical let us examine a specific prophetic text where people shift from one type or genre of Scripture to another. In this example we can see the plain meaning in portion "A" of Acts 1:11 yields the truth that

Christ truly was physically in a body that literally, materially, and spatially ascended to heaven.

If that is true of part "A" why would we shift interpretive methods to some symbolic or allegorical meaning in portion "B" of the same sentence and believe that his return would only be spiritual (non-physical) through the coming of the Holy Spirit at Pentecost or at his coming in judgment on Jerusalem in AD 70 (as full preterists assert)? *Allegorical methodologies leave us with austere anomalies that annul the authority of Scripture.*

As Dr. Paige Patterson has said of Acts 1:11, "First, orthodox Christianity requires a literal return of Christ. The angel who greeted the disciples at the ascension stated with crystal clarity, 'This Jesus, who has been taken from you into heaven, will come back in the same way you have seen him go into heaven (Acts 1:11). Jesus promised that after going to prepare a place, he would return to receive the disciples to himself John (14:3). This is a first-order truth that must be embraced to claim orthodoxy."[69]

But full preterists indeed deny that this text means that. They with this text, as well with many others, embrace a portion of Scripture in its historical grammatical (literal, plain) sense while "shifting horses" in midstream within the interpretive process to some symbolic or allegorical meaning.

From that one text we can see how objectivity (and thus the truth) is lost when a person inserts into Scripture some methodology that seeks to find some meaning beyond the actual words used in the text. Allegorical methods are "usually resorted to when the literal sense seems unacceptable to the interpreter. The actual words, then, are not understood in their normal sense but in a symbolic sense,

---

[69] Paige Patterson, *The New American Commentary: Revelation*, vol. 39, ed. E. Ray Clendenen (Nashville, TN: Broadman and Holman Publishers, 2012), 35-36.

which results in a different meaning of the text, a meaning that, in the strictest sense, the text never intended to convey." [70] Consequently, when someone applies this allegorical methodology, a system popularized by the Alexandrian Jews, Philo, and Origen,[71] "then objectivity is lost."[72] "Switching the hermeneutical base from literal to allegorical to semiallegorical . . . inevitably results in different, inconsistent, and often contradictory interpretations."[73]

The Dangers of Allegorical, Alexandrian, Sensus Plenior Interpretive Methods

The allegorical school of thought, which means there is some "hidden meaning [that is] to be deciphered by using a particular hermeneutical key,"[74] does not seem to display an honest effort to interpret the Bible. As Dr. Gerald Bray, an Anglican Professor of the University of Paris-Sorbonne, says in regard to allegorical literature: "it is doubtful whether

---

[70] Charles C. Ryrie, *Basic Theology* (Chicago, IL: Moody Press, 1999), 125.

[71] Mal Couch, *"The Allegorists Who Undermined the Normal Interpretation of Scripture,"* in *An Introduction to Classical Evangelical Hermeneutics: A Guide to the History and Practice of Biblical Interpretation*, ed. Mal Couch (Grand Rapids, MI: Kregel Publications, 2000), 95.

[72] Charles C. Ryrie, *Basic Theology* (Chicago, IL: Moody Press, 1999), 128.

[73] Ibid, 129.

[74] Gerald Bray, *"Allegory,"* in *Dictionary for Theological Interpretation of the Bible*, ed. Kevin J. Vanhoozer (Grand Rapids, MI: Baker House, 2005), 34.

any part of the Bible can be regarded as such."[75] If our epistemology is Scripture, which for true born again believers it is, and if we are serious and honestly seeking to know the God who we claim wrote that book, then by logical necessity we must interpret the book he inspired in words through a normal and plain methodology. As Dr. Norman Geisler correctly says,

> *Epistemological fundamentals* (e.g., inspiration and inerrancy) are tests of evangelical veracity. *Hermeneutical fundamentals* (e.g., literal historical-grammatical interpretation and its subsequent premillennialism) are tests of evangelical consistency.[76]

We ought not in one breath praise the God who wrote the Bible and in the next breath proclaim that God in honesty if we substitute or switch from a literal or plain interpretive method to some mystical, allegorical, or highly symbolic methodology disguised cleverly under some scholarly sophistry known as genre analysis.[77] To do so makes us dishonest teachers. When we do this we substitute the authority of God for our own reasoning and schemes. We become basically religious humanists, i.e. anthropocentric interpreters of Scripture rather than theocentric or Christocentric interpreters of Scripture.

In such times we break God's law of stealing and thus we are in sin. How serious of a sin is stealing and

---

[75] Ibid.

[76] Norman Geisler, *Systematic Theology: Church & Last Things*, Vol. 4 (Minneapolis, MN: Bethany House Publishers, 2005), 566.

[77] Robert L. Thomas, *Evangelical Hermeneutics: The New Versus the Old* (Grand Rapids, MI: Kregel, 2002), 323-348.

teaching falsehood? It is serious enough for God to remind us that "thieves" will not inherit the Kingdom of God (1 Cor. 6:10), and anyone who loves and "practices falsehood" will not be a part of the eternal family of saints (Rev. 22:15). Is it possible that we are stealing the truths of God from others by our false teachings? Even the thought of that is sobering!

Are we theologian-teachers somehow exempt from those reminders just because we are teachers of the word with advanced training in the field of theology? Are we exempt because we are sincere? Some seem to suggest such thoughts by the way they flippantly approach God's Word. I find that if we are trained such a fact increases our culpability instead of lessening it.

It would be like a Judge or Law Enforcement Official breaking some fundamental law and then saying that he or she is exempt from the law because of his or her vast training in the field of law. The logic is terribly skewed and is so because that is a spirit of one seeking to skirt the accountability we have towards God and the call to be faithful with his word (see 2 Tim. 2:15). As Dr. R.C. Sproul says to his seminary students,

> I often startle my seminary students by saying that theological errors are sins. They recoil from this charge assuming that there is no moral culpability for making mistakes. I argue that the primary reason we misinterpret the Bible is not because the Holy Spirit has failed to do his Work, but because we have failed to do ours. We fall short of loving God with our minds and neglect the responsibility to apply ourselves to rigorous study of the things of God.[78]

---

[78] R.C. Sproul, *Essential Truths of the Christian Faith* (Wheaton, IL: Tyndale House Publishers, 1992), xix.

We must ask ourselves from the beginning these two key questions. *Did God write the Bible in such a way that the original and succeeding saints could find his heart and mind through the message given to them? Or did he write the Bible in order to hide, conceal, and/or symbolize his message that would require additional tools in order to decipher the true hidden meaning that goes beyond the actual words themselves?* I agree with the great men and women like Dr. Couch and those who worked on the Chicago Statements, I emphatically affirm that the Bible is a real revelation of God's heart and mind to the original saints as well as to us today. As Dr. Charles Ryrie has said of the book of Revelation,

> John was commanded not to seal the book (Rev. 22:10), and those who read it are promised a special blessing (1:3). Apparently, therefore, the book was expected to be understandable and helpful to those who read it. It is an apocalypse (literally, a revelation), designed not to mystify but to clarify.[79]

It seems to me, and as Mal has instructed so many of us over the years, that when we depart from this natural, plain, and straight-forward methodology we discover some very strained attempts to revise the real meaning of Scripture. That to me reveals much about the character and honesty of the one interpreting the Scripture. Something else other than Scripture must be at work behind the scenes to lead one to such strained interpretations of Scripture where a person will interpret a portion of one sentence, passage, or book literally and then another portion of it allegorically.[80]

---

[79] Charles C. Ryrie, *Revelation: Everyman's Bible Commentary* (Chicago, IL: Moody Press, 1996), 7.

[80] It amazes me how the allegorists can interpret the first half of the book of Ezekiel and see it speaking of a real, literal, physical temple but then

Of course Jesus taught us that it is what is in our hearts that defiles us (see Matt. 15:10-20).

When someone does this (as I have done in my own life) it would be more honest if the person would just say that he or she does not believe this text to be inspired of God and to honestly say that such a text is in error. But, for a true born again Christian, such is not so easy when one realizes that to say such places him or her out of the faith and in direct opposition to the witness of Christ.

Therefore, many will simply opt to disguise their unbelief in fancy interpretations so as to hide their guilt just like Adam and Eve did with the fig leaves in the Garden of Eden. Instead of just being honest and admitting to the personal struggle in the heart because of unbelief many will resort to crafty interpretations, allegorical, figurative, or even mystical methodologies in order to use that as their own fig leaves to cover their unbelief in what the text really means if taken in its plain and straight forward manner.

Sometimes our sins in theological beliefs arise not so much because we are incapable of interpreting words within their given context. We often interpret natural realm magazines, books, and even future weather predictions with better accuracy than we do Scripture. How often have you ever seen a weather forecaster make a future prediction and the general population begin to look for some hidden, allegorical, or symbolic meaning to the future prediction just because the prediction (rather in word or print) was futuristic?

Reasonable people do not do that. Most reasonable people are able to take the plain words of others and interpret them in a way so as to arrive at sane, clear, and logical

---

interpret the last half of the book's discussion on a future restored temple as some spiritual, mystical, symbolic and non-literal event or entity of some sort. Of course, the plethora of theories abounds as to what it might mean once the allegorical method of interpretation is applied to the text.

conclusions that correspond between the words and reality. We do this each day and every day while also allowing for figures of speech and other symbols that retain a literal correspondence to the physical world in which we live. Why is it so that the majority of people can do this in human speech and written language outside of Scripture but often seem to lose this ability while interpreting Scripture?

In many of the cases it seems to me this is so because in those matters we are not being called to account by our Creator God. The Bible calls us to account and it hits us even more forcefully than between the eyes. The Bible hits us in the *heart, i.e. in our deepest recesses of our being.* Consequently, we sometimes read into the Bible our agenda in an effort to cover up our own sins. *We, like Adam and Eve with their coat of skins, clothe our insecurities through the actual revision of biblical terms, sentences, and even whole books.*

Character Flaws and Personal Agendas Can Influence one to Revise Bible Truths

Our character flaws or personal agendas can sometimes lead us in some cases to revise the Bible so that we can in our own minds regain control. We do not naturally like God being in control and thus through revisionist efforts we redefine terms, sentences, passages, and books of Scripture to fit our own ideas which make us more comfortable than does God's omnipotent orderings of his universe.

For instance, think of these possibilities with certain nuances of doctrinal thought. If our hearts are lazy could it not make sense to interpret prophecy in such a way that we assert the Kingdom of God is already here? Why do we need to work, labor, and strive when it is already here and Christ has already returned (preterism or amillennialism)?

Or, what if our hearts are prideful? If so, would we ever admit to the biblical truths about God's sovereignty over our lives? Will we admit our own destiny, salvation, and future judgments (sovereignty in salvation past, present, and future; read Romans 9:10-23) in a large part rest within the omnisapience of God and his providence? To admit that would mean we lose control and what natural human, who is born naturally selfish, wants to lose control?

What if we are angry and we want others to suffer for their injustices? Might that color the way we read prophecy, and could it lead us to even desire for the Bible to teach the view that all of God's people must suffer tribulation in order to be purified (post-tribulational premillennialism)? Have you ever heard someone say that about the purpose of tribulation? Some believe the body of Christ needs this to be purified of their sins.

Or what if we are afraid and fearful and so because of that fear we develop our theology and embrace the idea of the removal of the body of Christ before the time of God's wrath (pre-tribulational premillennialism)? Could some have embraced pre-tribulational theology due to that fear in their hearts?

What if we are workaholics and overly zealous with a spirit of self-sufficiency? Might that lead us to a post-millennial interpretation of Scripture where we think our efforts will usher in the Kingdom of God? Could that zealous spirit lead someone to embrace the idea that through such zeal we can usher in the golden age for all of earth?

Why do I pose such questions as this? For us to find certainty and clear answers, and to avoid being deceived by even our own hearts, we must embrace a solid, stable, and shiftless interpretive methodology to Scripture. Without such a hermeneutic we are prone to drift and interpret scripture (all of it not just eschatological portions) in whatever manner we believe best suits our personal interests. The better option, and I say the only valid one if we are honest interpreters, is to embrace a consistent historical-grammatical methodology to each and every text of Scripture.

That method applied consistently through all of Scripture serves as a safety net of objectivity. For those who reject it they have an astronomical burden of proof upon them to explain why is it that we interpret the literal prophetic predictions of Christ's first coming to earth as the God-Man and his literal physical death if we do not also interpret the texts about his second coming in the same light. Why do some interpret the first half of Ezekiel in a normal, plain, and literal way and then in the last half switch to some allegorical methodology? What justifies such fanciful exegetical gymnastics?

If the writer and prophet Ezekiel had thought such a shift were needed do you not think he would have told his readers something to guide them to that approach? If Genesis is truly a clear revelation about the beginnings of earthly history does it not make sense that God would also give to us a clear revelation about the ending of earthly history? I love what Mal's mentor, Dr. John F. Walvoord, taught us about these very preliminary issues. He said of our approach to prophetic Scripture this:

> As . . . hundreds of prophecies are studied, a pattern of literal prophecy is revealed with literal fulfillment already achieved. Unmistakably, the evidence is overwhelming that God means exactly what He says as prophecy after prophecy has already been literally fulfilled. When history has run its course, every prophecy will be fulfilled . . . . The revelation of prophecy in Scripture serves as an important evidence that the Scriptures are accurate in their interpretation of the future. Because approximately half of the prophecies of the Bible have already been fulfilled in a literal way, it gives a proper intellectual

basis for assuming that prophecy yet to be fulfilled will likewise have a literal fulfillment.[81]

A New Book with an Ancient Message for a Modern Journey

Indeed, the *Dictionary of Premillennial Theology* book I took home from that local Christian bookstore in the in the fall of 1996 introduced me to a world that has provided more clarity, conviction, courage, confidence, certainty, and camaraderie than what I had ever known before. Through that *Dictionary of Premillennial Theology* I found the roots to my spiritual heritage. I discovered a large portion of Christ's body devoted to an honest hermeneutic that led to honest interpretations that honored the holiness of God and Scripture.

Furthermore, it was through that divine providential guidance in selecting that book that I also found a home for discipleship. It was from that book that I learned of the man known as Dr. Mal Couch. In 1997 with numerous questions on my mind, and after digesting that dictionary, I sent him a letter with many questions in it. In November 1997 I received a detailed memo from him answering my questions along with another book, "*When the Trumpet Sounds.*"

Inch-by-inch I moved beyond some of my confusion within eschatology to a spirit of conviction. My persistence was slowly helping the puzzle pieces to come together in a more harmonious whole. My zealousness for the truth was now meeting scholars who were at a zenith point of church history for the doctrine of eschatology where a collaborative focus had engaged the topic more thoroughly than in prior

---

[81] John F. Walvoord, *The Prophecy Knowledge Handbook* (Colorado, CO: Chariot Victor Publishing, 1990), 7, 10.

ages. I would be the recipient of many blessings by the fruit of their labors.

And on a personal scale I had found an Apostle Paul like mentor in Mal for the next 15 or so years as I too traveled my faith journey towards Christ Jesus. The seeds other ministers had planted inside me began to sprout more fully, and those seeds were watered by Dr. Draper in my hermeneutics course to which Dr. Couch harvested and harmonized for me years later as I studied in a formal setting under him and his various colleagues.

I recall in one lecture Mal talking to us about his mentors, men like Dr. John Walvoord, Dr. Charles Ryrie, Dr. J. Dwight Pentecost, and others who led him to solid conclusions on the doctrine of end times. These lectures helped me to even see in a new light why discipleship from other more mature leaders remains a key to fruitful Christian growth. Jesus taught us this truth and I witnessed how Dr. Couch had lived it out in his own journey, a journey he had now invited me to with his spiritual father role in my own life.

I distinctly recall one lecture where he said his mentor Dr. Dwight Pentecost lectured his class on hermeneutics for an entire course of Bible prophecy. Mal could not understand why he was in a prophecy class when it seemed more like a class on hermeneutics. But to his surprise at the end of the course Dr. Pentecost leaned back in his chair and told his students something like this: "If you apply these rules of hermeneutics and interpret the Bible from Genesis to Revelation in a historical and grammatical fashion you will always see a pre-tribulational premillennial futuristic return of Jesus Christ."

Indeed one can read Dr. Pentecost's book, *Things to Come*, and see the first 65 pages of his book are devoted to the proper rules of biblical interpretation.[82] Overall in my assessment of this idea years later, this does seem to be true. The application of a literal hermeneutic to key portions of Scripture yields some clear essentials for an honest and intelligible faith. Though some would question if it always leads to a premillennial faith (I think that point has merit), it certainly does always lead to orthodox affirmations of the essentials related to the future return of Christ and his establishment of the New Heaven and New Earth.

Though our Evangelical Dispensational Zion of believers may have some healthy variations of the minors and particulars, we as a family have apparently found a safe haven of general unanimity in regard to seven areas of our eschatological faith. Additionally, even non-dispensational teachers can and do affirm at least five of the seven following points. Some even affirm six of the seven.

Furthermore, how one defines the wrath of God (hell or tribulation judgments) and the kingdom (1,000 millennial reign or beginning in the New Earth kingdom reign) means even some could almost agree to all seven even if not exactly in a dispensational premillennial model. For example, some conservative amillennial teachers affirm that God protects his bride from the final wrath of hell (or final judgments over the earth and unbelievers) and that the future kingdom on earth (New Earth) does mean God gives Israel her land in that New Earth (points #3 & #4).

These teachers would affirm God fulfills his promises to spare believers from God's wrath and that God's earthly land promises come to pass in a real tangible way on the New Earth where Christ physically rules and reigns. Though I differ with how they would define that (as I am a pre-trib, premillennial believer), I do recognize that some substantive unity can still exist here. Those positions by the

---

[82] J. Dwight Pentecost, *Things to Come: A Study in Biblical Eschatology* (Grand Rapids, MI: Zondervan Publishing, 1958), 1-64.

amillennial brethren do show reasonable efforts to retain the literal hermeneutic in regard to God's specific promises. That is commendable even if I still am not fully persuaded to their position. But our differences at this point relate more so to the time at which God's promises occur in reality, not if they actually do come to pass.

Nonetheless, an application of an honest hermeneutic to the biblical text has led to the following conclusions for us dispensational premillennialists:

- (1) At death all people consciously go immediately into the intermediate heaven or an intermediate hell;

- (2) Christ Jesus will in his physical body return to this earth in the future to consummate earthly history;

- (3) our LORD shall protect and preserve his bride from the Wrath of God poured out on the earth;

- (4) there will be a Christocracy, an extended physical kingdom reign of Christ, on this earth where he shall fulfill all promises to humanity, especially unto the elect nation Israel;

- (5) there will be a New Heavens and New Earth established for the saints;

- (6) Satan and his demons (including the anti-Christ, false prophet, and beast) will be defeated and eternally bound and will suffer eternal judgment and condemnation.

- (7) The elect saints shall dwell in peace, harmony, and safety with God for all of eternity.

The proper path to formulating those type of proper prophecy convictions rests upon one's dedication to (1) an inspired and inerrant Scripture as the highest authority, (2) a consistent application of the literal hermeneutic to all books of the Bible, and (3) a resolve to study the text thoroughly enough until the single sense of the text can be gleaned.

When a person embraces the proper epistemology (Scripture as the highest authority), and when a person interprets that piece of literature through a historical-grammatical (literal; plain) hermeneutic that recognizes the single sense of each text of Scripture (in contrast to sensus plenior) then the person will discover these major truths that so many other faithful bible interpreters have found before us from the earliest of days.

Later in this book, I'll examine each of those seven key truths that arise when those three essentials are followed consistently. However, when any of those three essentials are neglected interpretations of the text drift into areas that miss the mark of God's message to us. But when propery applied, believers discover great hope exists for the wonderful work of the Lord in the future as this world ends and a new one dawns.

Chapter 2.
Some Preliminary Philosophical Issues

In the first chapter we examined the preliminary issues of proper hermeneutics in order to rightly understand God's Word. In that section I also shared how I developed my eschatological convictions as I matured from a spiritual child into more of a spiritual adult. In this chapter we will now move into the meat of actual interpretation and application of the major prophetic truths of Scripture.

Eschatology has sometimes been the one section of theology that many fail to carefully study. All too often we theologians hear the joke about people being "panmillennialists," i.e. it will all pan out in the end. But that type of attitude, though certainly jovial in some senses and contexts, ought not to be the real attitude of a saint that desires to know God as revealed in Scripture. Eschatology comprises a large portion of Scripture. Surely God wants us to apply our minds to it so we can know as much as possible. Why else would God inspire so much of his word with eschatological truths if he did not desire for us to understand his heart and mind in these areas?

In fact, so serious is the study of eschatology that some theologians have even surmised that the fall of some seminaries from the Evangelical faith has been because of loose and liberal seeds that exist within the theological faculty in the field of eschatology. Commonly, what one professor holds without passion will become almost extinct in a student/disciple. A professor, which in some contexts is just another term for a teacher, elder, or shepherd within the academy, normally has a great influence over the student body. Often it only takes one generation for a truth to be lost when a prior generation does not hold to the essentials.

Therefore, when professors (or other ministerial leaders) hold liberal eschatological views those seeds often sprout liberalism in the students in more areas than what the professor may have exhibited. Liberalism in regard to biblical interpretation amounts to rebellion against God, just like when a child distorts his parents' words in order to fulfill his or her own selfish agenda. While a professor may love Christ, and affirm honorable and sound theology in 11 of the 12 doctrines of Scripture, a failure in the doctrine of eschatology, doctrine 12, may lead the subsequent disciples further towards ungodly, pagan, or liberal views in more areas beyond eschatology. Certainly if the methods used to interpret eschatological portions of Scripture by non-literalists are applied to other doctrines of Scripture falsity will occur with more regularity.

Dr. Couch believed that one of the key errors that led to the loss of the gospel in Princeton Seminary was that seminary's failure to emphasize and correctly teach biblical prophecy.[83] The seminary in its founding was a godly and honorable school. Sad to say that cannot be said of that seminary today where rank heresy and liberalism rules the day. The failure to apply a historical-grammatical hermeneutic interpretive scheme to prophetic portions of scripture seems to have blossomed and spread to more portions of the Bible as the years progressed. That methodology may have eventually produced a widespread liberal view of the overall text of Scripture, which now is the norm for those leading within Princeton.

Mal's theory was that liberal seeds in the area of eschatology could often lead to liberalism in other portions of Scripture. If one fails to interpret prophetic portions of Scripture carefully with a historical-grammatical method which yields interpretations in harmony with the text, what prevents that method from expanding to other portions of

---

[83] Mal Couch, "The Fall of Evangelical Seminaries: A Lesson from the Past," In The Conservative Theological Journal, volume 4, number 12, August 2000, 225.

Scripture? If the spiritual underworld has a goal to undermine the work of God, what better way than to lead interpreters to loose, liberal, and lazy methodologies that fail to properly decipher the text of Scripture?

On many occasions I and other theology professors have watched students and saints skirt God's authority and seek to wiggle out from under the plain teaching of Scripture through their allegorical, mystical, or non-literal interpretive methods. Often pastors, students, and ministers see the obvious conclusion of a verse or text when taken in its plain sense but they in turn resort to metaphorical or other symbolic meanings that allow the person to avoid the obvious meaning of the text. One of the easiest ways to escape accountability with a Word from God (at least perceived wise) is to write the verse off as some symbol or allegory.

Although sometimes presented as nonessential doctrine, eschatological truths have deep and significant ramifications for each human being. False ideas in regard to eschatological related matters are of no small significance. One need only contemplate this question to realize the serious nature of eschatology. How important is a correct knowledge of what happens to us beyond death for how we live our lives today? If the majority of my existence and your existence will occur after we leave this earthly world, would this not mean knowing what is to come constitutes a vitally important concept for us? Certainly this would mean that!

If that is not important I am not sure what *would* be important. If my decisions today impact my future in another world should I not make a serious study to know what is to come in that other world beyond this world? Dr. Paul Benware rightly says, "A two world view can be described as living well for Jesus Christ in this world because there is a clear focus on the world to come. When believers do have this clear focus on and understanding of the world to come, their lives will be lived with greater authenticity and with greater consistency."[84]

Therefore, as we move closer to examining those issues I will highlight two other final matters that require our attention as we prepare to discover what is to come in the future. I have discussed in chapter 1 the importance of properly studying language. In addition to that we have two other important preliminary issues that underlie a holistic theology in regard to eschatology. The study of life after death brings to light two of the most basic philosophical issues for all disciplines of thought: (1) *metaphysics* and (2) *epistemology*.

Metaphysics & Epistemology: God as Ultimate Reality Perfectly Revealed Himself in a Written Revelation

The first issue, metaphysics, has to do with "the features of ultimate reality, what really exists and what it is that distinguishes that and makes it possible."[85] Dr. Panayot Butchvarov says that metaphysics deals the field of thought that investigates the "nature, constitution, and structure of reality . . . . one of its traditional concerns is the existence of non-physical entities, e.g., God."[86] As Dr. James Sire also

---

[84] Paul Benware, *"Biblical Prophecy: An Essential Element in Living a Genuine & Useful Christian Life,"* in *Dispensationalism Tomorrow & Beyond: A Theological Collection in Honor of Charles C. Ryrie*, ed. Christopher Cone (Fort Worth, TX: Tyndale Seminary Press, 2008), 478.

[85] D.W. Hamlyn, *"History of Metaphysics,"* in *The Oxford Companion to Philosophy*, ed. Ted Honderich (Oxford, NY: Oxford University Press, 1995), 559.

[86] Panayot Butchvarov, *"Metaphysics,"* in *The Cambridge Dictionary of Philosophy*, 2nd ed., ed. Robert Audi (New York, NY: Cambridge University Press, 1999), 563.

adds succinctly of this issue, "What is prime reality—the really real? To this we might answer God, or the gods, or the material cosmos. Our answer here is the most fundamental."[87]

The second issue, epistemology, has to do with how we know what we claim to know. How do we know that which is ultimately real? This is a field of study "of the mind's capacity for knowing . . . . what can we legitimately claim to know, and what we cannot claim to know because our claims carry us beyond the limits of the powers of the mind."[88]

In a more brief definition Dr. Norman Geisler and Dr. Paul Feinberg explain that epistemology is "the theory of knowledge or how we know."[89] Dr. Ed Miller asserts that this issue of "how do we know" implies many other questions such as, "how is knowledge acquired . . . . can we be really certain of anything . . . . what is truth?"[90]

Dr. Miller has also noted that some philosophers "think that the fields of metaphysics and epistemology are, in a way, the pillars of all the rest. Why would one say this? Are the questions What is real? And how can I know it? in a sense the most basic questions of all? Is it possible that how you answer these questions will determine your whole philosophical outlook?"[91] Along with many others, I think

---

[87] James Sire, *The Universe Next Door: Basic Worldview Catalog* (Downers Grove, IL: InterVarsity Press, 2004), 20.

[88] Robert Paul Wolff, *Philosophy* (Engelwood Cliffs, NJ: Prentice-Hall Inc., 1989), 36.

[89] Norman Geisler and Paul D. Feinberg, *Introduction to Philosophy: a Christian Perspective* (Grand Rapids, MI: Baker Books, 1980), 431.

[90] Ed. L. Miller, *Questions that Matter: An Invitation to Philosophy* (USA: McGraw-Hill Companies, 1984), 5.

[91] Ibid.

these are the two most essential, fundamental, and most crucial issues for anyone. And for those who have been born again the issue has been eternally settled!

If we are a true follower of Christ Jesus we will accept a key non-negotiable essential that defines both our metaphysical worldview as well as our epistemological worldview. We as true followers of Christ believe that our LORD God exists and that he is the ultimate reality (see Romans 1:19-20 & Hebrews 11:6). Everything in the universe was created by him, through him, and for him (Col. 1:15-17). God is therefore the ultimate real for someone who has truly experienced the inward work of eternal grace from God. He is the ultimate real for all of humanity too, but due to the depravity of mankind those outside of the graces of Christ do not realize it.

Christ's True Believers Have Faith in His Scriptures

God's inward work of grace implanted in the heart and mind of each Christ follower leads a believer to the proper epistemological view of life. How does a true follower of Christ have knowledge about this world, about God, about life, about eternal life? We know because God has given to us an inspired revelation that transcends space, time, and the physical world. An omniscient God (unlike the pagan neo-theist who wrongfully claims God does not know the future) can give to us a perfect Word on what is to come because he is the Alpha and the Omega, the beginning and the end. He knows the future before it occurs because he is the God who transcends time and knows how every moment of history will move. We can have certainty to the degree in which we properly interpret and understand God as he has revealed himself in Scripture.

God gave to us a perfectly inspired Bible that enlightens us on matters that we who are finite cannot see or comprehend without such a revelation. Those who have experienced the regeneration work of Christ Jesus have implanted in their very hearts and minds a faith that brings with it a faith in the divinity of Scripture. By divinity of Scripture I mean that the scriptures are holy, of God. This is one of the fundamentals that all Evangelicals (gospel centered believers) affirm.

Dr. Fruchtenbaum has said, "one of the tests of saving faith is consistency of doctrine—doctrines which are key . . . there is no disagreement on the fundamentals of the faith among those who are truly evangelical believers, among denominations and different church groups. They disagree in other areas, but not on the fundamentals of the faith. There is always unanimity there."[92] *True conversion brings with it a degree of belief, trust, and spirit of submission to Scripture.* If such does not exist in the heart of the professing believer it is of paramount importance for the person to re-examine his or her conversion experience.

I love what the Medical Doctor D. Martyn Lloyd Jones stated of an Evangelical: "an Evangelical is one who is entirely subservient to the Bible. John Wesley said that he had become 'a man of one book'. This is true of every evangelical. He is a man of one book; he starts with it; he submits himself to it; this is his authority. He does not start

---

[92] Arnold G. Fruchtenbaum, *God's Will & Man's Will: Predestination Election & Free Will* (San Antonio, TX: Ariel Ministries, 2013), 79. Fruchtenbaum, like Ryrie, Couch, Geisler, Lightner, Chafer, Pentecost, and others would be in the redemptive grace view, or moderate free grace view (to use Geisler's terms). This position is not the same as the "ultra-free grace" view. Ultra-free grace teachers usually deny the truth all believers will produce some fruit at some point. They would also usually not agree that true faith means having some settled fundamentals of the faith implanted into the heart and soul of a person as described by Fruchtenbaum. Dr. Chris Cone was right to note that the standard or historic free grace (what I and Mal Couch termed the redemptive grace view) have enough "distinctions between the two" which are "monumental" and substantively "significant" (Priority in Biblical Hermeneutics, p. 112, footnote 145).

from any extra-biblical authority. He confines himself and submits himself completely to the teaching of the Bible . . . . we must believe the whole Bible. We must believe the history of the Bible as well as its didactic teaching. Failure here is always an indication of a departure from the true evangelical position."[93]

Jesus taught us this too. His true sheep (disciples of him), those dedicated to the gospel, will know his Word to be true and they will seek to follow it. He said:

> Truly, truly, I say to you, he who does not enter the sheepfold by the door but climbs in by another way, that man is a thief and a robber. But he who enters by the door is the shepherd of the sheep. To him the gatekeeper opens. *The sheep hear his voice*, and he calls his own sheep by name and leads them out. When he has brought out all his own, he goes before them, and *the sheep follow him*, for *they know his voice*. A stranger they will not follow, but they will flee from him, for *they do not know the voice of strangers* (John 10:1-5).

Though there are astronomical scientific, miraculous, archaeological, and other types of evidences that verify God exists,[94] the person who has been imparted with the new life from Christ Jesus, who is God in the flesh (see John 1:1; 14; Matt. 3:3; 1 Tim. 3:14-16), affirms the existence of God because that God indwells the person. Through the natural creative act of God all people are born

---

[93] D.M. Lloyd Jones, *What is an Evangelical* (Carlisle, PA: The Banner of Truth Trust, 1992), 42, 73.

[94] Kenneth D. Boa and Robert M. Bowman Jr., *20 Compelling Evidences that God Exists: Discover Why Believing in God Makes So Much Sense* (Tulsa, OK: RiverOak Publishing, 2002).

with an inner knowledge of a higher power, an inner perception that something or someone exists beyond us. As the great Protestant Reformer Dr. John Calvin said,

> There is within the human mind, and indeed by natural instinct, an awareness of divinity . . . . God himself has implanted in all men a certain understanding of his divine majesty . . . . all perceive that there is a God and that he is their maker.[95]

Scripture confirms this truth to us (see Romans 1:19-20). *And if people have that understanding through the mere natural created order how much more so after the person is supernaturally reborn into the new family order (John 3:1-8; 2 Peter 1:3-4)?* A born again saint has new or more powerful inner presuppositions and a disposition (divine nature according to 2 Peter 1:4) that is effectually inclined towards God. They know him because they are known by God, YHWH.

Literally, we who are born again have been "begotten" (ἀναγεννήσας - *anagennaō*) of God (1 Peter 1:3 NKJV). This new nature makes us share in or have the actual spiritual code of Christ the LORD-God who implants himself in us through the Holy Spirit (see Romans 8:9).[96]

---

[95] John Calvin, *Institutes of the Christian Religion*, Vol. 1, tr. Ford Lewis Battles (Philadelphia, Westminster Press, 1960), 43-44.

[96] Someone may at this point ask about the idea of someone then being the New Israel because of having been born of the Jewish Messiah. The new birth, however, is of the heavenly nature of God, not of Christ's earthly Jewish nature. We are born again as children of God and joined to Christ through Holy Spirit baptism much like a man is joined to a woman. Jesus in his earthly sense is Jewish and of the Abraham, Isaac, and Jacob line. We, however, as redeemed people are not sons and daughters of Christ but rather sons and daughters of God, YHWH. We are of Christ in the sense that Christ is God. But if we are speaking of some type of spirit/genetic code then it is not the Jewish gene but rather

Because of that a person with the Spirit and mind of Christ inside him will have a disposition that seeks to yield to Scripture as his or her authority. If that inner desire does not exist that is a sign of lacking the inner indwelling Spirit of Christ.

This point cannot be stressed enough as we approach this study of eschatology or any other doctrine. The one who has truly been born from above and who has received the divine nature implanted in him from YHWH, that person believes in the divinity and authority of Scripture. *Since Christ is the Word (John 1:1), as well as YHWH (see Matt. 3:3), and the Word became flesh (John 1:14) those who know this Christ also know and trust in his word.* As with the existence of God, there are scientific, miraculous, archaeological, and other types of evidence that verify the authenticity, accuracy, and authority of Scripture above and beyond all other sources of literature in human history.[97]

Yet beyond those evidences there remains the inward presupposition and disposition of a converted soul that has been by God's grace effectually inclined towards affirmation of Scripture as from God. Those who deny either God's existence or deny or persistently doubt the divinity and

---

the spiritual God "gene" (so to speak) implanted into us at the new birth. We non-Jews do not become Jews, or spiritual Jews or the New Israel or anything of the like because of the new birth into God. God as YHWH does not have a defined nationality. Thus, when Gentiles become sons and daughters of God that does not make them Jewish. A person's physical DNA code does not change when he or she believes in the Lord Jesus. In the resurrection people will have new bodies with the DNA codes of their ethnicity they had while on earth.

[97] Josh McDowell, *A Ready Defense* (Nashville, TN: Thomas Nelson Publishers, 1993). Norman Geisler and Peter Bocchino, *Unshakable Foundations* (Bloomington, IN: Bethany House Publishers, 2001). John Warwick Montgomery, *Faith Founded on Fact* (Newburgh, IN: Trinity Press, 1978).

authority of Scripture stand in a perilous position that speaks volumes about their inward spiritual disposition.

Scripture Provides for the Need for a Third Person Objective Eye

Because God exists outside of time, because he is eternal and infinite, and because he has written an inspired book that reveals matters we could not know otherwise, we can turn to this divine book to know for certain what comes after death on this earth. The Bible helps us escape the insurmountable dilemma of the third-person identity problem that philosophers wrestle with.

How can we who are bound by time ever get out of ourselves to see objectively? How can we humans ever have an objective, external, and reliable source to verify or establish our perceptions of reality if we all as humans are trapped in our own perceptions and sense experiences?

Umpires, Referees, & Ballgames

The reason we have umpires or referees during ball games relates to the need for objectivity. Two players involved in the game cannot see the event as clearly as the disconnected umpire or referee. We need umpires to see a player sliding into a base as the catcher grabs the ball. The catcher and the player are caught in the moment of the game and cannot objectively see as well both the ball and the plate at the same time. An umpire can (or should).

A football referee can observe if the offensive player (wide receiver) with a defensive tackler caught the ball inbounds or out of bounds. The defensive player, focused on the offensive player, and the offensive player focused on catching the ball, cannot objectively see himself and the other player at the same time. The players are trapped inside their own viewpoint.

But umpires and referees stand outside the game in a sense. They can see both players and the event transpiring in the game. They are not trapped in the game and stand in a sense outside of the event as a neutral observer. This is how God is with his revelation in Scripture. God is the ultimate Referee or the ultimate Umpire who stands outside the game (transcendent) while being able to see and record words of truth for us playing in the game of life. He can see it all objectively and give us a sure call as we play the game of life.

All people will answer the questions of life and reality through some *external source of reality* or through *some time bound sensory aspect of reality*. For the believer we have the answer of a reality beyond this earthly reality. Scripture testifies to the world beyond this world and it provides for us the highest and most reliable resource to have certainty in our knowledge. So convinced am I of scripture's integrity that if I opened the book today, read, and of course properly interpreted, that there were pink, purple, polka dotted unicorns on this planet, then that is what I would believe regardless of whether science, friends, or other acquaintances agreed with me or not.

I would not use my personal experiences or current scientific data to serve as my final authority. Though science and experience play a role in helping interpret the data and stimuli around us, our final authority must always reside in God as revealed in Scripture *correctly interpreted*.

Scripture and Scripture alone stands as our ultimate basis for belief for any area to which Scripture speaks. We should not ignore natural revelation as that must harmonize with special revelation as both are from God. Concordism[98]

---

[98] Concordism is the idea that the Bible's teachings about the natural world agrees with scientific discoveries. It's based on the belief that the Bible is completely truthful, so there can't be a contradiction between the Bible and science.

remains vitally important for a holistic worldview. God's special revelation and his natural revelation concur. Dr. Wolfhart Pannenberg correctly affirmed the importance of this in his wonderful work *Toward a Theology of Nature: Essays on Science and Faith.* The tendency to bifurcate special revelation and natural revelation has caused a chasm to exist in the fields of science and theology. Dr. Pannenberg has emphasized how this creates a real problem. "If the one God of the Christian faith is also the Lord of nature, then we will not be satisfied with this chasm."[99]

But special revelation, Scripture, is supreme to the areas in which it speaks. That has been, is, and will forever be the spirit of the pure saints of Christ Jesus. The words of the world renowned theologian Dr. Carl F.H. Henry (Th.D from Northern Baptist Seminary & Ph.D from Boston University), who with the support and aid of Billy Graham initiated the magazine *Christianity Today*, were on target when he said:

> The verdict of historic evangelical Christianity is unequivocal in these matters. Augustine, Aquinas, Luther, Calvin, and lesser expositors before and after them, held firmly to the revelatory character of the written word. The message of the Bible is not the message of men merely; it is the veritable Word of God, since all Scripture is God-breathed. . . . [too] the sovereignty of God must always be in the background from which Christian theology begins. He is Creator and Lord, and His freedom to reveal himself if and as he will must be maintained. He may write his glory in the stars, and, if he desires, he may inscribe Ten Commandments on stone. If he can

---

[99] Wolfhart Pannenberg, *Toward a Theology of Nature: Essays on Science and Faith* (Louisville, KY: Westminster/John Knox Press, 1993), 72.

create man, the communication to him of ideas and words in man's language is no great burden. If God's Spirit breathed into man the gift of unique life, qualifying him for an eternal destiny, that same Spirit assuredly can breathe out to sin-ensnared man the redemptive words of God.[100]

Consequently, if faithful expositors of God's Word we must maintain both the conviction of divine inspiration as well as the ability to interpret those words, even the words of *future prophecy*. Our view of metaphysics and our epistemological basis leads us to that conclusion. In some circles the doctrine of perspicuity of Scripture has applied to most of the Bible except eschatology. There are some truths about the future that God has revealed in words that we can interpret with confidence.

---

[100] Carl F. H. Henry, "*Divine Revelation and the Bible*," in *Inspiration and Interpretation*, ed. John F. Walvoord (Grand Rapids, MI: Wm. B. Eerdman's Publishing Co., 1957), 255, 271.

Chapter 3.
Seven Major Truths about the End of the World & New World to Come

Christ's Life, Death, & Resurrection: A Foundation for the Future End of World Truths

A Christian, who rests his belief upon a set of writings known as the Holy Bible, does not have to have a blind allegiance to Scripture. There is good reason to believe in life after death based upon empirical evidence. Christianity rests upon a documented historical account of the life of a person named Jesus Christ.

When seeking to determine truth in any area people normally study the historical accounts of what took place around the event in question. For example, in the court of law if a murder has taken place the event is basically reconstructed by reviewing the history of the lives of people that surrounded the time and place of the murder. The evidence presented establishes the reasonableness as whether or not a crime did or did not occur. "Trials are fought with facts supplied by witnesses and with inferences drawn from those facts."[101]

One legal scholar has simply defined evidence as "the means by which facts are proved."[102] This evidence is the means by which ones proves something either did or did not happen. In the court of law one uses evidence to prove

---

[101] Michael J. Saks, "*Evidence*," in *The Oxford Companion to American Law* (Oxford, NY: Oxford University Press, 2002), 280.

[102] Henry Wilbur Humble, *Principles of the Law of Evidence with Cases for Discussion* (Chicago, IL: Callaghan and Company, 1934), 2.

his or her case. The proof "is the establishment of a fact by evidence and is the effect of evidence . . . . Proof is the result of the evidence, evidence is the means of attaining proof."[103]

Of course it is wise to keep in mind that proof, which in this case is proof that there is life after death, does not mean absolute certainty. Prove here means to "give adequate evidence for" or to "provide good reasons for"[104] the fact of believing in life after an earthly physical death. Therefore, it is the premise herein that when looking at the evidence for the resurrection of Jesus Christ from the grave that this belief is more probable, reasonable, and coherent than to believe that he did not arise from the grave.

And consequently, since the evidence points to this fact that Christ did indeed come forth from the dead it leads one to recognize that life does exist beyond the grave. This establishes a foundation for all of the truths related to the end of the world and new world to come. Jesus Christ is the key introducing us to the end of life and new life to come.

If Jesus was truly a human, and if Jesus truly died, and then if he truly came back to life and lives today then this evidence proves the fact that it is reasonable to believe in life after death. A world exists beyond the end of this world and one's own life. It is unreasonable to believe life and this world is all there is now. Jesus' life, death, and resurrection reveals that even in death and the endings of this world another world exists for our future.

---

[103] Ibid, 5.

[104] Norman Geisler, "*The Need for Apologetics,*" in the *Baker Encyclopedia of Christian Apologetics* (Grand Rapids, MI: Baker Books, 19990), 41.

Jesus Christ Lived on Earth and Predicted His Return to Life After Death

Of all the world religions, faiths, sects, and cults, the prophecy and fulfillment of Christ's resurrection marks Christianity as not only unique but superior to any and all other faiths. The Christian worldview of life after death has empirical support because of the death and resurrection of Christ Jesus. The fact that Christ predicted his own death and resurrection means he marked himself as a prophet and laid his entire Messianic claim upon this one historical event.

No other religion or faith has ever had a founder that made such a bold claim. "The resurrection of Christ is therefore emphatically a test question upon which depends the truth or falsehood of the Christian religion. It is either the greatest miracle or the greatest delusion which history records."[105] And history indeed verifies whether or not such a claim came true or not. The evidence supports the worldview of a life beyond this earthly life. Josh McDowell writes of the uniqueness of Christianity's resurrection claim:

All but four of the major world religions are based on mere philosophical propositions. Of the four that are based on personalities rather than on a philosophical system, only Christianity claims an empty tomb for its founder. Abraham, the father of Judaism, died about 1900 B.C., but no resurrection was ever claimed for him. Wilbur M. Smith says in *Therefore Stand:* 'The original accounts of Buddha never ascribe to him any such thing as a resurrection; in fact, in the earliest accounts of his death, namely, the

---

[105] Phillip Schaff, *History of the Christian Church*, vol. 1, *Apostolic Christianity A.D. 1-100* (Peabody, MA: Hendrickson Publishers, 2002), 173.

Mahaparinibbana Sutta, we read that when Buddha died it was 'with that utter passing away in which nothing whatever remains behind.' 'Professor Childers says, 'There is no trace in the *Pali* scriptures or commentaries . . . of Sakya Muni having existed after his death or appearing to his disciples.' Mohammed died June 8th, 632 A.D., at the age of sixty-one, at Medina, where his tomb is annually visited by thousands of devout Mohammedans. All the millions and millions of Jews, Buddhists, and Mohammedans agree that their founders have never come up out of the dust of the earth in resurrection.'[106]

What does Christ actually say concerning his own resurrection? His words as recorded in history reveal his clear prediction. Matthew recorded these words of Christ in his gospel account: "As they were coming down from the mountain, Jesus commanded them, saying, 'Tell the vision to no one until the Son of Man has risen from the dead' (17:9 NLT)."

And again these words are recorded from the lips of Jesus Christ in Matthew 17:22-23: "One day after they had returned to Galilee, Jesus told them, 'The Son of Man is going to be betrayed. He will be killed, but three days later he will be raised from the dead.' And the disciples' hearts were filled with grief (NLT)."

Furthermore, the gospel writer John recorded what he heard from the mouth of Christ concerning the resurrection. John 2:18-22 records the testimony of Christ before the Jews when he prophesied about his resurrection. "'What right do you have to do these things?' the Jewish leaders demanded. 'If you have this authority from God,

---

[106] Josh McDowell, *The New Evidence that Demands a Verdict* (Nashville, TN: Thomas Nelson Publishers, 1999), 205.

show us a miraculous sign to prove it.' 'All right,' Jesus replied. 'Destroy this temple, and in three days I will raise it up.' 'What!' they exclaimed. 'It took forty-six years to build this Temple, and you can do it in three days?' But by 'this temple,' Jesus meant his body. After he was raised from the dead, the disciples remembered that he had said this. And they believed both Jesus and the Scriptures."

Luke 9:22-27 and Mark 9:9-10 recorded similar statements from Jesus Christ. Such statements as these verify the remarkable prediction that Christ made. Each writer of the four gospels witnessed these statements from Jesus Christ. These men were eyewitnesses to such predictions and they documented these statements. The eye witness accounts and the written historical documentation gives strong evidence for the fact that not only did Christ make such claims but that the claims were accurately recorded by various people at various times.

Did such an event happen? Does history support the Christian's claim that Christ arose from the grave? Does a world exist beyond this world? When life ends here does more exist after that? Is there a new world to come after this one?

Certainly the writers of the gospels, Matthew, Mark, Luke, and John all wrote of Christ's resurrection. And Christ's death and resurrection set the stage for all realities related to the end of this world and the world to come.

Apostle Paul recorded that after Christ arose from the grave "He appeared to more than five hundred brethren at one time" (1 Cor. 15:6). These people were eyewitnesses to this historical event. That is powerful testimony for the truth of the actual event in history and time. Yet some skeptics and antagonists towards Scripture will sometimes comment that these writers may have lied or were in error. Some assume that these writers were biased and therefore would have lied in their writings.

But such theories lose weight and deflate quickly when you have the non-Christian historian Josephus, who lived as a contemporary of Jesus Christ, speaking of Christ's historical resurrection. Josephus, a Jewish historian, who had nothing to gain by articulating and recording the history of the resurrection, wrote this of Christ's life, death, and resurrection.

> Now there was about this time Jesus, a wise man, if it be lawful to call him man; for he was a doer of wonderful works, a teacher of such men as receive the truth with pleasure. He drew over to him many Jews, and also many of the Greeks. This man was the Christ. And when Pilate had condemned him to the cross, upon his impeachment by the principal man among us, those who had loved him from the first did not forsake him, for he appeared to them alive on the third day, the divine prophets having spoken these and thousands of other wonderful things about him. And even now, the race of Christians, so named from him, has not died out.[107]

The resurrection of Christ did not only receive attention from the followers of Christ. This common knowledge of the day received attention even from secular historians. If such information had of been an outright lie, deception, or myth then why would not a person such as Josephus have exposed this story as a myth or deception? It does not seem as if Josephus had any reason to manipulate any historical facts. He simply documented history, as would any historian.

---

[107] Josephus, *Antiquities*, 18.3, quoted by Josh McDowell in *The New Evidence that Demands a Verdict* (Nashville, TN: Thomas Nelson Publishers, 1999), 213.

Also, if the resurrection did not occur why then would the disciples have included such stories in the gospel accounts since the official compilation of Christ's life and ministry were completed after the death of Christ?

If the resurrection were a hoax, myth, or an event that never transpired would not the writers have succumb to the temptation of leaving out such predictions? It would seem that a disciple when under severe persecution of that day at the hands of the Roman government and from some within Judaism [108] because of the confession and dedication to Christ who arose from the grave, and had he really not arose from the grave, would not have included Christ's predictions in the historical accounts.

Certainly any disciple could have easily omitted these references so as to avoid persecution. This is exactly the reason why Dr. Schaff said that the "Christian church rests on the resurrection of its Founder. Without this fact the church could never have been born, or if born, it would soon have died a natural death. The miracle of the resurrection and the existence of Christianity are so closely connected that they must stand or fall together."[109]

Furthermore, it would be very odd for the disciples who recorded these events to have done so knowing that in recording those predictions that it would do nothing to relieve the persecution they faced at that time. The disciples had nothing to gain whatsoever by including the resurrection predictions unless the resurrection actually occurred in history. Had Christ not risen from the grave they could have easily left out those accounts. By leaving out the accounts

---

[108] Henry Sheldon, *History of the Christian Church: The Early Church*, Vol. 1 (Peabody, MA: Hendrickson Publishers, 1999), 133-144.

[109] Phillip Schaff, *History of the Christian Church*, vol. 1, *Apostolic Christianity A.D. 1-100* (Peabody, MA: Hendrickson Publishers, 2002), 172-173.

they could have escaped severe persecution and covered up any false prediction that Christ made while with them.

It makes absolutely no sense as to why the disciples suffered as they did unless of course the resurrection actually occurred. They must have seen Christ alive with their own eyes. They realized the end of this life did not mean life ended. They realized that the death of Christ and his resurrection meant a new world existed beyond this world.

As Dr. Chafer wrote, "Once convinced of the reality of His resurrection, they were willing to die for their faith in Christ."[110] The disciples new a new world to come existed beyond this world they currently lived within now. That remains the most satisfactory explanation as to why the disciples would record such accounts even in light of the struggles they faced for documenting and compiling the life of Christ including his resurrection from the grave. They had a future hope.

Any skeptic has to face some other facts. If such a story as the resurrection were a lie then why did the disciples *die for a lie*? Certainly you will find many people throughout the world, such as with criminal trials in courtrooms, who will lie to try and keep from suffering consequences especially in light of crimes that require the death penalty. *However, how many people do you know who will lie in order to obtain the consequence of death?*

Yet, the disciples' story after the resurrection of Christ eventually cost them their very lives. Ecclesiastical writings in church history reveal "most of them sealed their testimony with their blood, nobly enduring their bitter trials and martyrdom."[111] The disciples were arrested, imprisoned,

---

[110] Lewis Sperry Chafer, *Major Bible Themes: 52 Vital Doctrines of the Scriptures Simplified and Explained*, rev. ed. John Walvoord (Grand Rapids, MI: Zondervan Publishing, 1974), 67.

[111] Herbert Lockyer, *All the Apostles of the Bible* (Grand Rapids, MI: Zondervan Publishing, 1972), 247.

beaten, and were eventually killed for not renouncing their faith in the resurrected Messiah.[112] They lived in such great hope of the world to come that it motivated their faith for today.

The government wanted to stop the disciples. Persecution was the only route possible because the government could not disprove the resurrection. Since they were not able to stop the spread of the gospel and news of Christ's resurrection, the government resorted to persecution. Why? The government resorted to persecution because they could not produce the body of Christ.

The body they placed in the tomb and guarded with their most elite soldiers of the day disappeared. Even the might and strength of the government did not stop God from raising Christ from the dead and fulfilling the predictions concerning Christ. The tomb was empty and Christ's body was not to be found on earth. As John Stott says of the government,

> They arrested the apostles, threatened them, flogged them, imprisoned them, vilified them, plotted against them, and killed them. But all this was entirely unnecessary if they had in their own possession the dead of body of Jesus. The church was founded on the resurrection. Disprove the resurrection, and the church would have collapsed. But they could not; the body was not in their possession. The authorities' silence is as eloquent a proof of the resurrection as the apostles' witness.[113]

---

[112] Josh McDowell, *The New Evidence that Demands a Verdict* (Nashville, TN: Thomas Nelson Publishers, 1999), 270.

[113] John R. W. Stott, *Basic Christianity* (Grand Rapids, MI: William B. Eerdmans Publishing Co., 1999), 51.

You would, at the very least, expect to find one of these early disciples denying the resurrection in order to save his life. But no such evidence exists. Neither the disciples, the government of that time, nor any other person of their era was able to produce the body of Christ.[114] The tomb was empty! This is a plausible explanation as to why the disciples lived as they did in light of peril.

These people were firsthand witnesses of the resurrection of Christ as documented in the Scriptures. They trusted the word of Christ and saw the evidence of his word being true by seeing the resurrection. This moved the men to great courage; this courage gave the men backbones of steel to face all the harsh persecutions even to the point of death for they knew Christ was indeed Lord. This is the hope that end times truths should produce in us.

Those disciples knew they would one day see this Lord again. The worldview of these early disciples shaped the worldviews of many to come, even many of this era today. The reality that Christ lived beyond the grave gave hope and courage to face the trials of their present day.

When evaluating the issue of the resurrection, you basically have only two options as to why the tomb was empty in Christ's day. Either someone removed the body of Christ, which means it was stolen or deceptively taken from the tomb, or a divine power removed Christ from the grave. As to the first option, why would the government steal the body when they actually guarded the body to keep a rumor of any type of resurrection from happening? The government crucified Christ because he was declared as the King. To remove the body would only promote the faith they so desperately wanted to silence.

In other words the government had no motive or reason to take the body. And if for some mysterious reason

---

[114] Ibid.

the government or even the other religious faiths of that day, such as with Judaism, had removed the body, why did they not produce it when trying to stop the faith and phenomenal expansion of Christianity (see Acts 4; 5:17-42; 7; 16:22-40; 26)? No such evidence of the body existed. They never once produced evidence that Christ was still dead and in a grave. This truth establishes the great foundation for our faith in the world to come as this world comes to an end. The end of our personal life and the end of this world at large is only the doorway to new world to come.

Summary: Unreasonable Explanations Examined

What might be the counter argument as to why the tomb of Christ's grave was empty. Many have speculated but the evidence and reasoning of such speculation leaves the person with unsubstantiated and unreasonable ideology. Something supernatural had to happen for the body of Christ to disappear from inside such a well-guarded tomb. If one rejects the idea of the Christian worldview of life after death as verified through Christ's resurrection from the grave, then basically the only two options left are: (1) The disciples or commoners of the community stole the body, or (2) the government stole the body.

Yet how could a commoner, a disciple or citizen steal the body by overpowering the most elite guard unit that stood watch over the tomb? That type of skepticism has no reasonable support. Such an idea lacks reason in light of the power the government exerted to protect the tomb.

Lastly, if the disciples had taken the body how would they have overpowered the most elite guards of that day who watched over the tomb? And if for some reason they did slip by arguably the best and most sophisticated set of officers, remove the enormous rock stone either while fighting off the soldiers or while they slept (of course which means they removed the stone without waking the soldiers), and/or over power any type of resistance from any officer and stole the body, then why would the disciples still die for that which they knew was a lie?

If they stole the body then would not at least one of the disciples have admitted the truth to save his life? And would not someone have come out publicly and documented this as history? If the body was stolen, then how come someone in the 3000 people converted to Christianity on the day of Pentecost did not have any contrary evidence to the resurrection of Christ (such as the actual stolen body)?

How could the disciples convince 3000 people if the resurrection was "merely a fiction?"[115] When you look at all the options, evidence, and historical documentation, the evidence decidedly stacks in favor of Christ's body being raised from the grave exactly as prophesied. Jesus Christ truly is Lord. And if he is alive, as the resurrection proves, then as Lord all humans are subject to his authority.

Christ's Resurrection Provides a Basis to Trust Future Prophetic Predictions

History does not lie. History is amoral in that regard. People when looking back can only evaluate what has taken place in time. To look back people must examine the documents of the time, the testimony of the time, and the succession of events that occur from any previous event. How is it that a person knows that George Washington (1789-1797) was the first President of the United States? A person can read documents that testify to him having such

---

[115] Lewis Sperry Chafer, *Major Bible Themes: 52 Vital Doctrines of the Scriptures Simplified and Explained*, rev. ed. John Walvoord (Grand Rapids, MI: Zondervan Publishing, 1974), 67.

an office in a certain period of time as well as see the effects that his life and actions produced from his era. A person can reasonably conclude that not only did George Washington exist but also that his existence had a profound effect on those people around him in that day.

One historian has even noted that his farewell speech is still to this day "one of the world's remarkable documents" and that this document "remains a wholesome political guide to the people of the nation to whom it was addressed."[116] No sane person with any degree of intellectual honesty reasonably doubts the life, history, and acts of George Washington. Yet the evidence for the life of George Washington does not compare to the evidence for the life, death, and resurrection of Jesus Christ.

There are as many or more New Testament manuscript documents to verify the historical authenticity of the disciple's account of Christ's life and death, testimony from lives, and effects from the life and acts of Jesus Christ than there are with the first President of the United States of America. So why is a person more likely to believe George Washington existed as the first President of the United States than that Christ died and arose again proving there is life after this life?

The reason is that even with all of the evidence presented, even with the ability to document, verify, and substantiate the claims of Christ historically, people come to the table with preconceived notions, ideas, irrational presuppositions (2 Cor. 4:4) that cloud the mind and the ability to rightly judge and discern facts. However this should not surprise the believer. This too was a truthful

---

[116] John C. Fitzpatrick, *Washington's Farewell Address,"* in the *Dictionary of American History*, Vol. 7, Eds. Harold W. Chase, Thomas C. Cochran, Jacob E. Cooke, Robert W. Daly, Wendell Garrett, and Robert Multhauf (New York, NY: Canada: Charles C. Scriber's Son, 1976), 252.

prophetic word that Christ taught his followers while he lived on earth. He explicitly stated that even empirical proof, such as one rising from the dead and coming forth from the grave, would not convince the people who will not listen to the truth already presented from a Christian viewpoint (Luke 16:31).

These people who refuse to believe the evidence would be equivalent to a set of jurors who hear first-hand testimony from the documents of eyewitnesses who saw the crime happen, they may even see the weapon used to commit the crime, they may see the fingerprints of the suspect on the weapon used, and yet even with all of the testimony that provides a very reasonable conclusion that the suspect did indeed commit the crime they still refuse to convict the person for the crime due to a prior presupposition that this simply could not be true. Though the other explanations may make little to no sense, they hold out that there must be some other explanation than to what has been offered. The preconceived bias clouds intellectual honesty.

However, for those who do indeed believe the evidence as presented then they realize and find true meaning to life. The people who do embrace the evidence for life after earthly death find that a new world opens before them. These people find hope and heaven (the home for the departed believers) as not only reasonable but also as intellectually satisfying. In comparison to all the other options that exist, philosophies such as materialism and humanism and other world religions that have no substantive proof of the afterlife, the argument and evidence for Christianity stands alone as the unique faith of all faiths.

Though there may numerous minor discrepancies, such as possibly tensions in consistency of the documents known as the Scriptures, or other tensions in how certain teachings within the faith coincide and correlate with one another, these problems should not and do not mitigate the clear reasonableness and consistency that the Christian worldview provides for the view of a life after physical death. No intellectually honest Christian denies that there are minor tensions within the faith, questions that still are left unanswered in some degree or another.

Yet those minor discrepancies and internal tensions are just like one might find when actually serving as a juror in criminal court. Though not every question may be answered in a criminal trial, the remaining questions one might have in light of the evidence given, evidence that leads one to be able to rest assured of the verdict beyond a reasonable doubt, do not warrant enough weight to overturn the weight of the major facts presented.

Likewise, in the case for life after death, the resurrection of Christ has written evidence to support it, eyewitness evidence to support it, changed lives to support it, no other plausible explanation to counter it, and no proof as to how any other option could exist as to why the tomb was found empty. The Christian worldview, though with its own set of nuances that require further exploration and explanation, provides the most stable and substantial answer as to the reality of life after death and the basis for the truthfulness of future predictions for the end of our world and the world to come.

Just as Christ predicted his own death and resurrection, which came true, so too will the predictions transpire of Christ's return for us and the end of this world with a new world to come. Seven major truths of the end of our world and the world to come have been given to us by our Lord and his Apostles.

Truth #1: Immediate Consciousness in Either Hell or Heaven at Death

None of us who are grace children, i.e. children redeemed by grace and beneficiaries of grace, find pleasure in the concept of hell. We generally like the idea of heaven. But the thought of hell troubles us, and it rightly should. It is a serious and solemn subject to discuss and contemplate life after death in some new sphere. Of course, if we are believers we embrace this truth because our LORD and his prophets and apostles taught us about this reality. To deny this reality places a person in direct opposition to the LORD himself. Any person who denies the existence or reality of hell mocks the testimony, witness, and revelation of our LORD Jesus.

The spirit of the anti-Christ works with vigor to infiltrate the minds of all whom he can seduce to minimize or extinguish the reality of hell. Ajith Fernando has noted that in 1986 only "23 percent of Europeans claimed to believe in hell."[117] Around 2017 another survey revealed about the same percentages with 19 to 22 percent who believe in hell in the European region.[118]

In the modern day, pluralism has strong roots in many spheres of society, especially in the Western World. Even in the United States of America a denial of hell existing as a real place is almost at 40 percent in recent polls.[119] Where will that number be in another twenty to fifty years?

---

[117] Ajith Fernando, *Crucial Questions About Hell* (Wheaton, IL: Crossway Books, 1991), 19.

[118] https://www.christiantoday.com/article/most-western-europeans-do-not-believe-in-heaven-and-hell-according-to-survey/120902.htm

[119] About 6 in 10 Americans (61 percent) say hell is a real place. Statistics provided by LifeWay Research:
http://www.lifewayresearch.com/2014/10/28/americans-believe-in-heaven-hell-and-a-little-bit-of-heresy/

This pluralism has led many to grow quiet or even ashamed of the doctrine of a literal hell where a portion of humanity receives due compensation of justice for their sin against their Creator God. When the spirit of postmodernism and pluralism seeks to unite all people the doctrine of hell offends such a spirit. The doctrine of heaven and hell vividly reminds us of an "irreversible division of humanity into two groups, the saved and the lost."[120]

But despite the uneasy feeling and emotion we may experience as we contemplate the doctrine of two spheres of existence, we must, if faithful to the entire witness of Scripture, teach the reality of this lest we undermine the witness of Christ while also failing to truly love our neighbors who need to hear of the reality that awaits them after they die. Hell and heaven serve to us the constant reminder that there remains established in the universe an eternal order of justice as well as an eternal order of grace. In other words, it reminds humanity of our ultimate accountability before our Maker and to the one whom we will experience either his love through divine justice or through divine grace for our decisions while here in the body.

Immediate Consciousness in Hell or Heaven after the Body Goes to Sleep/Death

When people die, do they go to sleep and remain unconscious for a period of time, such as until the return of Christ, or do they experience a consciousness immediately after transitioning from this world to the next (death)? Some who argue for a "soul sleep" do so because of a misunderstanding of the body and soul/spirit distinction. An

---

[120] Ibid, 22.

earthly body can die but the spirit/soul does not experience the same.

When texts speak of death as being asleep (John 11:11, 14; 1 Thess. 4:15) we must have that basic distinction in mind so as to harmonize all of the biblical texts. A body can sleep and be awakened (at the fullness of time for the final resurrection) but in the meantime a soul does not sleep but goes into the presence of the LORD in a realm of grace (heaven) or into the presence of the LORD in a realm for justice (hell). Numerous scriptures speak to the *spirit that leaves the body at death* or *that exists in a conscious state after death/sleep of the first earthly body* (Genesis 35:18; Ecclesiastes 12:5-7; Matthew 17:3; Luke 16:22-24; Revelation 6:9-10).

Two particular passages I will focus on herein: one text that pertains to the Old Covenant administration and one text that pertains to the New Covenant administration. First, in Matthew 17:3 we see that Jesus took the disciples to what has been called the Mount of Transfiguration. The text reads: "And behold, there appeared to them Moses and Elijah, talking with him" (ESV). Jesus and these two OT disciples were having a conversation. As Dr. Norman Geisler says, "Moses and Elijah, whose bodies had been dead for centuries, appeared and were speaking; they were in spiritual, disembodied form and conscious." [121] As I will explain later, I would lean, however, more to the idea that not only were they conscious but they also had some sort of body too, unlike Geisler who uses the term disembodied.

Our second text in Revelation 6:9-11 speaks of people living in the New Covenant administration who exist in a conscious state and who are even clothed with some form of physical coverings. The text reads: "When he opened the fifth seal, I saw under the altar the souls of those

---

[121] Norman Geisler, *Systematic Theology: Church and last Things*, Vol. 4 (Bloomington, IN: Bethany House Publishers, 2005), 250.

who had been slain for the word of God and for the witness they had borne. They cried out with a loud voice, 'O Sovereign Lord, holy and true, how long before you will judge and avenge our blood on those who dwell on the earth?' Then they were each given a white robe and told to rest a little longer, until the number of their fellow servants and their brothers should be complete, who were to be killed as they themselves had been." We clearly see two points from this text: (a) they were talking to God, and they had just been killed for their faith while on earth; (b) they had some type of body as they were clothed. *How does an unconscious soul talk, and how does a disembodied soul also wear clothes?*

As far as consciousness goes, the Bible is emphatically clear. As soon as the first earthly body falls asleep, a euphemism for death, the soul departs in its new bodily form to another place for dwelling. The term "sleep" in Scripture has confused some. But we ought to keep in mind that Scripture uses euphemisms at times to describe a reality.

Dr. Roy Zuck said of this: "This is the substituting of an inoffensive or mild expression for an offensive or personal one. In English we speak euphemistically of death by saying that a person 'passed on,' 'kicked the bucket,' or 'went home.' The Bible speaks of death as Christians falling asleep (Acts 7:60; 1 Thess. 4:13-15)."[122] Furthermore, to elaborate even more on this subject, Dr. Randy Alcorn adds to this discussion:

> At death, the human spirit goes either to heaven or hell. Christ depicted Lazarus and the rich man as conscious in Heaven and Hell immediately after they

---

[122] Roy Zuck, *Basic Bible Interpretation: A Practical Guide to Discovering Biblical Truth* (Colorado Springs, CO: Chariot Victor Publishing, 1991), 152.

died (Luke 16:22-31). Jesus told the dying thief on the cross, 'Today you will be with me in paradise' (Luke 23:43). The apostle Paul said that to die was to be present with Christ (Philippians 1:23), and to be absent from the body was to be present with the Lord (2 Corinthians 5:8). After their deaths, martyrs are pictured in Heaven, crying out to God to bring justice on Earth (Revelation 6:9-11). These passages make it clear that there is no such thing as soul sleep, or a long period of unconsciousness between life on Earth and life in Heaven. The phrase 'fallen asleep' . . . is a euphemism for death, describing the body's outward appearance. The physical part of us 'sleeps' until the resurrection, while the spiritual part of us relocates to a conscious existence in Heaven (Daniel 12:2-3; 2 Corinthians 5:8) . . . . Every reference in Revelation to human beings talking and worshiping in Heaven prior to the resurrection of the dead demonstrates that our spiritual beings are conscious, not sleeping, after death. (Nearly everyone who believes in soul sleep believes that souls are disembodied at death; it's not clear how disembodied beings could sleep, because sleeping involves a physical body.)[123]

A Major Error to Reject: The Heresy of Physicalism

One of the most serious heresies related to death has gained some new traction today. Some promote the idea that upon death the person ceases to exist. This is more than mere soul sleep that has been promoted by the false Seventh Day Adventist Church. Though in error, they at least admit the

---

[123] Randy Alcorn, *Heaven* (Wheaton, IL: Tyndale House Publishers, 2004), 46-47.

soul continues to exist during death, just in a sleep type of condition. In their view they claim "death is sleep. Death is not complete annihilation; it is only a state of temporary unconsciousness while the person awaits resurrection."[124] Some conservative Christians in history have embraced this idea of soul sleep. But this idea itself does not constitute per se a heresy.

The heresy emerges when people assert that upon death the person ceases to exist and experiences annihilation. A soul that sleeps means the soul still exists, the immaterial aspect of man. But the heresy of physicalism asserts that the soul is not some immaterial aspect of man that survives death. Upon death the person, which the term soul speaks of, ceases to exist. Death annihilates or ends the existence of that person until resurrection and judgment.

Often this idea has been adopted to bolster the doctrine of annihilation of sinners in hell. Consistent annihilation teachers build the case upon the premise of physicalism. If we are physical beings and we cease to exist in our first death it makes logical sense to argue that God can annihilate a person in the second death. Both deaths mean the person ceases to exist.

Annihilationists who reject phsyicalism do so with a major inconsistency in their theology. They argue souls leave the body during the first death, but that these souls remain actively conscious (or at least in existence if they embrace soul sleep) until the final judgment where God annihilates the person through the application of his eternal wrath which consumes the whole person. These are inconsistent annihilationists.

A consistent annihilationist, however, uses the death of Christ to build a case. And consequently, this leads the

---

[124] Ministerial Association General Conference of Seventh-day Adventists, *Seventh –day Adventists Believe: A Biblical Exposition of 27 Fundamental Doctrines* (Hagerstown, MD: Review and Herald Publishing Association, 1988), 352.

physicalist into a Christology heresy. This happens because the basic premise relates to the wrath of God that Christ Jesus experienced. Jesus on the cross suffered the wrath of God, hell for him. The physicalist argues that Jesus died and ceased to exist. He suffered annihilation.

Therefore, if you reject Jesus you too will experience hell as did Jesus, i.e. annihilation. You cease to exist in the first death and upon resurrection (recreation) you will be judged and the wrath of God will eradicate you from reality, i.e. annihilation. This idea, however, ruins a biblical Christology.

Two Modern Physicalists: Chris Date & Norman R. Gulley

Chris Date

Date has been a major voice of the modern Rethinking Hell movement. In 2021, I and Pastor Brannon Poore debated Chris Date in a public format on the issue of annihilation. Chris Date is currently a professor of Trinity Theological Seminary in Indiana. He is a graduate of Fuller Seminary and Liberty University. He is also now a teacher-preacher with Table of Hope, a Community Church in Washington State.

Chris Date believes "human beings are physical creatures comprised of only one kind of substance: the physical. They do not have non-physical souls that remain conscious between death and resurrection."[125] He stated in our debate too that this applies to Christ Jesus as well. Jesus Christ in his human nature (human soul) ceased to exist during death as he experienced annihilation.

---

[125] Chris Date, *Statement of Faith*, accessed on 1.11.25 @ https://www.chrisdate.info/statement-of-faith

In his worldview when he dies he too will cease to exist until God recreates him at the resurrection. For Date, he wrongly places this issue in the category of non-essentials. He foolishly also places the issue of inerrancy as a non-essential.[126] These highlight how closely he aligns with some modern progressive forms of Christianity.

Norman R. Gulley

Dr. Gulley was a professor of Theology with Southern Adventist University in Tennessee. He earned his PhD from the University of Edinburgh, Scotland. He served as a pastor has authored numerous books. He also served in the past as President of The Adventist Theological Society.

He too adopted the idea that the human upon death ceases to exist. He says, "nowhere in Scripture are there disembodied souls."[127] In this doctrine Dr. Gulley affirms the eradication of a person upon death. No intermediate state exists. "So souls can perish—they cease to exist."[128] Upon death the person no longer has any life. "There is no intermediate state between death and resurrection for an alleged soul."[129]

---

[126] Ibid.

[127] Norman R. Gulley: *Systematic Theology: Creation, Christ, Salvation* (Berrien Springs, MI: Andrews University Press, 2012), 116.

[128] Ibid., 119.

[129] Ibid., 120.

Seven Problems with the Unorthodox & Heretical Physicalism Doctrine

1. Ideology Born from Pagan Greek Philosophy

The idea we as humans have no immaterial soul arises from a false worldview. Early philosophers such as Heraclitus (around 500 BC) and Epicurus (341 to 270 BC) promoted this view. The Judeo-Christian worldview embraces the idea man has both a soul-spirit as well as a body. But these Greek philosophers developed a view in contrast to the ancient Hebraic idea of the biblical writers. Heraclitus taught that the soul and mind was a substance, a bodily kind of matter.[130] Epicurus adopted also a view of atomism for the soul. In his thought the body and mind of a person exists in the form of fine atoms. And upon death the substance is dispersed or dissolves.[131]

These philosophies focused on physical matter, and led to the empirical scientific method (empiricism), i.e. we determine reality by our five senses. Nothing exists but physical matter or dissolvable material which can be dispersed, eradicated, annihilated, or extinguished. *The soul (if one even exists) is not immortal.*

2. The Earliest Teachers of Church History Rejected Physicalism

Chris Date identifies himself with "physicalists."[132] He also says "there is not a shred of evidence that the soul is

---

[130] Stanford Encyclopedia, online.

[131] J.C. A. Gaskin, "Epicurus", in the *Oxford Companion to Philosophy*, ed. Ted Honderich (New York, NY: Oxford University Press, 1995), 240.

[132] Bible Brodown Podcast, "*What is Christian Physicalism*," 6:20 mark & ongoing; accessed at https://www.youtube.com/watch?v=lD60TM0JrVg on 4.6.25. Note, there is no Christian physicalism as physicalism is a pagan idea. Date

. . . naturally immortal."[133] Date added, "There is nothing {*about the mind & brain relationship*} that seems . . . to require that the mind actually be *some immaterial substance part of man like a soul.*"[134] Chris also defines life and death as "embodied and breathing" or "not breathing" (an empirical definition, reality defined by the five senses; like a medical doctor definition).

But these views show a clear departure from historic biblical Christianity. And sadly, some so-called conservatives have allowed this heretical view into their circles. Sometimes Date tries to use some early fathers to support his views on annihilationism and conditional immortality. The quotes he uses often are inaccurate, selective, and manipulated quotes.

In the public debate we highlighted these misquotes and errors in his research. The early fathers of church history were not physicalists, nor did they support the false idea that the soul lacked a type of immortality. These five fathers highlight just a small sample of early teachers that embraced a biblical view that man has a body and soul with the soul having a natural immortality to it.

---

says that Nick Quient, who claims to also be an egalitarian, is also a physicalist. Quient is more so practicing matriarchy in that he took on his wife's last name instead of her taking his last name. Egalitarianism is normally two people who retain their own last names when they marry.

[133] Warren McGrew, "*What is the Biblical View of Hell with Chris Date,*" *Idol Killer* Podcast, around the 45.05 mark, accessed at https://www.youtube.com/watch?v=sgsx7QRADik on 4.6.25. Note that Warren McGrew is also another unorthodox teacher. He denies the full omniscience of God as well as original sin that all are born with.

[134] Ibid., 52:30 mark.

- Ignatius (35-107): "thou art composed of both soul and body, art both fleshly and Spiritual."[135]

- Mathetes in the Epistle of Diognetus (117-130 AD): "The immortal soul dwells in a mortal Tabernacle"[136] (Mathetes was possibly an associate of Apostle Paul).

- Justin Martyr (100-165AD): "for the body is the house of the soul . . . ."[137]

- Irenaeus (130- 200AD): "the soul teaches the body" & "the soul possesses and rules over the body" and "The soul is **not** mortal, neither is the spirit."[138]

- Tertullian (145-220 AD): The soul has "natural immortality. . . ."[139]

3. The Wrong Definition of Immortality Used by those in Physicalism

The earliest disciples of the Apostles taught we had both a body (material) and soul (non-material element). Those caught in the deceptive physicalism worldview do not

---

[135] Ignatius, "Epistle of Ignatius to Polycarp," in *Ante-Nicene Fathers*, Vol. 1 (Peabody, MA: Hendrickson Publishers, 1994), 94.

[136] Mathetes, "The Epistle to Diognetus," in *Ante-Nicene Fathers*, Vol. 1 (Peabody, MA: Hendrickson Publishers, 1994), 27.

[137] Justin Martyr, "Justin on the Resurrection," in *Ante-Nicene Fathers*, Vol. 1 (Peabody, MA: Hendrickson Publishers, 1994), 298.

[138] Irenaeus, "Irenaeus Against Heresies," in *Ante-Nicene Fathers*, Vol. 1 (Peabody, MA: Hendrickson Publishers, 1994), 410 & 540.

[139] Tertullian, "On the Resurrection of the Flesh," in *Ante-Nicene Fathers*, Vol. 3 (Peabody, MA: Hendrickson Publishers, 1994), 570.

use Christ Jesus as the chief human to define humanity. This leads to them wrongly defining immortality. God's type of immortality and human immortality are not the same. God who is immortal has no beginning and no end. He is eternal. But man is not immortal in that sense. We must look to Jesus and his humanity to define our immortality or our status. Christ as God is eternal-immortal (no beginning and no end). Jesus as the human is everlasting-immortal (a beginning, but no end).

But the physicalists fail to see or rightly apply two types of immortality defined in Scripture. First, Christ (Son of God) is God & immortal: "the Word {Christ} was God" (John 1:1) and as Christ he is "King of kings and Lord of lords" with "immortality" (1 Tim. 6:15 & 16). Second, Jesus (Son of Man) has unending existence (everlasting) as the high priest and mediator for our salvation: "You {Jesus} are a priest forever, after the order of Melchizedek" (Hebrews 5:6-7 & 7:23-24). The human nature added to deity had a beginning point.

Then we also see that Jesus was mortal in his material body. Jesus had flesh, just like we do because he was a real human. He was mortal in his flesh. We see this because the human body of Jesus died (ceased to function correctly). The Bible says, "Christ put to death in the flesh" (1 Peter 3:18).

From this we can conclude that Christ is immortal in his deity, never-ending in soul-humanity-personhood, and was mortal in flesh. Likewise, since we are made in the image of God and Christ Jesus was the perfect God-Man, the perfect representative of mankind, we know that mankind is never-ending in human-personhood (soul/spirit) and mortal in the flesh, like Jesus.

There is a mortal aspect to us and an everlasting-immortal aspect to us. We are not eternal-immortal (no beginning and no end), but we do have an aspect to us that is everlasting-immortal (a beginning with no end).

The doctrine of Christ's humanity helps us to avoid the heresy of physicalism. But if we embrace physicalism we have a different Jesus than the Jesus of the Bible. Either the physicalist Jesus is the real one or not. If Jesus died and ceased to exist in his human soul-personhood then the Jesus we worship in historic Christianity is a false Jesus.

Or, if the Jesus we worship, whose flesh died and his soul continued on in the period of bodily death, is the real Jesus then the physicalist worships a false Jesus. This is indeed a fundamental issue of the faith as it relates to who is Jesus in death. Is he annihilated in death? Or did his body cease to function (death) while his soul remained in continuity with ongoing conscious activity with his deity? The seriousness of this issue cannot be overstated.

4. In Physicalism Christ's Priesthood is Broken or Non-Existent During his Death

Orthodox Christianity confesses that Christ is our high priest *forever* from the time of his incarnation. He lived for us, prayed for us, and died for us as our forever Human High priest who mediates our salvation (see Hebrews 5:5-10; & 7:23-24). His mediation role continued on during the period his body rested in the grave for the 3 days of bodily-flesh death. Yet his human soul that suffered for our sins remained alive though apart from his flesh. In this way, the mediator role continued on.

However, those like Chris Date and Norman Gulley insert a break into the priestly role of Christ. They either have to assert Christ Jesus did not begin his priestly role until resurrection, or that the priestly role ceased to function during those 3 days his soul experienced annihilation. Neither option helps them out of their serious Christological heresy.

If one asserts that the high priestly role of Christ did not begin until resurrection, that then divorces Jesus from his atoning work on the cross for the sins of the world. As our

High Priest, Christ carried out the work of being our high priest through his death on the cross. So this option undermines the priestly work of Jesus for us in his death. He mediated for us our reconciliation while dying on the cross for our sins.

However, if one confesses that Jesus functioned as our great High Priest on the cross by taking our sins to himself there, but then during death his soul ceased to exist, the priesthood has been broken and does not exist forever. For three days the mediation role and work of Jesus ended. One could say to those in that view, if so the world had a Savior for a moment, then lost their Savior for 3 days, and somehow regained another new or different Savior later. This impacts the doctrine of Christ as well as the doctrine of salvation.

Though some debate exists among godly believers on when prior to the cross that Jesus began his high priestly role, no debate exists for true Bible believing conservatives that when Christ went to the cross he functioned as our High Priest Savior. Dr. Arnold Fruchtenbaum believes that Hebrews 9:14 and 12:24 places the High Priest role beginning at the time of the cross for Christ.[140] Dr. Lewis Sperry Chafer seems to suggest Jesus began his High Priest role when set apart at his baptism by John the Baptist.[141]

However, his disciple and student Dr. John Walvoord, and 2nd President of Dallas Seminary, believed "it is better . . . to hold that Christ's priesthood was eternal" and that he exercised that role "before his dying on the cross" because during his life interceded "for man and acted as a

---

[140] Arnold G. Fruchtenbaum, *Messiah Yeshua, Divine Deliverer: Christology from a Messianic Jewish Perspective* (San Antonio, TX: Ariel Press, 2015), 103.

[141] Lewis Sperry Chafer, *Systematic Theology* (Grand Rapids, MI: Kregel, 1993), 7:256.

Mediator."[142] Dr. Michael Horton also has taken the route that Walvoord did in this matter. He has taught that "Jesus' priesthood does not . . . begin at Golgotha, but from eternity to his incarnation, life, and death all the way to his present intercession in glory."[143]

These minor differences among conservatives on when Jesus began the official priestly ministry remain a valid inner family conversation. But that Jesus did exercise the High Priestly role by the time he died on the cross has unanimity among Bible believing conservatives.

Sadly, those like Chris Date and Norman Gulley and others who adopt physicalism have no holy options on how to handle the High Priestly role of Christ. All conservatives agree that once it begins it never ends. All conservatives also agree it had to exist by the time Christ went to the cross because on the cross he exercised the priestly office to make the sacrifice of himself.

But if one adopts the heresy of physicalism, then either Jesus was not functioning as the High Priest in his death (not a possibility), or he functioned as the High Priest and then upon death Jesus ceased to exist and the High Priestly role ended which consequently negated the promise of it being eternal (also not a possibility).

Speaking to this matter of Jesus functioning as a High Priest in his death, Dr. Fruchtenbaum stated:

> Yeshua fulfilled both functions of the priesthood. In the area of sacrifice, he was both the sacrifice and the sacrificer (Heb. 9:11-15, 24-28; 10:12-14; 1 Cor. 5:7). The sacrifice of the Messiah accomplished

---

[142] John Walvoord, *Jesus Christ our Lord* (Chicago, IL: Moody Press, 1969), 242.

[143] Michael Horton, *The Christian Faith: A Systematic Theology for Pilgrims on the Way* (Grand Rapids, MI: Zondervan, 2011), 490.

redemption (Rom. 3:24-25), propitiation (1 Jn 2:2), and reconciliation (Rom. 5:10; 2 Cor. 5:18-21). When Yeshua fulfilled the first function of a priest, it was with a once and for all sacrifice . . . .[144]

Chris Date, Norman Gulley, and all others who also embrace physicalism, commit a serious fundamental error in their Christology. They are in heresy and outside of the historic orthodox Church. The idea that Jesus did not serve as High Priest until after his resurrection denies him of his rightful role as the Priest over the sacrifice.

To affirm he was functioning as our High Priest on the cross, but then in death he experienced annihilation (soul ceasing to exist) means the High Priest role had an end and was not eternal. If such were true then Jesus did not have the qualification to be the High Priest per the biblical qualifications. And lastly, it would mean our High Priest did not exist in the world for 3 days.

Could there be any more radical discontinuity in the doctrine of salvation than a Savior who is, then is not, and then is newly created again and not the same Jesus as before? These physicalists make a mockery of the Lord Jesus and do so with the promotion of their demonic doctrine.

5. Wrong Definition of Death in Physicalism

The definition of death from the physicalist teachers violates the biblical definition. Because these demonic-filled teachers have embraced the wrong idea of what constitutes a person, it leads to the wrong view of death. They embrace a Greek philosophy of naturalism. In their view a person does not have any non-material living aspect beyond the physical

---

[144] Arnold G. Fruchtenbaum, *Messiah Yeshua, Divine Deliverer: Christology from a Messianic Jewish Perspective* (San Antonio, TX: Ariel Press, 2015), 103.

matter. Once physical matter ceases to live the person ceases to exist. Life ends when the physical substance ceases to function.

Defining Personhood by the Trinity & Christ

The Bible reveals to us that personhood does not require physical substance for life to exist. First, the doctrine of the Trinity is at play here. Father, Son, and Spirit all existed as Persons in eternity prior to any creation. They were Persons and without a physical body. Until the incarnation all 3 members of the Godhead lived as Persons without any physical body. This gives us a solid theological basis to begin with in how we define living persons. A person can exist and live without any physical matter. The Trinity itself sets forth this truth.

Defining Death by Christ Jesus' Death

Christ existed as a Person within the Trinity prior to adding human flesh to himself. When he added human flesh to himself his human soul united to his deity nature (one Person with two natures). In the hypostatic union the deity and humanity joined to become one inseparable Person.

However, remember that God the Father and God the Spirit cannot die because they do not have a physical body. Christ as the Son in eternity also could not die. The Trinity in eternity has no susceptibility to death. But in this situation, once creation happened and the fall of mankind into sin transpired, the holiness of God had been offended and justice called for death. No member of the Trinity could in their eternal state die.

Therefore, for man to be redeemed, it called for a perfect man to die as a way to appease the wrath of God. But no sinless man would ever exist now on earth once Adam fell into sin. All from his sin forward would be born in his image, a sinful image.

Consequently, in the eternal omnisapience of God a covenant of redemption was agreed upon where the Son agreed to be born of a virgin by the Holy Spirit and to add to himself human flesh, flesh that could die. Note it is the flesh aspect that could die (cease to function). The Bible specifically tells us that Jesus was put to death in the flesh. At least three times in Scripture we see the specific focus being on the flesh of Christ dying. We see this in 1 Peter 3:18, Acts 13:34, and 1 Corinthians 15:45.

Why is the Bible so specific to say it this way? The specificity relates to the truth that souls do not cease to function when the flesh dies. Jesus as the perfect man, born from a virgin, suffered the wrath of God on the cross. He died. But his death related to his flesh. Death for Jesus meant the following: (1) broken or altered fellowship with another (his Father);[145] (2) a cessation of existence in one realm by a removal from that realm to another realm (earth to Hades, or another realm);[146] and (3) a break in the relationship with the

---

[145] I make a distinction between fellowship and union. The Trinitarian union did not end. But the peaceful relational fellowship did and the union existed under the justice code. While dying on the cross, Jesus related to God the Father through justice so that believers who unite to him do not have to relate to God through justice. Conservatives need to be careful here when they say the death of Jesus meant being separated in the sense that the union between Christ and the Father ended. That could very well be a Trinitarian heresy. A more biblical way to describe the forsaken status of Jesus could be by asserting it in the sense of the peace relationship transitioned into a momentary justice relationship. The union never ended, although the type of fellowship they had prior to the cross momentarily shifted from one of peace (harmonious union) to one of justice (wrathful union).

[146] Godly conservatives debate the realm Jesus entered upon his death. Some say he left earth and entered into paradise and/or hades, the place of OT saints, and from there declared victory and upon resurrection took those saints with him back to the now intermediate heaven. Other godly conservatives believe Jesus left earth and went to heaven until the resurrection. In either case, the definition remains valid because a movement from one realm into another realm took place.

131

soul/spirit and body causing improper bodily function. We call this the broken, removed, and ruined view.

Applying the Definition of Christ Jesus' Death to Adam's Death

God warned Adam that if he disobeyed him and ate of the wrong tree in Eden that he would suffer death on that day he sinned.[147] Upon his sin the following happened to Adam. His sin (1) broke his peaceful fellowship with God; (2) he was removed to another realm (out of Eden; eventually even cut off from earth); and (3) his spirit/soul

---

[147] Chris Date tries to make a case that Adam did not die on that day. He has ignored a large portion of Hebrew translators who translate this as a death on the day he ate. He has to do this to support his heresy of physicalism. Death in physicalism cannot occur until the body ceases to function. Therefore, if Adam died spiritually on the day he sinned his position is in trouble. Thus, he has to work very hard to build the case Adam did not really die on the day he sinned. These Bible translations of the Hebrew support the idea Adam did die on the day he sinned: 1. on that day (NASB 2020 edition); 2. on the day that you eat from it, you shall most certainly die (Amplified Bible); 3. on the day you eat from it, you will die (Common English Bible); 4. because on the day that you eat from it (Complete Jewish Bible); 5. If you eat any fruit from that tree, you will die before the day is over (Contemporary English Version); 6. on that day you will certainly die (Easy to Read Version); 7. on the day that you eat from it (Evangelical Heritage Version); 8. you will die the same day (Good News Translation)9. on the day you eat from it (Holman Christian Standard); 10. on the day you eat from it (Christian Standard Bible); 11. will certainly die during the day that you eat from it (International Standard Version); 12. in the very day, as soon as (NET translation alternative note); 13. for on the day when you take of it (Bible in Basic English); 14. for even ye same daye thou eatest of it thou shalt surely dye (Tyndale Bible); 15. on the day (Hebrew Bible by Robert Alter); 16. The moment you eat from that tree, you're dead (The Message); 17. for on the day that thou shalt eat of it, thou shalt die (Wycliffe Bible); 18. the day you eat the fruit of this tree, you will certainly die (The Voice).

broke from the Lord causing bodily dysfunction, even final dysfunction when the flesh ceased to function.

The physicalism doctrine, however, misses these truths about death. They define death from a naturalism worldview and not a Judeo-Christian worldview. They begin with a wrong view of personhood. Then from that wrong beginning they also wrongly define what death means to a person.

6. Violating the Historic Confessions & the Early Church View of Jesus' Activity During His Death

The historic, Bible believing, orthodox church has always affirmed some basic fundamental truths. These essential truths define the Judeo-Christian religion from false religions, cults, and unorthodox movements. Who is Jesus Christ constitutes one of those fundamentals of the faith. Physicalist teachers, as taught by teachers like Norman Gulley and Chris Date and even others associated with the Rethinking Hell (and Christ) movement, have created a new Jesus that does not align with the historic view of Christ Jesus.

Great confessions of our heritage and the earliest teachers of our heritage affirmed that Jesus' soul did not cease to exist during his death. This heresy promoted by Date, Gulley, others at Rethinking Hell Ministries, and beyond violates a core truth on who is Jesus Christ.

Two Creeds on Jesus' Activity During Death: (1) Apostles Creed & (2) Athanasian Creed

> *Apostles' Creed*: ". . .our Lord, who was conceived by the Holy Spirit, born of the Virgin Mary, suffered under Pontius Pilate, was crucified, died and was buried; *he descended into hell*; on the third day he rose again from the dead . . . ."

133

Athanasian Creed: "He suffered for our salvation; *he descended to hell*; he arose from the dead; he ascended to heaven." It also says, Christ was "completely human, with a rational soul & human flesh." {Christ had a soul and body; we also have a soul and body}.

These Creeds highlight a view of the early church on the ministry and activity of Christ during his physical death. His human soul nature and deity nature continued on in activity while his flesh lay in the grave. Though debate exists on this topic, the apparent later addition of this to the Apostles Creed emerged because of the consensus this idea had among the early church leaders. A common consensus among the Christians existed that the human soul of Christ, in union with his deity, "went to the place" of the departed "souls" and this event happened in between his fleshly death and resurrection.[148]

Speaking of this matter, Dr. Floyd Barackman noted that the personhood of Jesus continued on as his human soul left the dead flesh. "Upon his death Jesus' personhood and immaterial human nature (soul and spirit) went directly to the paradise region of hades to await the time of his resurrection . . . . While there, Jesus made an announcement of undisclosed content to the imprisoned fallen angels who had sinned in the days of Noah (1 Peter 3:19-20; Gen. 6:1-13).[149]

---

[148] Francis Pieper, *Christian Dogmatics* (St. Louis, MO: Concordia Publishing House, 1951), 314-320.

[149] Floyd Barackman, *Practical Christian Theology: Examining the Great Doctrines of the Faith* (Grand Rapids, MI: Kregel, 1998), 172.

Numerous church fathers taught this concept in the earliest periods of Church history. I will highlight four of those teachers who taught Jesus' personhood continued on after his flesh died and rested in the grave. Physicalist teachers promote a wrong view of Christ. Their Jesus they worship ceased to live during those 3 days.

The two different Jesus persons between the Orthodox Bible believing Christianity Jesus and the physicalist Jesus stand as different as night and day. The Jesus of the Bible laid his flesh to the side during the 3 days of fleshly death, yet he being in the image of God (as we are) his human soul continued on in existence (as ours will too) during death and even while under the wrath of God.[150]

> *Ignatius (35-107 AD):* Christ descended, indeed, *into Hades alone*, but he arose accompanied by a multitude. . . .

> *Irenaeus (130-200 AD):* It was for this reason, too, that *the Lord descended into the regions beneath the earth, preaching his advent there also.* And he declared the remission of sins received by those who believe in him.

> *Hippolytus (170-236 AD):* The jailers of Hades trembled when they saw him. And the gates of brass

---

[150] This highlights the inconsistency of non-physicalist annihilation teachers. If Jesus as our substitute endured the wrath of God and continued on in his personhood this means that when sinners experience the wrath of God in hell their personhood will continue on as well. The physicalist teachers have a more consistent form of annihilation doctrine. But in their consistency they consistently depart from Christianity and into heresy by embracing a false Christ Jesus. They worship another Jesus.

and the bolts of iron were broken. For, look! The Only-Begotten, God the word, *had entered Hades with a soul*—a soul among souls.

Alexander of Alexandria (d. 328 AD): Meanwhile, Hades was resplendent with light. *For the Star had descended to there.* Actually, the Lord *did not descend into Hades in his body, but in his sprit.*[151]

These teachers represent this idea from the first four centuries of our orthodox heritage. The idea that Jesus continued on in some form of life and activity while his flesh rested in the grave for 3 days has been the standard view of Bible believing Christians since the earliest disciples. Physicalist teachers such as Date and Gulley and others in this stream of thought have departed from the Bible and the great orthodox heritage of biblical Christianity.

7. A Newly Created Jesus at Resurrection Different from the Virgin Born Jesus of Mary

The Jesus the physicalist worships has been created (or recreated) at his resurrection. The Jesus who lived, died for our sins, and took our sins upon himself to then carry those sins away into the grave has, according to the physicalist teacher, disappeared and been eradicated (annihilated). This idea truly constitutes a false Jesus. In the physicalist view, Jesus has to now be created since he experienced annihilation. This poses many theological problems.

First, this new Jesus does not come forth from the virgin Mary. How can he be the Jesus prophesied of in the

---

[151] David W. Bercot, "Descent into Hades," *A Dictionary of Early Christian Beliefs* (Peabody, MA: Hendrickson Publishers, 1998), 206-207. All four quotes are from this source.

OT? How can he be truly human as we are if newly created from nothing? If the first Jesus came forth from Mary by the virgin birth, but then ceased to exist through eradication, where does this second new Jesus come from?

The physicalist has no biblical answer. The continuity of identity is lost between the first Jesus and the second Jesus because the first Jesus experiences eradication through annihilation. They have no answer and as is they worship a false Jesus. The new Jesus comes forth with no continuity to the virgin born Jesus where the humanity was added through the incarnation that brought about the hypostatic union.

Second, how can the newly created second Jesus of the physicalist be the Savior who took our sins to himself? The human soul of Jesus experienced the wrath of God during the cross. But this newly created soul of Jesus cannot be the same soul that experienced the wrath of God. How can this new Jesus of the physicalist be our substitute and worthy of our worship? This new Jesus in the physicalist religion does not have continuity with the Jesus that experienced the wrath of God for our sins on the cross. These are two different beings, the virgin born Jesus who took our sins to himself on the cross and some new Jesus that replaces the first Jesus that suffered eradication.

Third, the great transaction on the cross means that our sins were laid on Christ Jesus so that his righteousness could be placed on us. Well if this old Jesus was eradicated do we receive his righteousness upon the moment of faith in him? Or do we receive some righteousness of the new Jesus when we place faith in him? Or do we need to place faith in both of these beings, the Jesus who died on the cross and experienced eradication as well as the new Jesus who God created after the eradication of the first Jesus?

Fourth, how can the second newly created Jesus confer and impute his righteousness to us when his life began only at resurrection? This newly created Jesus in the physicalist religion did not obey the Law of God perfectly because this new Jesus did not actually live under the law of God for us. He is a new being created at resurrection without continuity to the life of the Jesus who lived under the Law of God.

These problems highlight the astronomical problem, the abomination, the pagan and demonic root to this ungodly physicalist religion. The gospel itself has been altered by this physicalist religion. To assert the personhood of Jesus ceases to exist because God has annihilated the person of Jesus in death establishes a new religion. Two distinct, separate, and different Jesus figures exist in the physicalist worldview.

Life After Death? An Important Question In One's Worldview

Every person has some type of worldview, a lens so to speak in how the world is viewed.[152] Furthermore, it may be safely accepted that most every person alive, at least those with rational capabilities, realizes that at some point this life ends. As the philosopher Vincent Barry has stated: "Any person who is conscious of death has wondered: will I continue to live after I die? This question has occupied humankind from the earliest times and perhaps penetrates the issue of self more deeply than any other."[153]

Certainly this question and its answer have major ramifications as to how one chooses to live his or her life. It was certainly for this reason that the writer of Ecclesiastes said: "It is better to spend your time at funerals than at

---

[152] James W. Sire, *The Universe Next Door: A Basic Worldview Catalog*, 4th ed. (Downers Grove, IL: InterVarsity Press, 2004), 17.

[153] Vincent Barry, *Looking at Ourselves: An Introduction to Philosophy* (Belmont, CA: Wadsworth Publishing Inc., 1977), 233-234.

festivals. For you are going to die, and you should think about it while there is still time . . . . A wise person thinks much about death, while the fool thinks only about having a good time now" (7:2,4 NLT). When one ponders death the application of that thought reflects in how one chooses to live today.

For example, Bertrand Russell (1872-1970) who was a "British philosopher, mathematician, Nobel Prize-winner (Literature 1950), civil-rights activist, and public figure"[154] articulated in many respects exactly why he did not embrace the Christian faith. In his work, *Why I am Not a Christian*, he expressed a denial of God and immortality.[155]

This denial led him towards a naturalist philosophy that placed much more weight in science and reason divorced from any supernatural elements. For the most part, much of the supernatural ideas, such as life after death, according to Russell were factors in religion designed to make men fear and consequently to embrace some sort of supernaturalism as found within the faith of Christianity. As Russell says of religion, "Fear is the basis of the whole thing—fear of the mysterious, fear of defeat, fear of death."[156]

This ideology for Russell followed suit with his philosophy of the constitution of man. When one ponders the idea of death normally two questions come to the table. First people usually ponder the possibility of a God, a being that is immortal and beyond the physical world. Yet inherent in that consideration is the actual subject of the physical world.

---

[154] Mark Sainsbury, *Bertrand Russell*, ed. Ted Honderich (Oxford, NY: Oxford University Press, 1995), 781.

[155] Bertrand Russell, *Why I Am Not a Christian and Other Essays on Religion and Related Subjects,* ed. Paul Edwards (New York, NY: Simon and Schuster, 1957), 4-11.

[156] Ibid, 22.

Philosophers have to wrestle with what exactly constitutes the nature of man. Is man only physical, molecular in nature? Is man nothing more than a succession of experiences that become engrained in the brain that form habits and patterns and recalled only by the course of memory?

Or is man composed of some type of mind that is distinct from the body yet intricately connected to it, a soul or spirit that transcends the molecular nature of the body? Russell adopted the materialist view. According to Russell, all "that constitutes a person is a series of experiences connected by memory and by certain similarities of the sort we call habit."[157] If that were not enough to verify Russell as a naturalist philosopher then his even more pointed criticism of any supernatural ideology can be verified by this blunt and serious challenge to the idea of any life beyond the dissolution of the brain, the central component of life for the naturalist Russell. He stated:

> We all know that memory may be obliterated by an injury to the brain, that a virtuous person may be rendered vicious by encephalitis lethargica, and that a clever child can be turned into an idiot by lack of iodine. In view of such familiar facts, it seems scarcely probable that the mind survives the total destruction of the brain structure which occurs at death. It is not rational arguments but emotions that cause belief in a future life. The most important of these emotions is fear of death, which is instinctive and biologically useful. If we genuinely and wholeheartedly believed in the future life, we should cease completely to fear death. The effects would be curious, and probably such as most of us would deplore. But our human and subhuman ancestors

---

[157] Ibid, 89.

have fought and exterminated their enemies throughout many geological ages and have profited by courage; it is therefore an advantage to the victors in the struggle for life to be able, on occasion, to overcome the natural fear of death.[158]

Such reasoning above from Russell aligns with the official religion known as secular humanism. The Humanist Manifesto, an anti-supernaturalist religious document, agrees with Russell that life develops through a "continuous process."[159] It also subscribes to the idea that life is organic, that is the "traditional dualism of mind and body" that allows for some type of soul or spirit that transcends the molecular structures must be "rejected."

Furthermore, the worldview of humanism, the frame of reference for Russell, advocates the "here and now" fulfillment of the person's personality because that defines the essence and end of life for the person.

In essence the worldview for Russell rejects any supernatural element. It defines the essence of life as the self-fulfillment of living that extends from continual processes that form habits and emotions, yet none of that rises to the level of a mind/body distinction where the mind or spirit ever has any meaning, existence, or survival beyond the life of the molecular cells in the brain.

In short, for the naturalist philosopher like Russell, the end of physical brain activity means the complete cessation of life. As he proposed, "the brain, as a structure, is dissolved at death, and memory therefore may be expected

---

[158] Ibid, 90-91.

[159] Paul Kurtz, *Humanist Manifesto I & II*, ed. Paul Kurtz (Amherst, NY: Prometheus Books, 1973), 8-9.

to also be dissolved." [160] Russell's worldview of death flowed from his previous worldview of what constitutes life. Russell defined death as the cessation of being instead of as a transition from one domain to another, as in a Judeo-Christian worldview. To properly understand death one must first properly understand life.

Alan Lacey has proposed two significant questions when evaluating death philosophically. The two main questions are: (1) "What is it," and (2) "Why does it matter?"[161] Russell has presented the case against survival after the moment of death occurs. In the naturalist philosophical worldview death of the physical means complete cessation of life. Nothing exists beyond the physical activity of the brain. Such a naturalist philosophy has been termed materialism.

Materialism is the view "that there is nothing in the world except matter."[162] If this worldview is correct, then logically it follows that any idea of life after death is fictitious and fraudulent for any serious rational being to embrace. In the materialist worldview death is the cessation of life. Therefore, what does it mean to the materialist? Though this worldview may manifest itself in a variety of avenues, much like symptoms do of a disease, it basically means that the subscriber of this philosophy had better make the best of this life because at the end of it no hope, reality, or domain exists for continued development, happiness, or purpose.

---

[160] Bertrand Russell, *Why I Am Not a Christian and Other Essays on Religion and Related Subjects,* ed. Paul Edwards (New York, NY: Simon and Schuster, 1957), 89.

[161] Alan Lacey, *"Death,"* in *The Oxford Companion to Philosophy*, ed. Ted Honderich (Oxford, NY: Oxford University Press, 1995), 177.

[162] Harold H. Titus, *Living Issues in Philosophy* (USA: American Book Company, 1959), 208.

Death within the naturalist worldview such as with Russell stems from the previous ideology that life is nothing more than molecular processes that flow from one moment to another, just like a river.[163] In Russell's own words, "I believe that when I die I shall rot, and nothing of my ego will survive."[164] Such a view of death as that logically flowed from Russell's prior understanding of what constituted life. For him a man's life was "a part of nature."[165]

A Christian Worldview Response to Death

Elisabeth Kubler-Ross made a profound statement once in her famous book concerning death. She stated: "Facing death means facing the ultimate question of the meaning of life. If we really want to live we must have the courage to recognize that life is ultimately very short, and that everything we do counts. When it is the evening of our life we will hopefully have a chance to look back and say: 'It was worthwhile because I have really lived.'"[166]

Yet in this technologically advanced age the norm is for people to avoid contemplation of death. Maybe it is because when a person thinks about death he or she has to come to terms with the most serious questions about life. Sometimes humans will laugh at death to cover the fear of it, or sometimes people will ignore the concept as if this can delay the inevitable. Nonetheless, death happens for every

---

[163] Bertrand Russell, *Why I Am Not a Christian and Other Essays on Religion and Related Subjects,* ed. Paul Edwards (New York, NY: Simon and Schuster, 1957), 89.

[164] Ibid, 54.

[165] Ibid, 48.

[166] Elisabeth Kubler Ross, *Death: The Final Stage of Growth* (Englewood Cliffs, NJ: Prentice-Hall, Inc., 1975), 126.

person alive at some divine moment. Billy Graham has correctly noted of the avoidance factor,

> Advertisers do all they can to help us deny the ultimate fact of life. Billions of dollars are spent on a cosmetic industry that promises creams and lotions will slow the aging process and make us look younger. Joggers line the roads, often before dawn, and workouts at health clubs have become popular ways to keep the body in shape to prolong life. Fiber is an increasingly prevalent part of some people's diets as physicians tell us of its ability to reduce the risk of cancer. Many people are giving up smoking to reduce the possibility of heart and lung disease. But the irreversible fact is that no matter what diet, no matter how much you exercise, no matter how many vitamins or health foods you eat, no matter how low your cholesterol, you will die—someday, some way. You may add a year, or even a few years to a life that could be shorter had you not been concerned about your health, but in the end death will conquer you as it has every person who has ever lived.[167]

The idea of death produces all kinds of various thoughts among humans. Largely one can tell what is the philosophy of a person by how he or she views death. For example, "to the materialistic thinker, death means complete annihilation. For the Hindu and the Buddhist, death means reincarnation. To the terrorist, death provides a way to be rewarded for his cause. Many Shiite Moslems believe that for every infidel they kill (especially Christians and Jews),

---

[167] Billy Graham, *Facing Death and the Life After* (Minneapolis, MN: Grason Publications, 1987), 10-11.

they will have incomparable sexual pleasures in paradise."[168] So how does the Christian view death?

First, the Christian contemplates death with a serious and solemn concern. Believers realize that "it is destined that each person dies only once and after that comes judgment" (Heb. 9:27). As often stated, "the examined life is better"[169] because the unexamined life is not worth living. The idea of death, as presented in the Christian set of Scriptures, motivates the believer to see the end as a means to live holy today in the immediate present (Eccl 7:2,4). The end empowers the believer today to make every moment count for eternity.

Second, a proper view of death helps the believer to understand his or her own mortality and the present need to depend upon God for every moment of life. It is Jesus Christ who sustains every moment of the believer's life. As Scripture says it is Christ who "sustains the universe by the mighty power of his command" (Hebrews 1:3b). The very breath people breathe comes from the providential hand of God. He owns us and he alone gives us life or takes life away. These are in essence the views that a believer has because of his or her allegiance to Scripture as a solid epistemological base for determining reality.

Truth #2: Christ Will Physically Return in the Future to Consummate History

Though some may not associate the future return of Christ to the gospel itself, it seems rather clear that the writers of Scripture saw the second advent of Christ through a redemptive lens. When each person dies he or she

---

[168] Ibid, 41.

[169] James Sire, *The Universe Next Door: A Basic Worldview Catalog* (Downers Grove, IL: IVP Press), 2004.

experiences either the grace of Christ or the justice of Christ. The elect experience glorification personally and begin their new eternal journey in that new estate of grace.

On a more global scale, beyond personal eschatology, the finality in the full advent of Christ ushers in a new era of God's perfect Kingdom rule over a regenerated universe. Apostle John taught us this in Revelation chapters 19-22. The results of that return usher in the consummation of the ages where history merges into eternity. A cosmological regeneration occurs in that era when Christ removes the curses placed upon this universe. Apostle Paul had this to say in Romans 8:18-25 about Christ's future physical return bringing redemption to the universe:

> For I consider that our present sufferings cannot even be compared to the coming glory that will be revealed to us. For the creation eagerly waits for the revelation of the sons of God. For the creation was subjected to futility—not willingly but because of God who subjected it—in hope that the creation itself will also be set free from the bondage of decay into the glorious freedom of God's children. For we know that the whole creation groans and suffers together until now. Not only this, but we ourselves also, who have the firstfruits of the Spirit, groan inwardly as we eagerly await our adoption, the redemption of our bodies. For in hope we were saved. Now hope that is seen is not hope, because who hopes for what he sees? But if we hope for what we do not see, we eagerly wait for it with endurance (NET).

This coming of Christ to reverse the curse upon the world has implications for a person's view of the gospel of redemption. The doctrine of salvation is, as Dr. Lewis Sperry Chafer rightly said, revealed in three phases. There is the completed action of salvation (past tense), there is the current work of salvation where grace reigns over the power of sin (present tense),[170] and then there is to come the full revelation of Christ where in the day of Christ the good work of grace Christ initiated will come to fruition (future tense).[171]

As the Protestant Reformer Dr. Martin Luther noted, this text highlights the universal work of grace where Christ brings in a New Heaven and New Earth (see 2 Peter 3:13 & Isaiah 65:17).[172] As Dr. Woodrow Kroll says,

> . . . one day God will remove the curse and save the earth from its pain when he establishes his millennial Kingdom here on earth (Rev. 20-21). The Millennium is when the wolf will dwell with the lamb and the little child will put his hand into the snake's nest and not be hurt (Is. 11:6-9). And as

---

[170] Dr. Chafer would be in the category we call moderate free grace (to use Norman Geisler's terms) or what Mal Couch & I termed the "redemptive grace" view. Some teachers in extreme lordship models seem to suggest that anyone who believes must surrender every sin and every area of one's life to Christ in order to be saved. That violates the gospel. On the other hand, some ultra or hyper free grace teachers believe that for one to be redeemed no repentance of sin needs to occur. Some even go so far to say all one needs to do is just believe the facts about the gospel. These in this camp sometimes also say one can be born again and never have any fruit. As with so many issues, the truth is in between these extreme positions. Dr. Chafer believed some fruit would occur in a believer's life. In his words, the Holy Spirit makes it natural or normal for fruit to occur if one is a believer. Fruit naturally occurs in a believer's life because of the work of the Spirit. But he did not think at conversion all sins had to be forsaken either. He held a balanced view.

[171] Lewis Sperry Chafer, *Major Bible Themes* (Findlay, OH: Dunham Publishing, 1926), 155.

[172] Martin Luther, *Commentary on Romans*, translated by J. Theodore Mueller (Grand Rapids, MI: Kregel Publications, 1954), 125.

glorious as that messianic age will be, it will be only a prelude to eternity when "creation itself also will be set free from its slavery to corruption into the freedom of the glory of the children of God" (Rom. 8:21). That's when "there shall no longer be any curse; and the throne of God and of the Lamb shall be in it [the whole earth]" (Rev. 22:3).[173]

This universal advent of Christ where he ushers in the Christocracy that culminates in the New Heavens and New Earth stands as a central, non-negotiable, fundamental doctrine for an overall biblical orthodoxy.

However, a minority of theologians today have embraced a corrupt view of Christ's return. This novel theory promotes the idea that the LORD Jesus Christ has *already* returned in the form of the Holy Spirit. Technically this damnable doctrine has been called "Preterism." Though there are some less radical forms of preterism, sometimes called mild and moderate forms, the full or consistent preterist view teaches that "all Bible prophecy was fulfilled in the destruction of Jerusalem in A.D. 70. The second coming occurred in A.D. 70."[174]

As J. Stuart Russell directly stated, no other sense "than the obvious and unambiguous one" can be gleaned from Scripture other than the one "that our Lord's second coming would take place within the limits of the existing generation"[175] of the apostles and first disciples. A modern

---

[173] Woodrow Kroll, *The Book of Romans: Righteousness in Christ in the Twenty-First Century Biblical Commentary Series*, gen. ed. Mal Couch and Ed Hindson (Chattanooga, TN: AMG Publishers, 2002), 136-137.

[174] Thomas Ice, *"Preterism,"* in *The Popular Encyclopedia of Bible Prophecy*, gen. eds. Tim LaHaye and Ed Hindson (Eugene, OR: Harvest House Publishers, 2004), 285.

[175] J. Stuart Russell, *The Parousia: The New Testament Doctrine of our Lord's Second Coming* (Grand Rapids, MI: Baker Books, 1999), 540.

day heretic who promotes this demonic idea is Gary Demar.[176]

Apparently some of these teachers, like my friend Kenneth Gentry (a partial preterist), have proposed the idea that we are actually right now living in some form of the New Heavens and New Earth.[177] Though his language is somewhat vague and open to an expansive range of time for precise fulfillment, he does seem to suggest that the New Creation that we read about in Revelation 21-22 has already arrived in history by the first century.

What makes his language confusing is that he apparently suggests that the "new creation/New Jerusalem imagery" actually "begins in the first century"[178] while it extends progressively throughout the globe until the full or final consummation. In his own words he says, "The new creation begins flowing into history before the final consummation (which will establish a wholly new physical order, 2 Peter 3:10-13)."[179]

That seems clear enough. However, when we read further we find him also saying that Revelation 21-22 applies to the current salvation experience of the body of Christ. Those chapters, especially 21, speak of a New Heaven and New Earth that has replaced the prior versions. What does Gentry do with these two chapters of Scripture? He says,

---

[176] See the appendix where a team of us confronted Gary Demar on his recent apostasy from the faith. Demar can no longer be seen as a brother in the Christian faith.

[177] J. Stuart Russell, *The Parousia: The New Testament Doctrine of our Lord's Second Coming* (Grand Rapids, MI: Baker Books, 1999), 288.

[178] Kenneth Gentry, "*A Preterist View of Revelation*," in *Four Views on the Book of Revelation*, eds. C. Marvin Pate and Stanley N. Gundry (Grand Rapids, MI: Zondervan, 1998), 87.

[179] Ibid, 88.

"the preterist believes that John is expressing, by means of elevated poetic imagery, the glory of salvation."[180] Gentry, therefore, seems to embrace what has been called partial preterism (mild or moderate preterism).[181] That view would still allow for a future visible return of Christ to this earth. For that I am thankful as he remains within basic orthodoxy by not denying the future return of Christ.

Yet if he consistently applied his language to current reality he would have to embrace the idea that Christ has already returned (spoken of in Revelation 19) and that chapters 20 through 22 speak of Christ presently ruling in the New Heavens and New Earth within which we all currently participate. *This is exactly what the more consistent versions of preterism do teach.*

Full preterists, who do seem to be more consistent in the articulation of their inaccurate theology, assert that Christ indeed has already returned and there will be no other future return of Christ. As Michael Fenemore, a full preterist, has stated,

> Since Rev. 1:7 clearly refers to the destruction of the Jews in A.D. 70, the book of Revelation must have been written no later than the late sixties. Furthermore, since this one verse from Revelation was fulfilled in A.D. 70, then *all* of Revelation must have been fulfilled by that time. And since all of Revelation has been fulfilled, then *all eschatological events* including the second coming, resurrection of the dead, rapture and judgment must have come to complete fulfillment as well.[182]

---

[180] Ibid, 89.

[181] http://www.theopedia.com/Preterism

[182] http://www.preterism.info/every-eye.htm

These modern views were largely promoted in an earlier pastor-theologian's writings by the name of J. Stuart Russell (1816-1895). Dr. Russell wrote a book in 1878 titled *The Parousia*. In that work he advocated for the idea of a first century fulfillment to the prophetic portions of Scripture regarding Christ's second coming.

But such views as this do not embrace the full witness of Scripture adequately. As the theologians Hays, Duvall, and Pate express, "The great weakness of the preterist view is its failure to deal adequately with predictive prophecy. Revelation is self-described as a 'prophecy' (Rev. 1:3; 22:7, 10, 10, 18, 19), and most interpreters view at least some of these proclamations as awaiting future fulfillment. All forms of the preterist view have been unsuccessful in locating historical referents for the return of Christ, the last judgment, and the new heaven and new earth in the first century."[183]

Christ's Return Will Be (1) Physical, (2) Visible, & (3) Climactically Miraculous

A Physical Return of Christ

First, the Bible teaches that when Christ Jesus does return that his return will be in physical form. The full preterist view that espouses the idea of a Christ that has already returned does so through a revision of "how" Christ Jesus is to return. Instead of Christ Jesus returning in a physical body they alter or revise the meaning of the second advent texts from a physical coming to a mystical, or spiritual, or non-physical coming. The coming of Christ in A.D. 70 (or whatever date they so choose, as it varies) by a

---

[183] J. Daniel Hays, J. Scott Duvall, and C. Marvin Pate, "*Preterist View of Revelation*," in *Dictionary of Biblical Prophecy and End Times* (Grand Rapids, MI: Zondervan, 2007), 348.

full preterist cannot be the LORD Jesus returning back to this physical earth in his physical body.

Numerous alternative explanations abound, but the one solitary option not allowed is that Christ will return in a physical body to this earth. Scripture, however, could not be any clearer than it is in saying our LORD will return in a physical body.

- Zechariah 14:2-4, & 9 says: "Then the LORD will go out and fight against those nations as when he fights on a day of battle. On that day his feet shall stand on the Mount of Olives that lies before Jerusalem on the east, and the Mount of Olives shall move northward, and the other half southward. . . . And the LORD will be King over all the earth. On that day the LORD will be one and his name one" (ESV).

- Matthew 24:29-31 & 25:31-32 says: "Immediately after the tribulation of those days the sun will be darkened, and the moon will not give its light, and the stars will fall from heaven, and the powers of the heavens will be shaken. Then will appear in heaven the sign of the Son of Man, and then all the tribes of the earth will mourn, and they will see the Son of Man coming on the clouds of heaven with power and great glory. And he will send out his angels with a loud trumpet call, and they will gather his elect from the four winds, from one end of heaven to the other. . . . When the Son of Man comes in his glory, and all the angels with him, then he will sit on his glorious throne. Before him will be gathered all the nations, and he will separate people one from another as a shepherd separates the sheep from the goats" (ESV).

It is interesting to also note that when we read Zechariah 14 further we see how it correlates to these Matthew 24 and 25 texts. Christ will actually be the King over the earth and people will travel to come to his presence to worship him while he is physically ruling over the earth. Zechariah 14 speaks of the terrible judgments over the earth and that "everyone who survives of all the nations that have come against Jerusalem shall go up year after year to worship the King . . . . and if any of the families of the earth does not go up and present themselves, then on them there shall be no rain; there shall be the plague with which the LORD afflicts the nations that do not go up to keep the Feast of Booths" (ESV).

These texts make it very clear that when Christ returns he will be on this earth in physical, bodily form. Christ will be here, ruling, and he will personally as King direct judgment and affliction upon "any dissentients who shall dare to refuse . . . to worship before him."[184] With Christ ruling here on this earth visibly and personally, the world will know it is the time has arrived where "God is directly governing the world." [185]

Furthermore, Zechariah specifically tells us where the Lord will be at his return. In 14:3-4 the Bible says, "Then the LORD will go to battle and fight against those nations, just as he fought battle in ancient days. On that day his feet will stand on the Mount of Olives . . . and the Mount of Olives will be split in half from east to west, leaving a great valley" (NET).

Dr. Stephen Miller rightly rebukes the preterists here in their futile attempt to revise these predictive promises. He stated, "all attempts to identify this invasion of Jerusalem

---

[184] H.A. Ironside, *Minor Prophets* (Neptune, NJ: Loizeaux Brothers, 1909), 430.

[185] Ibid.

with that of Nebuchadnezzar in 586 B.C. or the Roman General Titus in A.D. 70 are fruitless. No other war has been halted by the personal return of the Lord, and the Mount of Olives is still intact."[186]

Even interpreters not inclined to take a very plain or literal reading of prophecy realize this text gives us a very specific promise as to where the Lord will be located upon his literal, tangible, and physical return to this earth.

Joyce Baldwin of Trinity College noted that Zechariah 14:4 relates to Acts 1:11. "The ascension of Jesus on the Mount of Olives, and in particular the promise of the angel concerning his return (Acts 1:11), draw attention to the significance of this prophecy and suggest a literal fulfillment."[187] Preterism fails the test here and ignores the clear assertions of the text.

Redemption Includes the Physical Realms

For some reason, the physical or earthly aspects of Christ's return to rule and reign troubles some Bible interpreters. It should not cause any Bible believer trouble though. We are not Gnostics in the Judeo-Christian worldview. Too often the error related to preterism and other weak interpretations relates to some underlying presupposition that the earthly physical world here lacks spirit value. In other words, heavenly is non-physical and

---

[186] Stephen Miller, *Holman Old Testament Commentary: Nahum, Habakkuk, Zephaniah, Haggai, Zechariah, Malachi*, ed. Max Anders (Nashville, TN: B&H Publishing, 2004), 294.

[187] Joyce G. Baldwin, *Tyndale Old Testament Commentaries: Haggai, Zechariah, Malachi* (Downers Grove, IL: Inter-Varsity Press, 1972), 201.

more spiritual than the earthly physical realm. Dr. Randy Alcorn calls this the curse of Christoplatonism.[188]

Defining Christoplatonism: A Mixture of Greek Philosophy & Christian Theology

The idea that spiritual means nonmaterial has a long history running back to Greek philosophy. The Greek philosopher Plato thought the soul was good and the material realm was bad. "For Plato, salvation is salvation *from* the body."[189] This ideology spread into the Hebraic circles. It led to one Jew by the name of Philo (20 B.C. to around 54 A.D.) using Platonic ideology in how to interpret Scripture. He sought to find the hidden or spiritual meaning to texts. Philo thought the spiritual or more mature reading of the text went beyond the plain meaning of the words. The literal meaning of the biblical words were the "more immature level of understanding, corresponding to the body, whereas the allegorical meaning is for the mature, corresponding to the soul."[190]

This ideology continued to grow. A student of Philo's ideology, Clement of Alexandria (155-216), developed the methodology of Philo further in the post-apostolic era. "Clement taught that all Scripture speaks in a mysterious language of symbols."[191] Allegory led the way in his model of biblical interpretation, so much so these ideas

---

[188] Randy Alcorn, *Heaven* (Wheaton, IL: Tyndale House Publishing, 2004), 461.

[189] Norman L. Geisler, *A History of Western Philosophy: Volume 1 Ancient and Medieval* (Matthews, NC: Bastion Books, 2016), 64.

[190] Roy Zuck, *Basic Bible Interpretation* (Colorado Springs, CO: Chariot Victor Publishing, 1991), 32.

[191] Ibid., 35.

formed what has been known as the Alexandrian School of thought. For Clement, Bible texts may have numerous meanings: "(a) historical (the stories of the Bible), (b) doctrinal, with moral and theological teachings, (c) prophetic, which includes types and prophecies, (d) philosophical (allegories in historical persons such as Sarah representing true wisdom and Hagar representing pagan philosophy), and (e) mystical (moral and spiritual truths)."[192]

As this model spread deeper into church history, the idea that a spiritual view equals nonmaterial ideas gained traction. "Alexandria became the home of a new school of theological thought. Clement of Alexandria . . . was part of this movement, as was Origen (185-254)."[193] This school of thought developed an entire system in how to interpret scripture that moved away from the historical-grammatical hermeneutic. Through the Alexandrian school of thought and the teaching of Origen the Bible became a "three-part living organism, corresponding to body, soul, and spirit. The body was the literal or historical sense, the soul was the psychic or moral sense, and the spirit was—by far most important—the philosophical sense."[194]

In this new hermeneutic model, physical ideas or truths from Scripture were seen as less spiritual. The more holy meaning required interpreters to find some other meaning behind the physical meanings. But this poses serious problems for a Judeo-Christian worldview. God created the material and declared it good. Christ Jesus is the God-Man, with flesh. We affirm a physical resurrection and a physical New Earth to come.

---

[192] Ibid., 36.

[193] Randy Alcorn, *Heaven* (Wheaton, IL: Tyndale House Publishing, 2004), 461.

[194] Ibid.

The physical comprises key fundamental truths of historic Christianity. To deny these truths places one in heresy. As Dr. Geisler stated, "to Christians salvation is with (in) a body. It is called resurrection. In Genesis God made man from dust (Gen. 2:7), and he will return to dust and later is to be resurrected from dust (John 5:28-29)."[195]

However, when Christoplatonism presuppositions exist within the mind of an interpreter, the physical realities of Scripture often come under scrutiny and suffer from an effort to minimize those ideas for some other more spiritual and less earthly ideology. Dr. Randy Alcorn highlights the negatives of this model when examining the prophetic truth of heaven.

> Judged by Christoplatonic presuppositions, anytime the Bible speaks about Heaven in plain, ordinary, or straightforward ways, the assumption is that doesn't actually mean what it says. For example, the plain meaning of living as resurrected beings in a resurrected society in a resurrected city on a resurrected Earth cannot be real, because it doesn't jibe with Platonic assumption that the body is bad and the spirit good. Consequently, Heaven cannot possibly be like what Revelation 21-22 appears to say. There could not be bodies, nations, kings, buildings, streets, gates, water, trees, and fruit, because these are physical and what's physical is not spiritual. The prophetic statements about life on a perfect Earth are considered mere symbols of the promise of disembodied spiritual world.[196]

---

[195] Norman L. Geisler, *A History of Western Philosophy: Volume 1 Ancient and Medieval* (Matthews, NC: Bastion Books, 2016), 64.

[196] Randy Alcorn, *Heaven* (Wheaton, IL: Tyndale House Publishing, 2004), 461.

The Dangers of Christoplatonism with the Promises of Israel's
Land and New Earth to Come

The Bible presents a coming rule of Christ. All Bible
believing Christians affirm a future, literal, physical, second
coming of Christ to rule. For some this begins in the 1,000
year millennium. For others, this begins in the New Earth.
All affirm at least the coming rule on the New Earth with a
New Heaven. To reject that places one outside of historic
orthodox Christianity.

Consequently, for Christ to rule on Earth means he
will rule on and over a physical land. Throughout the Bible
dominion or rule over land exists as a central theme to the
promised kingdom of God. Dr. Alcorn noted that God "gave
management of the earth to Adam and Eve" and then later
"God made his covenant with Abraham" and committed
again through promise the right to have "land (Genesis
12:1,7). Though the whole Earth was under the Curse, God
granted Abraham a piece of land that could be lived on,
ruled, and managed in a way that would bring glory to God
and blessing to all other lands and nations."[197]

In the New Earth, the whole earth will be under the
immediate rule of Christ and his people. The "Earth belongs
to God and his people (not the unrighteous who sometimes
rule it now)" and when believers rise in the resurrection they
will "rule Christ's Kingdom on Earth (Daniel 12:2-3)."[198]

The idea of God giving an earthly, physical, tangible
inheritance to his believers constitutes a spiritual meaning. It
does not need some other allegorical interpretation. The
physical earth is good, spiritual, and holy as it was created

---

[197] Ibid., 203.

[198] Ibid.

by God and will be home to where Christ rules in the future with his redeemed people who live and dwell here in physical resurrected bodies. The Bible does not denigrate the physical world.

This issue connects not only to how we see the New Earth to come, but also to Israel's land promises. Some dismiss these promises through the idea that some other meaning exists beyond the plain promises that God will give his believing ethnic Jews the land promised to them. This for some is too earthly, carnal, and not the real meaning. But if we applied that concept to the New Earth we would cut off a key essential of biblical orthodoxy. Why should we apply that to the promises made to Israel for the land God specifically promised to them with exact boundaries given to them for it?

The Reformed Covenant theologian Dr. Walter Kaiser rightly challenges his own heritage on this matter. He reminds us of the holistic focus of the Lord in his redemptive work. God is not just saving souls and working with the non-physical realms in his kingdom redemptive rule. The Lord is redeeming the whole universe and bringing it under his rule. Dr. Kaiser offers a corrective word here to those who try and "spiritualize" the Bible by removing from it the earthly physical elements included within the redemptive scope. Some interpreters forget or ignore that the Lord's "kingdom has both spiritual and material aspects."[199]

> While many Christians find it difficult to see how God's work of salvation should have any attachments to geography, the fact remains that God himself linked the two from the very beginning with

---

[199] Walter C. Kaiser Jr. "Kingdom Promises as Spiritual and National," in *Continuity and Discontinuity: Perspectives on the Relationship Between the Old and New Testaments*, ed. John S. Feinberg (Wheaton, IL: Crossway Books, 1988), 303.

the call of Abraham in Genesis 12. This is simply another way of affirming that God's activities do not take place in an abstract vacuum but in the midst of the concrete space and time of human history. The events of our salvation have strong attachments to Canaan, Bethlehem, Jerusalem, Nazareth, the Mount of Olives, and Golgotha.[200]

The return of the Lord does not happen in a symbolic, ambiguous, or vague manner. Zechariah makes it crystal clear that "after all Israel and the world have endured, finally God will arrive in person of the Messiah and bring order, peace, security, joy, and the utopian age that human beings have long dreamed of."[201]

Also we have other texts that clearly speak of his physical return. I have already interpreted Acts 1:11 earlier in this eschatology study so I shall not repeat that again. Other texts like 1 Thessalonians 4:13-18 and Revelation 19-20 reveal a physical and bodily return of the Messiah to this earth where he will rule and reign.[202]

---

[200] Walter C. Kaiser, Jr., "The Land of Israel and the Future Return (Zechariah 10:6-12)," in *Israel, The Land, and the People: An Evangelical Affirmation of God's Promises*, ed. H. Wayne House (Grand Rapids, MI: Kregel Publications, 1998), 223-224.

[201] Stephen Miller, *Holman Old Testament Commentary: Nahum, Habakkuk, Zephaniah, Haggai, Zechariah, Malachi*, ed. Max Anders (Nashville, TN: B&H Publishing, 2004), 294.

[202] Premillennialists & Postmillennialists believe the rule and reign begins 1,000 years prior to the New Heaven and New Earth reign (though still with differences in how that rule exists; Premills believe it is with Christ presently here. Post mills believe it is through the church and gospel). Amillennialists believe the rule and reign begins in the New Heaven and New Earth. But all three schools affirm a future, literal, bodily return of Christ to the earth to establish his final and ultimate rule and reign. Not to affirm that future, literal, bodily return to rule and reign places one outside of orthodox Christianity.

More will be said about this physical return and physical rule over the land and earth in section #4: A Christocracy where Christ Jesus Rules Over the Earth as King. In this kingdom the earth, including Israel's promised land will exist and all the promises of God shall come to pass and be fulfilled.

A Visible & Universally Recognized Return

Second, when Christ does return to this earth the event will not occur without universal acknowledgement of what has taken place. The text in Matthew 24:30 reveals this event as global in nature. The text reads: "Then will appear in heaven the sign of the Son of Man, and then all the tribes of the earth will mourn, and they will see the Son of Man coming on the clouds of heaven with power and great glory."

Dr. Ed Hindson and Dr. James Borland have noted, "What this sign . . . will be is not explained here. Ancient commentators (e.g. Chrysostom) thought it to be the appearance of a cross in the sky, whereas Lange suggests it will be the Shekinah glory of Christ himself. In some way a visible manifestation will mark the visible . . . return of Christ in judgment at the end of the Tribulation. As the earth revolves, the various nations and tribes will be able to see this sign."[203]

The early church father/bishop (episcopas) Irenaeus affirmed that truth as he stated, "When he comes from heaven with his mighty angels, the whole earth will be

---

[203] Edward Hindson and James Borland, *The Gospel of Matthew: The King is Coming in the Twenty-First Century Biblical Commentary Series,* ed. Mal Couch (Chattanooga, TN: AMG Publishers, 2006), 214.

shaken, as he himself declares, 'There shall be a great earthquake, such as has not been from the beginning.'"[204]

This thought aligns too with Revelation 1:7 which says, "Look, he is coming in the clouds, and *every eye will see him*, even those who pierced him; and *all the peoples of the earth will wail on account of him*." The text could not be any plainer about the global visibility of Christ's return to this earth.

A Supernatural, Climatic, & Miraculous Return with Cataclysmic Global Impact

Third, the return of Christ will occur through a sovereign display of supernatural and miraculous events. The return of Christ culminates in a series of events that reveal the glory of God in his sovereignty over the nations. When Christ returns some dramatic, cataclysmic, and earth altering events take place. Dr. John Walvoord has accurately stated that "Jesus' second coming will probably be the most dramatic event of history and prophecy."[205] When we read a text like Revelation 19:11-16 we discover the climactic and magnanimous supernatural events that surround Christ's descent to this earth. That text says:

> Then I saw heaven opened, and behold, a white horse! The one sitting on it is called Faithful and True, and in righteousness he judges and makes war. His eyes are like a flame of fire, and on his head are many diadems, and he has a name written that no one

---

[204] Irenaeus, *Against Heresies, In Ante-Nicene Fathers, Vol. 1. The Apostolic Fathers, Justin Martyr, Irenaeus,* ed. Alexander Roberts and James Donaldson (Peabody, MA: Hendrickson Publishers, 1994), 510.

[205] John F. Walvoord, *End Times: Understanding Today's World Events in Biblical Prophecy* (Nashville, TN: Word Publishing, 1998), p. 148.

knows but himself. He is clothed in a robe dipped in blood, and the name by which he is called is The Word of God. And the armies of heaven, arrayed in fine linen, white and pure, were following him on white horses. From his mouth comes a sharp sword with which to strike down the nations, and he will rule them with a rod iron. He will tread the winepress of the fury of the wrath of God the Almighty. On his robe and on his thigh he has a name written, King of kings and Lord of lords.

Dr. Arnold G. Fruchtenbaum has shown how the second coming of Christ will develop with *eight key events* that God supernaturally orchestrates as he draws history to an ultimate climactic pinnacle before the inauguration of the Christocracy. As we examine these though we would do well to keep in mind that the comings of Christ, the first and second, occur in a *process*. His first coming lasted 30 or so years. His second coming lasts as well for a set number of years. As the Calvinist and Dispensational Presbyterian scholar and Bible Teacher Dr. Donald Grey Barnhouse said, "the second coming of Christ is a series of events, even as the first coming of Christ was a series of events."[206]

This point by Barnhouse is important because sometimes a clash occurs by those who charge some premillennialists with error because they see a series of events within the stages of Christ's second coming (rapture & revelation). No such controversy needs to exist here. All of us who are orthodox see the 1st coming of Christ as a single event with many phases to it (birth, childhood to youth, adult ministry, death, & resurrection). Likewise, orthodox believers can see his second coming as a single

---

[206] Donald Grey Barnhouse, *The Invisible War: The Panorama of the Continuing Conflict Between Good and Evil* (Grand Rapids, MI: Zondervan, 1965), 267.

event with distinct phases to it as well. Just as we all can see one first coming with multiple events to it we all can also see one second coming with multiple events related to it as well.

As to these events, one cannot miss that these are nothing short of miraculous and providential by the hand of the Almighty. As Fruchtenbaum says, "the two climactic events of the Great Tribulation are the Campaign of Armageddon and the Second Coming."[207]

Therefore, I will set forth these eight events in brief form. However, I encourage the reader to examine these texts listed in detail and to even read the full treatment of this in Fruchtenbaum's work as he does a thorough and very detailed presentation of these eight events. I will only give you the highlights here.

1. **"Assembling of the Allies of the Antichrist**." Revelation 16:12-16 speaks to this matter. In this phase the false Trinity, the Dragon (Satan; a counterfeit father), the Beast (the anti-Christ; a counterfeit son), and a False Prophet (the counterfeit holy spirit) move the kings/leaders of the earth to assemble their armies together against the nation of Israel. Two other texts speak to this as well: Joel 3:9-11 and Psalm 2:1-6.[208]

2. **"The Destruction of Babylon**." Zechariah 5:5-11 and Revelation 18:9-19 teaches us about a future world economic center. Scripture calls this Babylon. The "city of Babylon is to be rebuilt and become the world capital of the Antichrist" as well as the world's

---

[207] Arnold G. Fruchtenbaum, *The Footsteps of the Messiah: A Study of the Sequence of Prophetic Events* (Tustin, CA: Ariel Ministries, 2004), 309.

[208] Ibid, 309-313.

"economic capital." [209] In this phase of Christ's return Gentiles will wage war against this economic and political capital and will destroy it (see Isaiah 13:1-14:23 & Jeremiah 50-51).[210]

3. **"The Fall of Jerusalem**." Though during this phase of Christ's coming Satan's economic capital will be destroyed, his focus remains thoroughly upon the destruction of the Jewish race and nation. It seems that in Satan's mind that if he can destroy the Jews he has succeeded in nullifying a promise of God and thus this remains his ardent passion. The satanic armies of the anti-christ will move against Jerusalem and seek to annihilate the capital city of the Jewish nation. Zechariah 12:1-9, 14:1-2, and Micah 4:11-5:1 speak to this subject.[211] "From the valley of Jezreel the armies of the Antichrist will move south, and all the armies of the nations will gather against Jerusalem. Once again, Jerusalem will fall into Gentile hands, and half of the Jewish population will be taken into slavery while the other half will be allowed to remain in the city to await another fate."[212]

4. **"The Armies of the Antichrist at Bozrah**." During these heavy battles that take place the soldiers of Israel's Army, and the remnant of Israelis, will gather in a place known as Bozrah, or what is "present-day

---

[209] Ibid, 313.

[210] Ibid, 313-327.

[211] Ibid, 327-330.

[212] Ibid, 328.

southern Jordan."²¹³ Jeremiah 49:13-14 speaks of this as well as Micah 2:12 which refers to the remnant of Jews gathered there.²¹⁴

5. **"The National Regeneration of Israel.**" During this time the efficacious work of the Spirit through various means will move the Jewish people to "recognize the reason why the Tribulation has fallen on them" as they will "come to a realization of the national sin" that brought them as a nation under judgment.²¹⁵ As Isaiah 53:1-9 speaks of their national confession of sin and as Zechariah depicts in 12:10-13:1 along with Isaiah 64:1-12 the Jews will plead for the grace of the LORD and beg for deliverance.

6. **"The Second Coming of the Messiah.**" Though many of us associate Christ's second coming to the Mount of Olives, the Bible speaks of his coming to earth at the place of Bozrah and from there he will make his triumphant march up to the Mount of Olives. Isaiah 34:1-7, Isiah 63:1-6, Habakkuk 3:3 (referencing Teman and Mount Paran which are both in the area of Bozrah), and Micah 2:12-13 "clearly pinpoint the place of the Second Coming as being in the land of Edom and at the city of Bozrah."²¹⁶

It is at this place where the final battle of Christ and the Anti-Christ shall take place. Revelation 19:1-16 speaks of Christ battling and

---

²¹³ Ibid, 330.

²¹⁴ Ibid.

²¹⁵ Ibid, 331.

²¹⁶ Ibid, 339-342.

defeating the anti-christ. The actual and literal slaughter of the King against the evil forces will be so severe that Revelation 19:17-18 tells us that "birds will eat the unburied carcasses of many who participated in the Campaign of Armageddon."[217]

7. **"The Battle From Bozrah to the Valley of Jehoshaphat**." The battle that begins at the place where Christ descends upon this earth continues as Christ makes his way towards eastern Jerusalem. Along this journey Christ will slay the anti-Christ with his breath (2 Thess. 2:8) and this miraculous and swift defeat will cause widespread "disbelief that he died so suddenly and easily, considering he had shaken the kingdoms of the world and the earth trembled in his presence."[218]

   Following the death of the anti-Christ our Lord and King shall utterly pulverize the armies of the nations. He shall march "through the land in indignation" and as he does he shall "slaughter" the armies of the anti-Christ. The texts speaking to this include: Joel 3:12-13, Zechariah 14:12-15, Jeremiah 49:20-22, and Revelation 14:19-20.

8. **"The Victory Ascent up the Mount of Olives**." After fighting off the enemies and first saving the tents of Judah (Zech. 12:7), Christ shall make his way to the Mount of Olives for his victory ascent and proclamation as King over the entire earth (Zech. 14:3-4). At this time several cataclysmic events will occur as the Great Tribulation ends. The seventh Bowl Judgment in Revelation 16:17-21 will cause

---

[217] Ibid, 346.

[218] Ibid, 353.

the "greatest earthquake ever to occur in history of the earth (vs. 18). This will cause the city of Jerusalem to split into three divisions, while the city of Babylon will suffer the full wrath of God (vs. 19). Many geographical changes will take place (vs. 20) and hail weighing 120 pounds will fall (vs. 21). . . .

Not only will Jerusalem be split into three divisions, but the Mount of Olives will be split into two parts, creating a valley running east and west."[219] At this place Christ shall begin his Kingdom reign over all the earth. The earthquake that occurs will also create the necessary topography for the new massive Temple where Christ will rule from as King.

Truth #3: Christ Shall Rescue his Bride before the Time of God's Wrath

One of the most well-known marks of most all dispensationalists has been that they see the coming of Christ marked by a length of time instead of a very short moment in history. Just as Christ's first coming lasted about 30 or 33 years (depending on which calculation one adopts), so his second coming and the events surrounding that will last several years. Despite the vast amount of unity we do have in this area, dispensationalists have some variations in the precise timelines for these events.

We are not monolithic in the minor details surrounding the time and duration of the great tribulation (God's wrath). But overall we do all agree that God will spare his bride from the time of the wrath (however long that will be, 7 years, 3.5 years, or something else).[220]

---

[219] Ibid, 355-356.

[220] John Walvoord believed the first 3.5 years were a time of peace with the final 3.5 the time of God's wrath. Charles Ryrie believed the entire 7

Some of us believe that texts like 2 Thessalonians 2:3 could be, or is, a clear reference to the departure of the body of Christ from earth before the Day of the Lord. For example, Dr. David Olander says of this text: "This is the rapture and a legitimate use of the word for departure, stand apart, or apostasy. Historically the word can mean this. Once the church has departed (been raptured) there is not one believer left on the planet. This would be total or complete apostasy in at least several ways. In essence, one departure or apostasy causes the other and Paul could easily have used the word he did referring to the secondary part (those left behind on the planet) in total." [221] Another teacher, Dr. Wayne House, seems to also hold that position on the meaning of the Greek word and its implications for a departure of the church.[222]

Others who may not see that text in that light see other texts like 1 Thessalonians 1:10 and 5:9 as a clear teaching on Christ delivering us from the great time of wrath that God pours out upon the world. But beyond those texts we Dispensationalists have some variation on the other aspects related to the doctrine of the rapture and tribulation (though still all within the pre-tribulation model).

For example, Dr. John Walvoord, the 2nd President of Dallas Theological Seminary, believed that Christ would snatch away the church and then there would be 3 ½ years of peace and then 3 ½ years of great tribulation before Christ

---

years were a tribulation period. Both affirmed a rapture prior to the 7 year final period of history before the millennial reign. Morgan Edwards in the 1700s also seems to have taught the tribulation period was only 3.5 years. He too taught a pre-trib rapture view.

[221] David Olander, *The Greatness of the Rapture: The Pre-Day of the Lord Rapture* (FT Worth, TX: Tyndale Seminary Press, 2009), 118.

[222] H. Wayne House, "*Apostasia in 2 Thessalonians 2:3: Apostasy or Rapture*," in *When the Trumpet Sounds* (Eugene, OR: Harvest House Publishers, 1995), 261-296.

sat down on the earth to rule and reign. [223] Dr. Walvoord believed that there was at least a 7 year period between the resurrection of the ecclesia (Christ's body/bride) and the coming of Christ to earth for Israel and the world. He, however, placed the entire tribulation period into the last 3 ½ years of the 7 year period. He saw the first half of Daniel's 70th week as a time of peace (see Daniel 9:27).

However, one of Walvoord's professors under his administration, Dr. Charles C. Ryrie, believed that the entire seven year period (the 70th week/seven of Daniel's 70 weeks/sevens prophecy) is a part of the great tribulation. [224] He too, like Walvoord, was a student of Lewis Sperry Chafer. Yet he differed slightly from Walvoord on how long the tribulation would actually last.

The founder of what later became Brown University also had a different view of the timeline. In contrast to both Ryrie and Walvoord, this early Baptist leader in the 1700's, Morgan Edwards (1722-1792), believed that Christ would come for his bride and then there would be only a 3 ½ years interval for the entire tribulation period before Christ returned to the earth. [225] Some would classify that as a mid-tribulation rapture view. But that would not be an accurate description because Edwards saw the *entire tribulation* happening not within a 7 year period, but rather he saw it all concentrated in 3 ½ years of time. Thus he placed the rapture before the 3 ½ years of tribulation/wrath. So for him, he still held to removal prior to the time of tribulation.

---

[223] John F. Walvoord, *The Revelation of Jesus Christ* (Chicago, IL: Moody Press, 1966), 123, 131,135.

[224] Charles C. Ryrie, *Revelation: Everyman's Bible Commentary* (Chicago, IL: Moody Press, 1996), 53.

[225] Thomas Ice, *"Morgan Edwards,"* in the *Dictionary of Premillennial Theology*, Gen. Ed. Mal Couch (Grand Rapids, MI: Kregel Publications, 1996), 100-102.

These differences illustrate for us that there is some healthy debate within the Dispensational family of theologians. Yet within these differences there are key areas of unanimity. *The key area of agreement has to do with the fact Christ will take his bride away before the great time of judgment (the Day of the Lord) and then after this time of judgment (whether it be 7 years, or 3 ½ years, or another time frame), Christ will then come down to earth to judge the nations and inaugurate his Kingdom.*

Clear exegesis of at least two passages of Scripture[226] seem to prove with clarity that Christ's coming in the air is not the same as his coming to the earth to rule and reign. The differences between what is described in Matthew 25:31-46 and what is described in 1Thessalonians 4:13-18 and John 14:1-4 cannot be overlooked as minuscule. All of us dispensationalists, and even some who would not embrace a full or consistent Dispensationalism but see a time frame in between the coming of Christ for the church and his descent down to earth to rule and reign, believe that the second coming of Christ will unfold in a length of time that allows for a removal of the bride of Christ, a great time of tribulation and wrath (and within that time for people's conversion,

---

[226] I would also assert that 2 Thessalonians 2:3 seems possibly to be a clear statement referring to the rapture (departure) of the church. This is a minority position among our Dispensational family. But the context appears to support this idea as well because Paul tells the people not to "be quickly shaken in mind or alarmed." Clearly his goal is to comfort the people. Too, we also see that he opens this section with a word about "concerning the coming of our Lord" and "our being gathered together to him." This is a contextual clue showing us that Paul was encouraging these believers with the idea of the doctrine of Christ's coming for them. He used this doctrine to comfort (see 1 Thess. 4:18). But how encouraging would it be to tell his audience that their future involved seeing the faith of Christianity disappear from the earth while witnessing the rise of the "man of lawlessness" who opposes God? How does that promote the theme of encouragement and comfort? See next footnote for further explanation.

such as with the nation of Israel), and a descent down to earth to establish the kingdom of Christ here on this earth.

In these passages we have a teaching or doctrinal message that Christ will come for his own and he will take them back to heaven with him (John 14:1-4). In 1 Thessalonians 4:13-18 there is a great separation of the believers from the unbelieving world. The believers are *caught up in the air* and are translated into glorified bodies. This separation takes place *in the air*. The next chapter is about the Day of the Lord. Dispensationalists are unified that Christ will take his bride home before the Day of the Lord.[227] We may differ in exactly how long the Day of the Lord is, but wherever one places that time frame is also where we would teach that the Bible has declared the community of Christ as exempt. This distinction is clearly seen in that some saints are separated in the air.

However, reading Matthew 25:31-46, we see that in this time of separation Christ is *actually on the earth*. Christ is not separating the sheep from the goats in the air like what is described in 1 Thessalonians, nor is he moving a people with him back to heaven as in John 14. In Matthew's gospel,

---

[227] David E. Olander, *"The Pre-Day of the Lord Rapture,"* in *Dispensationalism Tomorrow & Beyond: Articles in Honor of Charles C. Ryrie, ed. Christopher Cone* (Fort Worth TX: Tyndale Seminary press, 2008), 269-291. I also tend to think 2 Thessalonians 2:3 is a text that speaks of the rapture. The term apostasia (often translated as apostasy) has the base single meaning of departure. I think this term has two referents to it. It refers to the departure of the body of Christ from earth as well as the departure of faith from the earth causing a total apostasy (departure) of faith on earth since the body of Christ is gone. Dr. Olander also agrees with this view. He says, "Once the church has departed, there is no 'faith' as an embodiment of biblical truth on earth. . . . The fact there will not be 'the faith' on earth has never happened since Adam's departure from God. There is most definitely a connection between the rapture (apostasy) and the departure of faith (apostasy)" (p. 275). Many translations of early years translated this term apostasia as "departure."

172

Jesus is actually sitting on his throne and he has all of the nations to come before him and his throne. The saved, the sheep, he separates to his right, and the unsaved, the goats, he places on the left. The sheep are allowed into the kingdom (the 1000 year earthly kingdom) whereas the goats are excluded and sent off into eternal judgment.

If all of these texts in Matthew, John, and 1 Thessalonians 4, occurred all in one short moment of time, as the amillennialists and post-day of the Lord rapture premillennialists suggest, then where would the sheep come from in Matthew 25 who are separated from the goats before the throne? *If all of the sheep (believers) are translated in the air and separated in translation into glorified bodies in the air then when is there time for another group of people to believe and become sheep mixed in with the goats that need to be separated from the goats before Jesus on his throne on the earth?*

The only explanation for this is that there has to be a time period in between Christ's coming for his bride and Christ's coming to earth to rule and reign from his throne in Jerusalem. [228] During that time other people believe and come to faith. These are those sheep separated from the goats

---

[228] I must give credit of this teaching to my theology professor Dr. Ron Clutter of Trinity Theological Seminary. Clutter, a former student of Ryrie, taught us this in class lecture on Christology and I had never seen this so clearly before. He shared with us that even if one were not a dispensationalist, which he is, that basic exegesis of these two texts requires some time lapse in between the two events. Even non-dispensationalists who see Israel and the bride of Christ as all being one solitary or unitary entity must come to terms with this when doing honest exegesis of the text. Exegesis of these texts alone does not tell us how much time is between the two separations, one in the air and one on the earth, but it does show two distinct acts/events that require enough time for some to become believing sheep after the first translation that takes place in the air and subsequently requires for them to be separated from the goats when before Christ's throne when he returns to earth to rule and reign.

before the throne of Christ. This truth highlights the facts that Jesus takes his bride away, a time period elapses, and then he comes to the land of Israel at his coming down to the earth where he then establishes his kingdom rule.

These texts reveal to us that "Israel must come into judgment (Ezek. 20:33-44; Matt. 25:1-13)" yet on the other hand we see that the ecclesia "will not come into judgment"[229] as she has been chosen to be spared by this time of trouble simply by a sovereign act of mercy from God towards the Son; he will snatch away his bride and consummate the union with her in heaven (1 Thess. 1:9; 5:9). These sheep in Matthew 25 who enter into the kingdom are the non-glorified saints who enter the kingdom in natural bodies. The community/family of Christ, already by that time in glorified bodies, enters the kingdom to rule and reign with Christ over the whole earth.

Post-Tribulation Premillennial, Post-Millennial, & Amillennial Options for Escaping Wrath

The Bible promises that the people of God will be spared from the wrath of God. 1 Thessalonians 1 and 5 give the people of God great hope. I think the pre-tribulational premillennial view best explains these texts. However, for those in other positions, they too can still preach and teach God's faithfulness in keeping his promises.

Sadly, some who are very antagonistic towards a pre-tribulation rapture doctrine become so obsessed in trying to prove that view wrong that they fail to see they too must give some reasonable explanation as to what God has promised to his people. Explaining why one thinks the pre-trib rapture doctrine is wrong does not constitute a positive view on what Paul actually did promise the believers. If a pre-trib rapture

---

[229] Lewis Sperry Chafer, *Systematic Theology*, vol. 2 (Grand Rapids, MI: Kregel, 1993), 52.

doctrine were wrong, then the believer must still explain what God means in this promise to spare the believer from the wrath to come.

So what should non-pretrib teachers do? Well, of course I would love to persuade them to see the text as I do. It was a Reformed theologian, Dr. Timothy George, who helped me see these promises as a basis to the pre-trib view. I will never forget him walking me through the book of 1 Thessalonians at North Greenville University in the library. He helped me begin my journey towards embracing the pre-trib rapture view. But, I know neither I nor many other pre-trib teachers will convince everyone this is the best view. So how can you explain it and still affirm the promise of God? If you are a Bible believer you must accept God's promise and apply it the best way you know how.

The mandate to encourage believers remains an important task of the preacher and pastor here. Even if not subscribing to a pre-trib rapture doctrine one still has to explain how this promise of God applies to a believer. The next best step if one is not convinced of a pre-trib view would be to make sure that the believer realizes that the final judgment, the wrath of God that will consume the enemies at his return when he judges the world, shall not come down on the believer.

This could be one way to read these Thessalonian promise texts. Though I still do not find that view the most satisfactory in light of the fact in Christ we already have that hope (we have already escaped it {see Romans 8:1}, so this wrath seems to me to be the wrath of Revelation 6-19), that view would still give believers a real hope for the promise of God for their lives. The intended goal of Paul to give comfort and to remove fear could still occur to a degree for those using the text this way.

An example of this approach can be found in the teacher James Grant. As a Reformed brother he is not a dispensationalist.[230] Yet he argues for believers being spared from the wrath of God too. For him, this promise of God gives us hope because when Jesus returns he will bring in the day of the Lord, a time of judgment. He rightly sees that "the day of the Lord will be a day of judgment and fire, a remaking of the heavens and the earth."[231] That judgment to come should be preached along with this next point for encouraging others towards hope for them to have an eager heart to see Christ.

The next point after noting this judgment to come must be that "when the final and great day of the Lord comes, we will not receive wrath if we are children of God . . . . we do not have to fear that day, for it is the day of our salvation."[232] The right use of the biblical promises of God to protect us from wrath requires all of us from all millennial persuasions to explain the text with the goal to encourage believers towards joy and hope in the great day of his coming for us.

Though I think a pre-tribulational and premillennial perspective gives the fullest amount of hope, if one does not hold that view the obligation still remains from the text for

---

[230] I do believe that Dispensationalism was born from the Reformed heritage. In fact, some would see Dispensationalism as a wave of the Reformation. For many years, Reformed Dispensationalists ministered side-by-side with their other Reformed brethren in the academy, church, and beyond. It was the sad split in the 1940s that breached their wonderful fellowship. That breach needs to end. It began with a false idea that Dispensationalists believe in multiple plans of salvation. This is not true. See my book: *The Calvinism of Dispensationalism*. We would do well to repair those divisions by joining together again in the academy, church, and missions to carry out Great Commission work.

[231] James H. Grant Jr., *1-2 Thessalonians: The Hope of Salvation, Preaching the Word*, ed. R. Kent Hughes (Wheaton, IL: Crossway Books, 2011), 134.

[232] Ibid.

the believer, preacher, or teacher of the Word to explain what wrath will God spare us from because two texts in 1 Thessalonians 1 and 5 explicitly promise believers a divine exemption. All conservative, Bible believing, orthodox believers can line up together in affirming there is some future wrath to come that believers can escape. The particulars of how we define that wrath and the timing of it may differ, but even if so we can all still proclaim with great fervency that God will spare us from the wrath to come if we know Christ who is going to return to judge the world in the future.

Whatever debates we have on those points, let us all remember "we cannot lose sight of the focus: we will be with Jesus forever . . . . No matter what our eschatological arguments are concerning the details of this event, let us not lose sight of the fact that our ultimate desire is to be with Jesus Christ, our Lord and our God."[233]

Truth #4: A Christocracy where Jesus Rules Over the Earth as King

The term Christocracy is another term for the Messianic or Millennial Kingdom. The Messianic or Millennial terms have been chosen because both are descriptive terms of the kingdom. The term Messianic reveals that it is a kingdom mediated directly through the rule of Jesus Christ the Messiah. The word Millennial reveals the idea of the kingdom lasting for 1,000 years. This kingdom was promised in the OC. God promised King David that there would come an "eternal house, an eternal kingdom, an eternal throne and an eternal descendant."[234]

---

[233] Ibid., 128.

[234] Lewis Sperry Chafer, *Systematic Theology*, vol. 2 (Grand Rapids, MI: Kregel, 1993), 611.

Hundreds of scriptures prophesy about this kingdom. The specific Davidic covenant promises come from 2 Samuel 7:11-17 and 1 Chronicles 17:10-15. It was this kingdom that Christ offered to the nation of Israel with his first coming. He did not have to explain or redefine any concepts of the kingdom because it was such a prominent theme in the OT that the announcement of the kingdom to the people of Israel could only mean the golden era whereby the nation Israel was restored.

> The hymn of thanksgiving voiced by Mary (Luke 1:46-55) makes it also clear that Mary so understood the angelic announcement. Elizabeth spoke prophetically of the advent of "my Lord" before His birth (Luke 1:43) as moved by the Holy Ghost (Luke 1:41). To Simeon, who was "waiting for the consolation of Israel" (Luke 2:25), the fact was revealed and the Person of Christ was clearly discerned, as we observe from his prophecy (Luke 2:29-35). Anna, the prophetess, who "looked fro redemption in Jerusalem" (Luke 2:38), saw the fulfillment of her hopes in the Messiah who has appeared. The wise men came looking for the one "that is born King of the Jews" (Matt. 2:2) and were given divine attestation that they had found the One in whom their hopes could be realized. Matthew, writing to present Jesus as the Messiah to Israel, begins his record with the genealogy which traces the lineage, not, as might have been expected, to Abraham alone, in whose lineage He might come to redeem, but to David, in whose lineage He might come to reign. All the events associated with His birth attest His Messiahship.[235]

---

[235] J. Dwight Pentecost, *Things to Come* (Grand Rapids, MI: Dunham Publishing, 1958), 448-449.

When Israel as a whole nation repents (Rom. 11:25-32) Christ will at that time establish this millennial kingdom on this earth (see also Acts 3:20-21). Christ from his throne will gather all of the nations before him (Matt. 25:31-46) and from there he will begin his 1,000 year reign over the whole earth from Jerusalem (Zech. 14:1-9; Revelation 20:1-6). Dr. Fruchtenbaum says of this kingdom era:

> The Messianic Kingdom will be administered through an absolute monarchy with a definite chain of command and lines of authority. The absolute monarch will be the person of Jesus the Messiah. The delegated authority will be split into two branches: a Jewish branch of government and a Gentile branch, each in turn having a chain of command. It can be charted as follows:

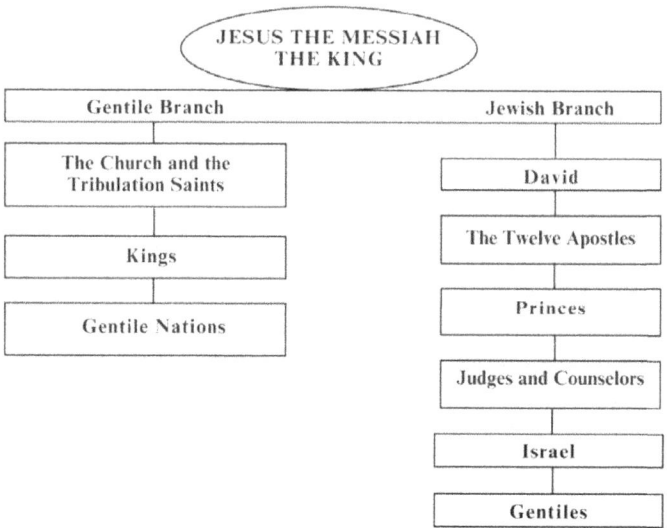

```
              ┌─────────────────────────────┐
              │   JESUS THE MESSIAH          │
              │       THE KING               │
              └─────────────────────────────┘

Gentile Branch                        Jewish Branch

The Church and the
Tribulation Saints                         David

                                    The Twelve Apostles

Kings
                                         Princes

Gentile Nations
                                  Judges and Counselors

                                          Israel

                                         Gentiles
```

This last dispensational era of earthly history where God providentially moves earthly history in earthly time culminates here where the rule of God, his kingdom rule, comes down to earth to rule perfectly over the earth. What Lucifer failed to do over the mineral Garden, what Adam failed to do over the Garden of Eden, what the people failed to do under the rule of conscience, what Noah and the governmental law did not do, what the patriarchs did not do, what Moses and Israel failed to do, and what the body of Christ at large failed to do through discipleship will now culminate in the kingdom of Christ on earth when Jesus fulfills all the promises and does what none before him have ever done.

Jesus Christ will physically bring down the perfect rule of heaven to the actual earth itself (see Matt. 6:10). He will rule perfectly as King of the world and under him will be delegate princes and leaders who administer his sovereign rule throughout the entire world. Of this kingdom era Dr. Alfred Eade has well stated this:

> It is very evident that if this coming Kingdom of heavenly rule is to take place of all previous dominions in the earth (Dan 2:35), it must be a real, visible, tangible Kingdom; with a King, a form of government, and subjects over whom the King shall rule—just as real a Kingdom as those which preceded it, but with one wonderful difference: it will be righteous in character and in government (Psalm 72; Matthew 6:10; Isaiah 11:3-5). It will be, at last, the only truly Universal Kingdom in world history (Daniel 2:35; 7:14; Zechariah 9:10). Unity, Peace, and Prosperity, the ideal system of world government so coveted by every passing generation, is at last realized in the Kingdom of "the Prince of Peace" (Micah 4:1-4). . . . All lines of Scripture lead us to the King and the establishment of His Kingdom.

180

"Thy Kingdom come" has been the unceasing prayer of the people of God throughout the ages.[236]

In this dispensation God will fulfill all of his promises to the nation of Israel. The land promises he made to Abraham and the physical ethnic descendants will be fulfilled in this era. All of the promises about a kingdom will be fulfilled here. Earthly history will find its culmination point here in this climactic period where God's sovereign rule comes down to earth and is administered in person by Jesus Christ and his representatives that he will appoint throughout the world to rule in his name and in his power.

We see this teaching in particular with Daniel 7 and especially in verses 25-27. Dr. Randy Alcorn says of this, "We will forever please our Father by ruling over the earth that he'll refashion for us to live on forever. As co-rulers with Christ, we'll share in the glory of the sovereign ruler himself. . . . We will become the stewards, the managers of the world's wealth and accomplishments. . . . Some will rule over cities; others will rule over nations."[237] Also as Dr. Ryrie stated:

After the second advent of Christ the millennial kingdom will be set up in fulfillment of all the promises given in both Testaments and particularly those contained in the Abrahamic and Davidic covenants. The Lord Jesus Christ, who will personally take charge of the running of the affairs of the world during that age, will be the chief personage

---

[236] Alfred Thompson Eade, *The Panorama Bible Study Course: From the Creation of the Angels to the New Jerusalem* (Grand Rapids, MI: Fleming H. Revell, 1961), 176.

[237] Randy Alcorn, *Heaven* (Wheaton, IL: Tyndale House Publishers, 2004), 217, 223.

of the dispensation. It will continue for a thousand years, and man will be responsible for obedience to the King and His laws. Satan will be bound, Christ will be ruling, righteousness will prevail, overt disobedience will be quickly punished.[238]

The Promised Covenant Stipulations for the Kingdom Era where the Land Covenant & Davidic Covenants Are Applied

For any person to understand God's Word rightly and to be able to love people and lead people correctly, there must be a proper understanding of God's progressive revelation whereby the interpreter of the Word recognizes God gradually and incrementally fulfills his promises exactly as prescribed. Many pastor-theologians and many saints fail to grasp the precision to God's faithfulness. Many fail to see that God can do multiple tasks at one time with various people or groups. Many fail to see that God's order in his household universe is broader and more comprehensive in nature than just with the saints that come to faith during the time of the New Covenant.

As often the case with bad theology, it first is often a bad heart that causes the poor doctrinal thinking. Poor doctrine in the head is in a portion of cases a result of a poor heart. For example, when pride fills the hearts of people it often leads these people to think that God has set aside the nation of Israel and the OT promises made to them as a people. This seems rather absurd and likely a visible manifestation of a prideful and aloof spirit.

Paul specifically said this would be an issue when he said: "do not be arrogant toward the branches [ethnic Jews]. If you are, remember it is not you who support the root, but

---

[238] Charles C. Ryrie, *Dispensationalism* (Chicago, IL: Moody Press, 1995), 56.

the root supports you" (Rom. 11:18). The replacement theology theory, or suppressionism, as it has sometimes been labeled, occurs when arrogance fills the heart and in turn controls the interpreter as he or she reads the sacred text.

Many of these people claim to be "Reformed" but in reality are not "Reformed" in the pure sense of where Reformation theology is today. Why do I say that? To be truly Reformed means that one will apply the essence of Reformation theology to the *whole Bible*, which means applying a historical and grammatical method of interpretation to all portions of the Bible. If this is done, it naturally yields a view that Israel will come to faith, the past Israelite forefathers including Abraham, Isaac, and Jacob and others will be resurrected, and they will all receive the geographical land that God promised to them as Christ rules from the throne in Jerusalem. God sovereignly elected that nation. How can that ethnic election ever be undone?

According to Romans 11:28 God's act of election cannot be altered. Those that reject this viewpoint do so often because they are filled with pride, which is what Paul said would be the problem (Rom. 11:18-20, 25) for those who do not understand their position and Israel's position in the overall family of God. The Dispensational view is the fruit of the continual work of the Reformation principles applied to the doctrines of Israel and eschatology.

Some people cannot easily accept that we Gentiles in the body of Christ are not the solitary or only focus of God. Jealousy is a tough sin to overcome. God having a love relationship with us in the body of Christ and also a love relationship with the elect nation of Israel (two peoples/members in one family or household by way of God's covenant(s) and/or promise(s)) causes some to cringe when jealousy arises in the heart. But if we take the text of Scripture seriously we do see God having a covenant relationship with both Israel and with the ecclesia.[239] And in his covenant relations with Israel God will fulfill his

[239] Some dispensationalists, like J.N. Darby, Lewis Chafer, Chris Cone, and George Gunn see the New Covenant as only being with ethnic Israel and not the body of Christ. Others, like J.R. Graves, C.I. Scofield, John Walvoord, Mal Couch, Arnold Fruchtenbaum, William Luck, and myself see the New Covenant as originally for Israel but with the progress of revelation God brought into the fold a new entity "to partake" (to use Arnold Fruchtenbaum's terminology) of the covenant blessings by union with Christ. For me this issue is simpler than what some make it out to be. God can do more than he promised, but he can never do less. God adding the body of Christ to the New Covenant of Grace is an additional grace blessing (planned in eternity past but revealed in history only by the NT writings). Too, I do not see how we can be in Christ and not in the New Covenant of Grace. Christ is the author or the one who the covenant rests within. The bride of Christ is one with Christ Jesus. To be in Christ is to participate in the will of promise (promise or covenant relationship; New Covenant of Grace) and thus to be related to the one who administers the covenant. Granted, people may be related to the Lord by different historical periods, but from Genesis to Revelation there is only one family of the redeemed. Those who partake of redemption participate in the eternal covenant of grace. There is only one family of God, those eternally elected. But in that family are different members who are born again in different historical periods of the various dispensations. For example, John the Baptist stated he was distinct from the bride (John 3:29). The bride of Christ is the unique and distinct people of God redeemed since the time of Christ's death and resurrection. John the Baptist was a part of God's people before the bride of Christ developed. He was part of the one family of God but not the same as the bride of Christ. We must think in terms of a family. Just as a physical family has various members in it, so too God's family has various members in it. I know others have argued for multiple New Covenants, one for Israel and one for the Church. Though that is theologically possible it does not seem to be textually possible in light of texts like Ephesians 3:6 and Romans 15:27. We actually do "partake" in the covenant/promise that God made originally with Israel. We are blessed because we are in the person from whom all covenant blessings flow from, i.e. in Christ Jesus the Lord and author of the covenant. Too, if the New Covenant is an expression of the Covenant of Grace (a part of the eternal covenant mentioned in Hebrews 13:20), i.e. the Tri-une plan of the Father, Son, and Spirit to redeem a family through an election unto grace, then it seems exegetically and theologically sound to see the

promises to that nation. The following provisions exist for the era where the Land and Davidic Covenant come to fruition in the earthly Kingdom of God.[240]

Seven Provisions of the Land Covenant from Deuteronomy 29:2-30:20

1. Moses prophesied that Israel would disobey God and would be scattered from her land and into all the regions of the earth (Deut. 29:2-30:1).

2. After this there will come a day when Israel will repent and turn from her disobedience (30:2).

3. The Messiah will deliver them and gather the children of Israel from all over the earth (30:3-4).

New Covenant of Grace as one solitary promise that is applied to different peoples progressively throughout revelatory history. There is only one family of God, the redeemed of all the ages (the spiritual elect) but in the family of God are different classifications of peoples just like there is in any family unit today. Does it not make more sense to see God as planning to redeem all of the elect of all the ages (one plan or eternal covenant of Grace) while placing those various elect peoples into different categories of the family of God according to the time in which they are redeemed (pre-Israelite saints, Israel, the Church, post-church saints)?

[240] For those who still use the old and worn out phrase that God's kingdom is not earthly but "spiritual," let it be known and remembered that Jesus Christ was spiritual and sinless yet he had an *earthly body*! Those who have fallen into this sinful mode of thinking have embraced a form of "*Christoplatonism*," which means they embrace forms of Christian theology but also forms of Greek philosophy that separate the soul and spiritual world from the physical world. The truth is that "earthly" does not mean sinful or unholy. Eden was earthly yet holy before Adam sinned and in the kingdom era the political, spiritual, and physical rule of Christ on earth will be a glorious rule and blessed time of peace and goodness for the world.

4. The Jews will possess the land (30:5) that was promised to the forefathers (Gen. 12:7; 15:18-21; 17:7-8).

5. The Lord will circumcise the hearts of the Jews. This is known as regeneration (30:6).

6. The enemies of the Jews will be judged and cursed by God (30:7).

7. The whole nation of Israel will be blessed in the time of restoration where God will provide them with many blessings (30:8-20).

Seven Provisions of the Davidic Covenant from 2 Samuel 7:11-16 & 1 Chronicles 17:10-14

1. David is promised an eternal dynasty. Nothing in all of the creation can alter or destroy this "House of David" (2 Sam. 7:11b, 16; 1 Chr. 17:10b).

2. From the loins of David would come an earthly king, Solomon, and only he would have the right to rule on the throne of his father David (2 Sam. 7:12).

3. David's son Solomon would be the one to build the temple (2 Sam. 7:13a).

4. This throne would have no end to it. The throne, the rule of God in this particular earthly sphere, would continue past Solomon and will last forever (2 Sam. 7:13b, 16).

5. The covenant made with David and his royal heritage could not be altered due to sin. The kingdom of God

186

was removed from Saul due to his sin. However, no sin, even the sins of Solomon, would ever cause God to change his promises or plan with the kingdom. Discipline would occur due to sin, but the discipline would never and will never alter the purpose and sovereign plan of God in fulfilling his kingdom rule (2 Sam. 7:14-15).

6. In the offspring of David, not from within his own body but from the offspring (later generations), will come the Messiah, the king who will rule on the earthly throne of his father David in the kingdom age that merges into eternal kingdom (1 Chr. 17:10-14; Matt. 25:31; Luke 1:32-33; Rev. 19:11-16; 20:6; 22:1,3,5).

7. There will be a time when the *King*, the *throne*, the *house*, and the *kingdom* will be established forever. This takes place when Christ comes to earth to rule and reign as the King of the earth and universe (1 Chr. 17:12-15). In this text, unlike the text in 2 Sam. 7, there is no reference to any sin because the Messiah is and will always be sinless. The emphasis in the 1 Chronicles passage is on the Messiah's everlasting rule, not just the everlasting presence of the throne as in the 2 Samuel text.

An Affirmation of Israel's Land Promises in Non-Dispensational Millennial End Time Models

The view of a mass conversion of the ethnic nation Israel and a gathering to their land has not been taught only by Dispensational Premillennial believers. Conservative believers from other end time positions have rightly recognized these promises will come true with ethnic Israel.

Historic premillennial, postmillennial, and amillennial believers have affirmed these promises.

The OT and NT both confirm God will give Israel the land sworn to the forefathers Abraham, Isaac, and Jacob. Conservative Bible believers who reject liberalism affirm God keeps his promises. Some promises, of course, are conditional. But in relation to Israel the promises made to Abraham were sworn in oath by God alone, i.e. God alone promised he would make sure the terms for fulfillment come to pass. In Genesis 12, 13, 15, and 17 God speaks of these covenant promises.

Most see these promises as unconditional. Yet even if one thinks the promises are conditional the Word still reveals the conditions one day by Israel will be met (by the providence working of the Lord in Israel) so that the conditions for fulfillment come to pass and then the blessings for Israel (Romans 11).

Post Millennial Jonathan Edwards: Israel Receives Her Land Promise and National Salvation

Few will argue against the massive impact of Jonathan Edwards' preaching and influence on America. Some have even said that he may be the "most significant and influential evangelical Christian in the history of the United States."[241] Dispensationalist Dr. Kevin Stilley agrees with this assessment and concurred saying Edwards "is generally recognized as America's greatest theologian and philosopher."[242]

---

[241] Barry E. Horner, *Future Israel: Why Christian Anti-Judaism Must Be Challenged* (Nashville, TN: B&H Publishing, 2007), 333.

[242] Kevin Stilley, "Jonathan Edwards," in the *Dictionary of Premillennial Theology*, ed. Mal Couch (Grand Rapids, MI: Kregel Publications, 1996), 100.

In the postmillennial thought of Edwards, the Jews would experience a national conversion to Christ. With this national conversion the ethnic believing Jews will receive their specific land promises that God made to the forefathers. Upon conversion to Christ the

> Jews will return to their own land again, because they never have yet possessed one quarter of that land, which was so often promised to them, from the Red Sea to the river of Euphrates (Exod. 23:31; Gen. 15:18; Deut. 11:24; Josh. 1:4). Indeed, it was partly fulfilled in Solomon's time, when he governed all within those bounds for a short time; but so short, that it is not to be thought that this is all the fulfillment of the promise that is to be. And besides, that was not a fulfillment of the promise, because they did not possess it . . . .[243]

Edwards affirmed a distinct role for the Jews in that they will receive their promised land as specified by God to the nation in the OT. He did not allegorize, revise, or seek some other symbolic or hidden meaning to these plain promises made. He rightly let the promises stand. Upon their national salvation the Jews will continue as a "distinct nation . . . {and} after their conversion . . . they {will} still be a distinct nation, that they might be a visible monument of God's wonderful grace and power in their calling and conversion."[244]

---

[243] Jonathan Edwards, *Apocalyptic Writings* (New Haven, Yale University Press, 1977), 5:133-134.

[244] Ibid, 5:135.

189

Dr. Charles Hodge served for many years at the then conservative Princeton Theological Seminary. He is considered as one of the greatest intellectual Reformed theologians of history. He too affirmed God would honor his promises to Israel.

> The second great event, which, according to the common faith or the Church, is to precede the second advent of Christ, is the national conversion of the Jews. . . . That there is to be such a national conversion may be argued. . . from the original call and destination of that people. As the rejection of the Jews was not total, so neither is it final. First, God did not design to cast away his people entirely, but by their rejection, in the first place, to facilitate the progress of the gospel among the Gentiles. And ultimately to make the conversion of the Gentiles the means of converting the Jews. . . . Because if the rejection of the Jews has been a source of blessing, much more will their restoration be the means of good. . . .The restoration of the Jews to the privileges of God's people is included in the ancient predictions and promises made respecting them . . . . The future restoration of the Jews is, in itself, a more probable event than the introduction of the Gentiles into the church of God.[245]

---

[245] Charles Hodge, *Systematic Theology*, (Grand Rapids, MI: Wm. B. Eerdmans, 1960, reprint), 3:805

The legendary preacher and pastor from London did not hesitate to take the plain reading of God's word in regards to the promises made to Israel. As a historic premillennialist, Spurgeon still rejected the idea that God's promises to the Jews would fail. He did not revise, alter, and jettison the promises of God made to the ethnic Jews. For Spurgeon, Christ would regain control of this earth over Satan in the millennium. This reveals God conquers this earth over Satan and that the end of this world does not end with Satan still in control. Pastor Spurgeon said,

> Yet this much we have ever learned most clearly— that on this earth, where sin and Satan gained victory over God through the fall of man, Christ is to achieve a complete triumph over all his foes; not on another battle-field, but on this. . . . Do not think the Lord will allow Satan to have even so much as one battle to call his own. . . . There shall be victory in every place and spot; and the conquest of Jesus shall be complete and perfect.[246]

Not only does Christ win on this earth in the millennial model of Spurgeon, unlike other models where victory does not occur until the eternal state, but the Jewish people also experience victory. Satan's efforts to keep them blinded, unconverted, and unable to experience the victory with Jesus fails as Jesus conquers their unbelief and brings the ethnic Jews to belief in the Messiah. Victory occurs as Jesus prevails and keeps the promises of God to the Jewish people. Spurgeon added:

---

[246] C.H. Spurgeon, "The Lamb: The Light," in *Spurgeon's Sermons in 10 Volumes* (Grand Rapids, MI: Baker Books, 1999), 8:280.

We believe that the Jews will be converted, and that they will be restored to their own land. We believe that Jerusalem will be the eternal metropolis of Christ's kingdom; we also believe that all nations shall walk in the light of the glorious city which shall be built at Jerusalem.[247]

Amillennialist R.C. Sproul: God Restores Israel

And so all Israel will be saved. The context indicates that Paul must be speaking of the Jewish people. He does not mean every Jew that ever lived, but the nation of Israel. Now why do I say that 'Israel' in this phrase refers to the Jews? All through his discussion Paul is talking about Israel in part: part of Israel has been blinded, part of Israel has been cut away, part of Israel has been stubborn, part of Israel has been excluded from the kingdom of God and its blessings. The Jews as a people are presently under judgment. But as there was a national judgment, so there will be a national restoration. Their rejection, even though it was a national rejection, did not include the rejection of every individual. So the restoration doesn't necessarily mean that every individual Jew will be saved, but the nation as a nation will be restored to God.[248]

---

[247] Ibid., 8:281.

[248] Phil Layton, *Noted Theologians in History who believed in a Future Conversion of National/Ethnic Israel*, accessed at https://www.monergism.com/noted-theologians-history-who-believed-future-conversion-nationalethnic-israel ; See also Sproul affirming this @ https://www.youtube.com/watch?v=8ahheVv6Wcw

Recognition for a More Earthly & Holistic Amillennial New Earth Model that Has a Place for Israel

Some non-premillennial teachers today have moved towards a more palatable model in regard to Israel's land promises. Though I believe the premillennial model best reflects the witness of Scripture, some teachers now from a non-premillennial model at least rightly affirm a place and role of Israel in the New Earth. Whereas premillennialists place the land promises of Israel beginning in the 1,000 year Christocracy (millennium) some amillennialists now recognize those land promises shall occur even though for them those fulfillments begin in the New Earth.

In such cases, the issue of fulfillment becomes a matter of time and not one of actual fulfillment. This movement has merit and ought to be encouraged by us premillennialists towards our amillennial brethren in the faith. This move is a step out of the more Christoplatonic forms of amillennial theology where the earthly or land idea has been presented as carnal or less spiritual. It also takes more seriously the unconditional promises made by God to ethnic Israel. Discarding a promise of God has enormous negative repercussions for one's theology and life. The recognition that the land promises to ethnic Israel must find a real, tangible, and actual fulfillment reveals more honest and faithful handling of the Scripture.

Two amillennial theologians have been more receptive of God's land promises for Israel and have promoted this idea of Israel receiving their land in the New Earth. Dr. Anthony Hoekema and Dr. Sam Storms. Of this matter Dr. Sam Storms has stated:

> I would argue that the land promise will yet be fulfilled *literally* and on the *earth*. But the question is 'When'? . . . . The . . . answer, proposed by amillennialists such as Anthony Hoekema and

myself, is that Old Testament prophetic promises of God's rule over his people in the land will be fulfilled in the new earth, which inaugurates the eternal state.[249]

Though some differences still exist on the millennium and possibly the distinct functional role of believing ethnic Israel in the New Earth, at the minimum we can praise the Lord for this monumental shift in the amillennial school of thought. This directional move towards recognition that the land promises still must come to pass highlights a substantive shift away from the Alexandrian, allegorical, and Christoplatonic hermeneutic errors.

Twelve Reasons to Accept a 1,000 Year Rule of Christ in the Millennium

The golden rules to all honorable, consistent, Bible interpretation are basically twofold: (1) accept the words in the text in their natural historical meaning, and (2) look for the single meaning/sense of each text. Those two rules govern the entire process of sound, solid, and sanctified Bible interpretation. If we read the book of Revelation and chapter 20 in a plain and normal method that text provides at least twelve internal clues and reasons that show we should accept the 1,000 reign of Christ as a righteous, real, actual, earthly spiritual rule of King Jesus over this earth.

Those who do not accept this reign of Christ as a real, actual, and earthly rule of Christ show inconsistencies as they pick out six references and assert it as symbolism when they, as do most others, interpret everything or most

---

[249] Sam Storms, *Kingdom Come: The Amillennial Alternative* (Scotland, UK: Mentor Press, 2012), 3466-348.

everything else around those references as actual realities (not metaphorical or symbolical). A plain reading offers good reasons why to affirm a real earthly Christocracy. Remember, earthly or physical does not mean less spiritual.

One of the best Evangelical Confessions of faith on how to interpret Scripture in the 1970s remains a great guide today. The Chicago Statement on Hermeneutics provides a healthy confession of faith (produced by over 300 scholars). In it we find these words on how to interpret Scripture: "Article XV: We affirm the necessity of interpreting the Bible according to its literal, or normal, sense. The literal sense is the grammatical-historical sense, that is, the meaning which the writer expressed. Interpretation according to the literal sense will take account of all figures of speech and literary forms found in the text. We deny the legitimacy of any approach to Scripture that attributes to it meaning which the literal sense does not support." If we use that method of interpreting this text the best view remains that Christ will rule over this earth for a thousand years.

Granted, many who helped to create that great confession, were not premillennial (ex: Sproul & Packer). In such cases, we believe they had the right confession, but failed to properly apply that confession in practice to this text in Revelation.

Twelve Textual Clues

The biblical text itself gives us twelve clues or reasons as to why we should not understand this term 1,000 years as symbolic or figurative. Many who interpret Revelation 20:1-6 accept everything else in this section of text as actual, real, or tangible realities. In fact, if they do not in a few places, as in regards to Christ and Satan, that interpreter would fall into serious, egregious, and detestable views. Thankfully, most accept the terms Satan and Christ in this text as actual, tangible, real beings. But they reject one idea in this text as an actual tangible reality and embrace it more so as a symbol. And the multiple meanings offered by those who reject a literal interpretation reveal how highly subjective the interpretations become once the normal hermeneutic has been abandoned.

This text reveals a grand and glorious moment in earthly history when Satan loses and God's people conquer sin more than ever. Christ Jesus moves from mediating his authority through believers while he is in heaven to him coming to earth to directly mediate his authority. Dr. Swindoll reminds what this wonderful transition means:

> Jesus is not yet {prior to this period} exercising direct authority over the earth. Christ personally sits at the right hand of the Father (1 Pet. 3:22). He has received all authority over heaven and earth (Matt. 28:18), but in the present age he has not yet fully exercised his authority to reign (Heb. 2:8; 10:12-13). Because Jesus has not yet established his kingdom on earth, governments remain corrupt and sinful. For the world to be turned right side up, Jesus must take his throne and reign . . . . The good news is that the book of Revelation promises a golden age in which all weapons of warfare will be fashioned into implements of peace. Prosperity will be shared. Peace will be the banner of all people. The light of justice will illumine every corner of the world. . . . True global transformation will occur only when Satan and his minions are ousted, allowing Jesus Christ and his glorified saints to rule over the earth.[250]

---

[250] Charles R. Swindoll, *Swindoll's Living Insights New Testament Commentary: Revelation* (Carol Stream, IL: Tyndale Publishing, 2014), 282.

Twelve reasons in context show us why viewing this period as merely a symbol lacks theological support. A natural, historical-grammatical hermeneutic applied that discovers the single sense of the text yields solid reasons why a future victory era for Christ and his believers shall occur.

Reason One

First, the text speaks of an actual angel. The text says, "an angel coming down" (Rev. 20:1). Should we interpret this as some symbol and not a real, actual, literal angel? I do not think we can see this as some symbol. The OT and NT mentions angels who carry out the work of God in time and history. From Genesis to Revelation we see angels in Scripture around 90 or so times. These angels are real, actual, literal, spirit-beings who serve the Lord's purpose in some way or another (see Hebrews 1:14).

Reason Two

Second, we see this angel descending out of "heaven" (20:1). Certainly, Evangelicals would not think of this text as symbolic. There is a real, actual, literal, tangible heaven right now that Christ and his saints live and function in right now (see Hebrews 12:22-24). Saints who die today ascend to this actual place somewhere in God's grand universe. They reside there until Christ returns and then establishes a New Heaven and New Earth.

Reasons Three through Six

Third, fourth, fifth, and sixth reasons we see the description of the angel as (3) having a hand with a (4) key to the (5) bottomless pit with a (6) great chain (Rev. 20:1). Angels through Scripture manifest themselves in physical or corporeal form. They are created beings. So, it is not abnormal or strange to see the angel as actually having a hand and holding some type of key and chain in his hand. Some will quickly resort to the earthly type chains we have here now and claim this cannot be a real chain. It is not an earthly chain (one we humans have created). A chain created by humans could not hold a powerful being like Satan. But cannot God create a real eternal chain that he uses to bind a created being? The composite material of this chain may be unknown to us, but certainly not unknown to God. Dr. Paige Patterson reminds us

> The intention of the angel having a chain and a key to the Abyss is to apprehend Satan and confine him in chains to the Abyss. Prisoners in antiquity as now were bound with chains. One might reasonably ask how a spiritual being can be bound with a physical chain. But there is no indication as to the exact nature of the chain. While a literal event is portrayed, the precise nature of the chain that binds Satan remains unknown.[251]

Analogy of Faith

This is where we use the analogy of faith rule in hermeneutics. Does any other Scripture help us understand what this key and chain is? The analogy of faith means we interpret Scripture by Scripture. Scripture is clear and it is its own best interpreter. If we turn to Jude we see God mentioning these types of chains that he has used in the eternal spirit realm. Jude 6 says, "And the angels who did not stay within their own position of authority, but left their

---

[251] Paige Patterson, *The New American Commentary: Revelation*, Vol. 39, ed. E. Ray Clendenen (Nashville, TN: B&H Publishing, 2012), 351-352.

proper dwelling, he {God} has kept in eternal chains under gloomy darkness until the judgment of the great day."

Unless someone adopts a Christoplatonic ideology, then why could not God create a set of eternal chains that embody the power of Christ in it that he uses to bind a created being like demons (Jude 6) and Satan (Rev. 20)? Is God unable, not powerful enough, wise enough to create such a chain (open neo-theists would struggle here as they worship a finite god who may not know what a demon would do)?

Can God create an entire universe, even Satan and all the angels too and yet not have the power to create such a real, literal, and powerful eternal chain? It seems best to see this truly as a type of chain "that would be necessary to shackle a spiritual being such as Satan."[252]

As to the bottomless pit reference, does that refer to some mystical, unreal, intangible place? No it does not mean that. Again, if we look carefully at other places in the Bible we see this place mentioned. We have an actual, real, tangible, literal demon to explain for us that this place exists. In Luke 8 we read of Jesus healing a man under demonic influence. Jesus then spoke directly to this demon. He asked him his name. The demon spoke to Christ and said, "Legion" (Luke 8:30). Then look at what this demon begged of Christ. Legion, the demon, says to Jesus Christ the Lord that he desired not to be thrown "into the abyss," or what we sometimes translate as the bottomless pit.

The demons understood this place actually exists somewhere in God's universe. Legion did not desire to be cast into that place either. We see this term in various places through Scripture. Romans 10:7 and Revelation 9:1 also mention this real, actual, literal place. And at some point, at Christ's return he will use his powerful eternal chain that in

---

[252] Robert Thomas, *Revelation 8-22: An Exegetical Commentary* (Chicago, IL: Moody Press, 1995), 406.

some sense visualizes Christ's lordship in concrete form, to bind Satan to cast him into this pit that the demons were well aware of and even mentioned.

Reason Seven

Seventh, the text teaches that this angel "seized the dragon, that ancient serpent, who is the devil and Satan" (Rev. 20:2). Is the serpent in the Garden of Eden only a figure of speech? Was not Satan and a serpent literally, tangibly, and really in the Garden of Eden (Gen. 3)? Did not Eve literally with her senses experience of voice and hearing interact with this real being? Did not God curse the serpent and in that ordain the serpent to crawl on its belly from that point forward (Gen. 3:14)? Too, did not Christ meet with Satan and interact with him face to face (see Matt. 4)? Satan is an actual being. Originally created as an angel (see Ezek. 28 & Isa. 14), who later chose to rebel (through original freedom), Satan exists in a real, literal, tangible, corporeal body of some sort. Nothing in this text, or anywhere else in Scripture, should make us think Satan refers to a mere symbol or figure of speech.

Reasons Eight & Nine

Eighth and ninth, in this text we read that some people on some thrones will exercise their authority to judge. The Bible says, "I saw thrones, and seated on them were those to whom authority to judge was committed" (Rev. 20:4). Are these real, tangible places where people exercise authority granted to them from Christ? Yes, these are certainly such places. Again we see that many other texts speak of Christ's people exercising authority per his designation in a future era of time. In Matthew 19:28 Christ promised his twelve disciples that they would "sit on twelve thrones" as they "judge the twelve tribes of Israel." We see

Paul stating in 1 Corinthians 6:2-3 Paul mentions that "saints will judge the world."

Jesus Christ mentioned in Revelation 2:26-28 and 3:21 that he will give his faithful believers "authority over the nations" and that they will sit with Christ on his "throne." These descriptions paint for us a tangible, real, actual structure and organization where Christ's people will rule from positions that show or signify Christ's kingly authority.

These thrones are actual places, structures, or tangible realities where the redeemed carry out their righteous authority in behalf of the King Jesus as they exercise authority over the nations. Just as judges sit on seats behind a bench in their courtrooms exercising authority today, or as leaders have chairs and desks from where they make executive decisions, so too there will come a time when believers will do that over the nations and over the spheres Christ appoints them. Today legislative bodies, presidents, and governors, and other similar type government leaders around the world appoint judges to rule for the cause of justice.

In this era, Christ, the King of kings and Lord of lords will appoint his judges throughout the universe. Nothing in this text requires these to be only figures of speech or some symbol any more than saying the terms "bench trial," which refers to a judge ruling from the bench, means he does not have a real chair and bench from where he or she rules. Dr. John Gill, the prolific and famous 1700s Calvinist Baptist theologian said of this text, "Besides the throne of God the Father, and the thrown of glory, on which the Son of God sits, and the twelve thrones for the twelve Apostles of the Lamb: there will be thrones set, or pitched, for all the saints, Dan. 7:9; who will sit on them, in the character of kings, and as conquerors . . . . power, dominion, regal authority, possession of a kingdom" belongs to them as they sit as "kings" in their "position" as they are "sitting on thrones."[253]

Reasons Ten through Twelve

Tenth, eleventh, and twelfth we also see real, literal, actual people who have died for their faith in following after Christ. John stated he saw "the souls of those who had been beheaded for the testimony of Jesus and for the word of God" (Rev. 20:4b). These were mentioned earlier in the book of Revelation in chapter 6. We read there that John saw "souls of those who had been slain for the Word of God and for the witness they had borne. They cried out with a loud voice, 'O Sovereign Lord, holy and true, how long before you will judge and avenge our blood on those who dwell on the earth?'" (6:9-10). Are we to believe this earth is not the real earth, i.e. the actual tangible earth where these people testified and gave their lives for the real, actual, tangible Jesus Christ? Were they not standing before the presence of God crying out to him in a real, literal, actual heaven? In these verses we have (10) literal souls who have (11) experienced death through martyrdom.

Additionally, (number 12) is not the reference "the testimony of Jesus" and the "word of God" actual, literal, real, and tangible realities? What is the testimony of Jesus? In John 15:18-25 Jesus Christ spoke of persecution for his name and for following him. In John 16:2 Christ spoke of a persecution so strong that it leads to the physical death of the disciples.

Is not the word of God an actual, tangible, reality that we have in print preserved for our instruction? Did not Paul even as he approached his dying hours desire to have the

---

[253] John Gill, *Gill's Commentary*, Vol. VI: *Romans to Revelation* (Grand Rapids, MI: Baker Books, reprinted in 1980 with original 1852-1854 copyright), 1064.

physical scrolls/parchments (Scriptures) so as to comfort him as he neared his departure for glory (2 Tim. 4:13)? The souls that died did so because they gave their lives for a real, tangible, actual, literal Lord and Savior Jesus Christ who left for us real, tangible, actual, literal words we call the Holy Scriptures. Nothing in this text here offers any idea we ought to approach this text as some figurative or symbolic text.

Summary of the Twelve Reasons

If we can easily and with biblical support interpret those twelve realities in this text in a normal, historical, plain, or literal way, why would we not do so also with the verses that mention the OT prophesied kingdom age that is to last one thousand years? The disciples were still expecting this kingdom to come as Jesus departed for heaven at his ascension (Acts 1:1-11). Jesus affirmed to them that their hope was right though he instructed them to have patience on when it would arrive (Acts 1:7). Dr. Wiersbe explained the matter.

> Jesus did not rebuke them when they 'kept asking' about the future Jewish kingdom (Acts 1:7). After all, {Jesus} had opened their minds to understand the Scriptures (Luke 24:44) so they knew what they were asking. But God has not revealed his timetable to us and it is futile for us to speculate. The important thing is not to be curious about the future but to be busy in the present, sharing the message of God's *spiritual* kingdom.[254]

The kingdom of God comes to this earth through a holistic means. The disciples expressed to Jesus their hope

---

[254] Warren W. Wiersbe, *The Bible Exposition Commentary*, Volume 1 (Wheaton, IL: Victor Books, 1989), 403.

for the coming Chistocracy, the millennial kingdom and eternal Kingly rule of Jesus. The time for the return of Christ to rule cannot be known. But the means that leads up to that moment remains central to the kingdom work. Dr. W.A. Criswell offered one of the most balanced views of this matter related to the disciples question in Acts 1:7.

His wisdom helps us to avoid two extremes. We must avoid date setting on when this millennial and eternal kingdom shall begin. But we must also avoid becoming lazy and lethargic because we know it will miraculously occur. Instead, we must work for the spiritual kingdom while we also wait for the ultimate kingdom to arrive. Dr. Criswell explained it well.

> There is a day coming, a time set when the kingdom will be seen visibly and our King will appear personally. There is a strategy in God's kingdom work that is cataclysmic. Without announcement . . . the heavens will suddenly be rolled back like a scroll, and God will descend and the kingdom will come. There is another character in the strategy of almighty God regarding his coming kingdom. The second part is not cataclysmic, it is not suddenly bursting, but rather it is gradual and progressive . . . . The strategy of God is his coming kingdom is twofold. It is cataclysmic and sudden but it is also gradual and progressive. It is not just that we are waiting for the coming king, but it is also that we are working and evangelizing, teaching, training, witnessing, and discipling.[255]

Peter continued to hope for that kingdom to come while he also worked for it by preaching that the times of

---

[255] W.A. Criswell, *Acts: An Exposition*, in One Volume (Grand Rapids, MI: Zondervan, 1980), 31.

restoration for Israel was at hand and would arrive if the nation as a whole would repent and receive the Messiah (Acts 3:19-21). Jesus did not correct, redirect, and rebuke the disciples for their understanding of the Old Testament earthly millennial kingdom reign view and hope. It is not a matter of "if" Israel will be restored when the kingdom arrives, but "when" because "the issue is not the fact of restoration, but the timing: 'When is it going to happen?'"[256]

These truths from Acts help us as we interpret Revelation. If the disciples hoped for this coming kingdom, why should we not read Revelation with that same hope they had? Why would this one thousand year reality not also be interpreted as a real, tangible, actual, literal rule of Christ for that many years in a world where he is King? Why would it also not be a real period that takes place prior to the eternal state of Revelation chapters 21 and 22? The Reformed Baptist Dr. John Gill gave a great summary of these verses in Revelation 20. He said this section teaches the following:

> This chapter contains the binding of Satan, the saints' thousand-year's reign with Christ, the loosing of Satan again, the destruction of him . . . . the angel that is to bind Satan is described by his descent from heaven: by his having the key of the bottomless pit, and a great chain in his hand; and by the use he made of them, laying hold on Satan, binding him, casting him into the bottomless pit, and then shutting it up, and setting a seal on him; by which he will be prevented from deceiving the nations for a space of a thousand years.[257]

---

[256] Arnold Fruchtenbaum, *Ariel's Bible Commentary: The Book of Acts* (San Antonio, TX: Ariel Ministries, 2022), 44.

[257] John Gill, *Gill's Commentary: Romans through Revelation* (Grand Rapids, MI: Baker Book House, reprint of the William Hill London 1852-1854 edition), 6:1061.

For those who reject this interpretation, I want to ask what could Christ or any apostle have said to make a 1,000 year rule plain had he wanted to really say it? If Apostle John said it six times here that the kingdom would last 1,000 years, how many times would he need to say it for it to be real and not merely symbolic? Or if John had not wanted it to be a symbol, what way do you think he would or could have written it to convey it was literal instead of symbolic? Too, what words could have Christ used had he wanted to actually teach a real, tangible, literal one thousand year rule on earth? How else could a writer of Scripture have said that if he truly wanted to say that?

Furthermore, if these verses mean just a symbolic long era, no real definite period, why did not John say something like he did in Revelation 7:9 where he said it was such a large number that it could not be counted? Or why did he not say it would be "like a thousand years," which were common ways to introduce to the reader some type of approximate or figurative account? It seems through the book of Revelation we have many numbers that are exactly that, fixed, determinate, actual, literal real numbers.

For example, it is not hard to accept that there were three unclean spirits in Revelation 16:13, three angels in the last three woes (8:13), and seven churches in Revelation 2 through 3. Those numbers do not signify some incorporeal symbol or refer to something that is innumerable and symbolic of something else. Why should we from this text, with so much immediate context around it that speaks of literal realities, convey something non-literal and merely symbolic?

Furthermore, if these verses mean just an symbolic long era, no real definite period, why did not John say something like he did in Revelation 7:9 where he said it was such a large number that it could not be counted? These contextual matters lead us to see how John spoke when he

206

wanted to convey symbols or approximations versus when he wanted to convey precision and literal concepts.

A Wrong Presupposition that Hinders Prophetic Interpretation

Throughout this work the importance of hermeneutics has been emphasized. When we read any document we ought to apply the normal or plain hermeneutic to the text. In this process the definition of words becomes key. Though we do not have an inspired dictionary in scripture to define all of the words used by the Lord, the interpreter can still discover the meaning to words through examining context, using Bible dictionaries, lexicons, and other linguistic tools.

One reason why some interpreters misunderstand prophetic portions of scripture relates to the underlying presupposition that the physical constitutes carnality and so we should seek the spiritual. The term spiritual then becomes one of the most problematic terms in scripture. Often the wrong definition of this one term creates some of the greatest confusion in matters related to prophetic truths of scripture.

Improper Definition of Spiritual

Sometimes interpreters believe the term "spiritual" must mean something other than a real, physical, or corporeal, tangible reality. When these who are often infected with Christoplatonism ideology read their Bible and they see the term spiritual they often read/interpret that as something intangible because the tangible (literal, real, physical like structures) is not as good as the spirit world, which they interpret as better than physical. Again this relates back to the Greek philosophy that adopted the wrong idea of the spirit world being good and the physical world being bad, a Gnostic idea.

207

The failure to rightly define the word spiritual seems to have been a serious stumbling block to some of the older and weaker amillennial teachers of the past. Their criticisms against premillennial believers often revolved around the idea that to affirm an earthly millennial rule of Christ missed the more heavenly and spiritual form of the kingdom.

To those amillennial teachers an earthly kingdom lacked spirituality. This can be found in the writings of the older amillennial teacher Dr. Oswald T. Allis (1880-1973). He and Dr. John Walvoord (1910-2002) had an ongoing sharp debate throughout their ministerial lives. I am sure they now rejoice and worship Christ together in glory. But for Allis, he viewed the idea of an earthly kingdom as a problem.

Allis raised the issue of the nature of the kingdom. To him this question had great weight in pointing to the proper view of the kingdom.[258] In his view, the idea of a physical kingdom on this earth with Jesus ruling over the world and Israel obtaining her promised land constituted a "worldly kingdom."[259] Instead, he believed the real kingdom offered by Jesus "was primarily and essentially a moral and spiritual kingdom." [260] For Allis when Jesus said his kingdom was not of this world (John 18:36), such a statement precludes a physical rule of Christ on this earth, i.e. the premillennial view.

In this weaker and more platonic amillennial worldview, Christ's kingdom does not primarily relate to this physical world. For it to be holy or spiritual the kingdom must not have strong associations with this earth or the

---

[258] Oswald T. Allis, *Prophecy and the Church* (Phillipsburg, NJ: Presbyterian and Reformed Publishing Company, 1947), 69-70.

[259] Ibid., 71.

[260] Ibid., 70.

physical world. Some amillennial writers view this as a carnal form of kingdom theology. But the problem relates to the idea of what it means to be spiritual.

Solution: A Biblical Definition of Spiritual to Understand the Holiness of a Millennial Kingdom

The right definition of spiritual resolves the concerns here with the platonic amillennial models. Dr. Charles Ryrie noted many years ago that believers will use the term spiritual without giving a definition to the term. He recognized that one can search "in vain for a concise definition of the concept itself."[261] This lack of precision and objectivity in the definition causes trouble when dealing with prophetic matters related to Israel and the kingdom.

An example of this definition confusion with Dr. Louis Berkhof and his idea what it means for the kingdom of Christ to be not of this world. His confusion on the definition of spiritual hinders his ideas here. Dr. Berkhof, like Allis, has argued that John 18:36 means no earthly kingdom here shall exist because Christ's kingdom is not of this world. Instead, Christ's kingdom is a spiritual kingdom. For Berkhof Jesus "never had in mind" the ideas of the Old Testament theocratic kingdom, but instead declared "the introduction of the spiritual reality, of which the Old Testament kingdom was but a type."[262]

However, the biblical definition for spiritual primarily means "maturity," or under "Spirit-control over a

---

Charles C. Ryrie, *Balancing the Christian Life* (Chicago, IL: Moody Press, 1994), 12.

[262] Louis Berkhof, *Systematic Theology* (Louisville, KY: GLH Publishing, 2017), 614.

period of time."[263] Therefore, when thinking with the wrong definition the amillennial believer fails to realize the millennial kingdom can be earthly and spiritual at the same time. Just as Jesus was in this world and spiritual while being of this world so too can the people in the Christocracy.

Believers, resurrected and non-resurrected believers, can be rightly under the control of the Spirit with Christ ruling in that period. It can be a spiritual kingdom in the sense that the people obey the Spirit's rule and walk under the authority of Jesus. Speaking to this issue Dr. Fruchtenbuam gave a helpful clarification to the problems in the more platonic (Christoplatonism) amillennial models.

> As for John 18:36, Berkhof rests his case on Christ's statement, *My kingdom is not of this world.* Amillennialists interpret the statement *not of this world* to mean that Christ's kingdom will not be *in* this world. A denial of the kingdom being *of* this world is for them a denial of the kingdom being *in* this world. That this cannot be so is clear . . . . Speaking of himself Jesus, Jesus said, *I am not of the world* (17:14,16); but several times he did say that he was *in* the world (17:11, 12, 13). . . . Not to be of the world means the believer is no longer *of* this world's nature, though he may very well be *in* the world still. By the same token, Christ's Messianic Kingdom may be in the world, but will not be of this world's nature.[264]

---

[263] Charles C. Ryrie, *Balancing the Christian Life* (Chicago, IL: Moody Press, 1994), 13.

[264] Arnold Fruchtenbaum, *Israelology: The Missing Link to Systematic Theology* (Tustin, CA: Ariel Ministries, 1989), 192.

Dr. Fruchtenbaum also in line with Ryrie defines the term spiritual. For one to be a spiritual person that means the person "is under the control of the Holy Spirit."[265] This applies to the nature of the kingdom too. Because Christ will be present, and the Holy Spirit will be present with glorified believers and born again saints, this kingdom will be a spiritual (holy) kingdom. It is not sinful, or carnal, or "of this world."

In fact, it will have a miraculous inauguration because it begins when Christ Jesus descends from heaven to earth to establish it with his immediate presence. How much more climatic and miraculous can it be? The millennial kingdom is spiritual, holy, and established from above as Christ Jesus returns to rule and reign. Hardly can this be seen as less than holy or spiritual. Once a person drops platonic ideology (the earthly world is less holy) then these matters become much clearer to the Bible reader.[266]

---

[265] Ibid., 700.

[266] The confusion with the term spiritual occurs also with the term spiritual Jew. Some wrongly believe that when a Gentile believes in Christ that one becomes a spiritual Jew. This is wrong. A believing Jew is a holy (spiritual) Jew. A believing Gentile is a holy (spiritual) Gentile. When one reads or speaks the term spiritual another good way to read or speak that is to use the term holy or righteous. People sometimes commit this error with Romans 2:28-29. The text speaks of a Jew as one who is one "inwardly" from the circumcision "of the heart, by the Spirit." If one understands by the Spirit to refer to being holy or righteous the text will make sense. To be circumcised in the heart is to be made righteous. An ethnic Jew is a spiritual or righteous or holy Jew when the Spirit circumcises the heart. This text does not say a Gentile becomes a spiritual Jew upon conversion. Ethnicity does not change upon belief in Christ. Paul does not begin to speak directly to Gentiles again after Romans 2 until Romans 3:29. The context thus in no way supports the idea that Paul was saying 2:28-29 that Gentiles become Jews inwardly upon conversion.

The Premillennial View is the Most Ancient View of the Historic Church

When we examine the major truths related to the end of the world and the world to come, one ought to root their views in ancient Christian history as much as possible. Sadly, Dr. Shelley has correctly noted that "many Christians today suffer from historical amnesia." And as a "consequence" many have a real "ignorance concerning Christian history."[267]

This ignorance comes to light with the doctrine of End Times, i.e. eschatology. Many seem unaware at best or willfully opposed at worst to the reality that the earliest disciples of the apostolic age affirmed a future Christocracy where Christ returns to rule and reign for 1,000 years over this earth. Amillennial theology and postmillennial theology are the new kids on the block so to speak. They lack the great antiquity that the premillennial doctrine carries with it. Though variations, nuances, and more developed models of premillennial theology have emerged through the 2,000 years of historical reflection, the fundamental foundations of premillennial theology have solid roots back to the earliest of disciples in the evangelical church.

Whether one is a historic premillennialist, classical/traditional dispensational premillennialist, revised dispensational premillennialist, progressive dispensational premillennialist, Reformed Covenant premillennialist, promise kingdom premillennialist, or some other hybrid form of premillennialist, all versions of premillennialism have their roots back to the earliest of disciples in church history. The seeds and even some substantive forms of premillennialism were taught by some of the most faithful

---

[267] Bruce Shelley, *Church History in Plain Language* (Nashville, TN: Thomas Nelson Publishing, 1995), xv.

brethren in the early church era. And some who taught premillennial theology even learned directly from the Apostles of Christ.

All believers that reject premillennialism theology and embrace some newer model (amillennialism or postmillennialism) must realize they have embraced a novel development in church history. Antiquity and apostolic connection rests with the premillennial view. Consequently, if antiquity matters (and it should), and if historical roots to our forefathers matter (it should), then all believers should have a deep appreciation and respect for the premillennial model of end times.

Historian Dr. Phillip Schaff commented on the predominance of the premillennial doctrine in the earliest periods of church history. He stated,

> The most striking point in the eschatology of the ante-Nicene age is the prominent chiliasm, or millennarianism, that is the belief of a visible reign of Christ in glory on earth with the risen saints for a thousand years, before the general resurrection and judgment.[268]

Esteemed church Historian Dr. Henry Sheldon has affirmed this same view of history with our earliest forefathers of the faith. In his review of church history he claims that in this earliest period the "millenarian views were more widely prevalent" than at any other "subsequent era" of church history. [269] For these first few years following

---

[268] Phillip Schaff, *History of the Christian Church: Ante-Nicene Christianity A.D. 100-325* (Peabody, MA: Hendrickson Publishers, 1858), 2:614.

[269] Henry Sheldon, *History of the Christian Church: The Early Church, Volume 1* (Peabody, MA: Hendrickson Publishers, 1895), 238.

Christ's Apostles till the 4th century or so, the premillennial view "came to find increasing support among Christian teachers."[270]

Not only do church historians recognize and admit this, but even those who do not embrace premillennial views recognize this historical fact. Dr. William G.T. Shedd, who opposes premillennial views and tries to minimize how prevalent this doctrine was in the early church, still admitted that the premillennial view was "flourishing" in the early church between 150 and 250."[271]

After explaining the general main tenants of premillennial theology with even the Jewish centricity view of it where "Jerusalem will be rebuilt," Dr. Louis Berkhof references the ancient historicity of this view. He stated, "in general this representation" of premillennial doctrine "is the typical" model of eschatological views of the "early Christian centuries."[272]

Historical theologian Dr. Gregg Allison traced the premillennial views through the early church and noted that the view extended all the way back to Papius who was a student of Apostle John. "This premillennial hope . . . was strong in the early church" until "church leaders from Alexandria, Egypt—Clement and Origen—offered an alternative eschatology that undermined premillennialism."[273]

---

[270] J.N.D. Kelley, *Early Christian Doctrines* (New York, NY: Harper Collins Publishing, 1978), 465.

[271] William G.T. Shedd, *Dogmatic Theology*, ed. Alan W. Gomes (Phillipsburg, NJ: Presbyterian & Reformed Publishing, 2003), 863.

[272] Louis Berkhof, *Systematic Theology* (Louisville, KY: GLH Publishing, 2017), 610.

[273] Gregg Allison, *Historical Theology: An Introduction to Christian Doctrine* (Grand Rapids, MI: Zondervan, 2011), 685-687.

The shift from the historical-grammatical hermeneutic to the allegorical model led to the dilution and "undermining" of "premillennialism" as the interpreters discarded the physical realities for some supposed "spiritual meaning" and "spiritual blessings."[274] These shifts led to "Tyconius and his chief follower Augustine" to establish a new and novel view of "amillennialism" where they argued the prophecies of Scripture would be fulfilled "spiritually" and not "literally" as the early church leaders had taught prior to this shift when the premillennial doctrine prevailed.[275]

When examining the history of the church, the record of facts reveals clearly that the disciples closest to the original Apostles of Christ affirmed some form of premillennial views. So strong was the view in the early church Dr. Tim LaHaye rightly could say: "Early Christians were unquestionably premillennialists" and this "dominant view held during the first three centuries of the early church."[276] Even a stern critic of the premillennial model of theology, C. Norman Kraus admits to this early church reality. He could not deny that some of earliest fathers of the church were "leaders" who "taught that the Kingdom of God would be climaxed in history by the reign of Christ on earth for one thousand years (a millennium)."[277]

As noted earlier, various versions of premillennial views exist. Some claim two models exist, others see three

---

[274] Ibid., 687.

[275] Ibid., 687-688.

[276] Tim LaHaye, "Millennial Views," in *The Harvest Handbook of Bible Prophecy*, eds. Ed Hindson, Mark Hitchcock, & Tim LaHaye (Eugene, OR: Harvest House Publishers, 2020), 255.

[277] C. Norman Kraus, *Dispensationalism in America: Its Rise and Development* (Richmond, VA: John Knox Press, 1958), 24.

models that exist, and some of us see four or five types of premillennial theology. Yet in all models some basic keys unite the stream of thought. This historicity of this has been properly summarized by Dr. Millard J. Erickson.

> The view that we today term premillennialism has a long history, having roots in the early church. Probably it was the dominant belief during the apostolic period, when Christians believed strongly in the approaching end of the world and the parousia of Jesus Christ . . . . This hope was exceedingly intense at times. . . . {and} in the postapostolic period the eschatological hope was still strong . . . .[278]

A Brief List of Early Church Premillennial Leaders

In the 1800s George N.H. Peters (1825-1909) served as a Lutheran minister and penned one of the largest "compilations of quotes from all the writings of the last two thousand years dealing with the kingdom and the literal return of Christ to earth."[279] In his 3 volume set titled *The Theocratic Kingdom* he compiled over four thousand quotes" as he defended the premillennial view of prophecy.[280] He too recognized that premillennial views were the original views of the earliest leaders of the historic church. He offered a massive list of teachers who promoted premillennial doctrine.

---

[278] Millard J. Erickson, *Contemporary Options in Eschatology: A Study of the Millennium* (Grand Rapids, MI: Baker Books, 1977), 94.

[279] Mal Couch, "George N.H. Peters," in the *Dictionary of Premillennial Theology* (Grand Rapids, MI: Kregel Publications, 1996), 302.

[280] Ibid.

1st Century Premillennial Teachers

Dr. Peters noted that Papias (AD 80-163) recognized the following as teachers of premillennialism in the 1st century. Granted, some will obviously object to the listing of the original Apostles. But, if Papias was correct on this historical account, then the weight in favor of premillennialism becomes so overwhelming one could not oppose it without being in opposition to the actual NT authors.

- Andrew,

- Peter,

- Philip,

- Thomas,

- James,

- John,

- Matthew,

- Aristio,

- John the Presbyter,

- Clement of Rome (AD 40-100),

- Barnabas (AD 40-100),

- Hermas (AD 40-140),

- Ignatius (AD 50-115), &

- Polycarp (AD 70-167).

Of this 1st century era, Dr. Peters summarized saying that "not a single name can be presented, which (1) can be quoted as positively against us, or (2) which can be cited as teaching, in any shape or sense, the doctrine of our opponents."[281]

2nd Century Premillennial Teachers

Of the 2nd century Dr. Peters listed these as premillennial teachers:

- Ponthinus (AD 87-177),

- Justin Martyr (AD 100-168),

- Melito (AD 100-170),

- Hegisippus (AD 130-190),

- Tatian (AD 130-190),

- Irenaeus (AD 140-202),

- the Churches of Vienne and Lyons,

- Tertullian (AD 150-220), &

---

[281] George N.H. Peters, *The Theocratic Kingdom*, 3 Volumes (Grand Rapids, MI: Kregel Publishing, originally published by Funk & Wagnalls of New York in 1884), 1: 494-495.

- Hippolytus (AD 160-240).

Dr. Peters goes on to say of this 2nd century era, "not a single writer can be presented, not even a single name can be mentioned of any one cited, who opposed chiliasm (premillennial doctrine) in {the 2nd century}. Now let the student reflect: here are two centuries . . . in which positively no direct opposition whatever arises against our (premillennial) doctrine, but it is held by the very men, leading and most eminent, through whom we trace the church."[282]

3rd Century Premillennial Teachers

As we move into the 3rd century, the premillennial views continued to remain the standard view of the main teachers. Of the 3rd century, Dr. Peters continues to cite early fathers who taught premillennial views.

- Cyprian (AD 200-258),

- Commodian (AD 200-270),

- Nepos (AD 230-280),

- Coracion (AD 230-280),

- Victorinus (AD 240-303),

- Methodius (AD 250-311), &

- Lactantius (AD 240-330).[283]

---

[282] Ibid., 1:496.

[283] Ibid., 1:496.

219

Summary: Non-Premillennial Views Lack Historical Continuity with the Early Church

When one studies church history it becomes very clear that any theology that totally rejects premillennial views has lost substantive continuity with the earliest period of church history. That poses a real problem for all non-premillennial teachers. This may be why Justin Martyr (AD 100-168) stated, "right minded Christians know that there will be a resurrection of the dead and a thousand years in Jerusalem, which will be built, adorned, and enlarged as the prophets Ezekiel and Isaiah and the others declare. . . . And, further, a certain man with us, named John, one of the Apostles of Christ, predicted by a revelation that was made to him that those who believed in our Christ would spend a thousand years in Jerusalem. . . ."[284]

Further weight is given to the premillennial view in the connection back to Apostle John. Justin Martyr thought this doctrine of the millennial reign of Christ had been passed down to them from Apostle John. He stated, "there was a certain man with us, whose name was John, one of the Apostles of Christ, who prophesied by a revelation that was made to him, that those who believed in our Christ would dwell a thousand years in Jerusalem."[285] This rule of Christ and resurrection would then be followed by "the general resurrection . . . eternal resurrection and judgment of all men would likewise take place.[286]

---

[284] Justin Martyr, "Dialogue of Justin, Philosopher and Martyr, with Trypho a Jew," in *Ante-Nicene Fathers* (Peabody, MA: Hendrickson Publishers, 1999), 1:239.

[285] Ibid., 1:240.

[286] Ibid.

Whatever one believes or finds helpful from other views (some emphases from other eschatology models have some benefit), to totally reject the premillennial faith equals a divorce from the first 300 years of church history. Such theologians wear the name novelty on their theology. They lack continuity with the ancient church. Only premillennial teachers have historic continuity to the earliest teachers of the evangelical body of Christ.

Dr. Peters was correct, based on this historical data, to ask what should be the reasonable conclusion of the historical data? His answers were: "(1) that the common faith of the Church was Chiliastic {premillennial}, and (2) that such a generality and unity of belief could only have been introduced . . . by the founders of the Church and the Elders appointed by them."[287]

Truth # 5: A New Heaven and a New Earth including a New Jerusalem

One of the unique aspects of our Christian faith is that God comes down to man. In all false world religions you have people seeking to move in some way towards God to meet him and/or to obtain favor with him. Our theology is radically different in the Christian faith. Not only did God come to us in the form of flesh through the incarnation, but in the future our God will also renew the earth and bring the New Heaven down to a New Earth where we shall rule and reign forever with Christ our King and LORD.

The entire cosmos, which includes Earth, will be renewed and recreated. The old will transition into the new

---

[287] George N.H. Peters, *The Theocratic Kingdom*, 3 Volumes (Grand Rapids, MI: Kregel Publishing, originally published by Funk & Wagnalls of New York in 1884), 1:496.

as the old order that has the marks of the curse on it will vanish and the new order will replace it (2 Peter 3:10-13).

Isaiah 65:17 and Revelation 21:1-2 also speak of a New Heavens and New Earth. Dr. Randy Alcorn says of this, "The new heavens will surely be superior to the old heavens, which themselves are filled with untold billions of stars and perhaps trillions of planets. . . . The Bible's final two chapters make clear that every aspect of the new creation will be greater than the old. . . . the new heavens will include new galaxies, planets, moons, white dwarf stars, neutron stars, black holes, and quasars. . . . the whole universe was intended to be under mankind's dominion . . . .[and] the new entire universe will be ours to travel to, inhabit, and rule— to God's glory."[288]

Additionally, God will recreate the earth and form this earth into a New Earth for us to live, dwell, and work with as we rule under him. People sometimes struggle to understand what the New Earth will be like. Much of that has to do with the Gnostic ideology of Greek platonic thought that has infiltrated the fields of sacred theology. Early in church history through Philo's (20 BC-AD 54), Clement of Alexandria's (150-215), and Origen's (185-254) allegorical biblical interpretative methodologies (Alexandrian school of thought) people were deceived by ideologies that the physical was bad and the non-physical was good.[289]

As Dr. Mal Couch properly noted, this allegorical mysticism had roots from the Greek philosophers like Xeophanes (570-475 B.C.), Plato (427-347 B.C.), and others

---

[288] Randy Alcorn, *Heaven* (Wheaton, IL: Tyndale House Publishers, 2004), 253-254.

[289] Ibid, 460-461.

who interpreted the poems of Homer allegorically.[290] These philosophers thought Homer's poems could not be read to children safely or taken in their literal meanings. Thus they resorted to allegorical, symbolic interpretations.

Subsequent to those philosophers, Philo, a Jew who loved both the Mosaic Law as well as Greek philosophy, sought to blend aspects of biblical revelation with Greek philosophy. Philo influenced the likes of Clement of Alexandria and Origen who took his mysticism further into the history of Christ's body. As Dr. Couch highlighted:

> Philo taught that the milk of Scripture was the literal but the meat was the allegory. Thus, there was a hidden meaning. The Word of God had two levels: the literal was on the surface, but the allegorical represented the deeper, more spiritual meaning. Therefore, anyone who simply interpreted the Bible in its most natural, normal way was simple and missing the great meanings of the Scriptures.[291]

The essential basis of Gnostic thought, which is that the non-physical soul is good while the physical material is bad, is Platonic dualism.[292] Such thoughts "profoundly influenced the early church"[293] as well as the church today. A person's view on Christ's physical body and spirit, our body now and in the resurrection, sexual relation laws

---

[290] Mal Couch, *An Introduction to Classical Evangelical Hermeneutics* (Grand Rapids, MI: Kregel Publications, 2000), 95.

[291] Ibid, 97.

[292] Louis P. Pojman, "*Gnosticism,*" in *The Cambridge Dictionary of Philosophy*, second edition, ed. Robert Audi (New York, NY: Cambridge University Press, 1999), 346.

[293] Ibid.

(morality of it; celibacy, monogamy, the levirate law, and promiscuity in contrast to purity) are all issues where Platonic dualism has influenced or likely will influence biblical interpreters towards various conclusions.

Additionally, views on eating (dietary laws), the more physical or less physical views of the millennial kingdom, styles of music acceptable to God, alcohol, and as particularly noted here, heaven itself will likely be shaped by one's underlying presuppositions in this area. These preliminary ideologies that one brings to the biblical text can impact how one understands these issues.

For example, a Gnostic ideology undercuts the biblical view of pleasure, which robs us of a proper view of the new life to come in the New Heavens and New Earth. Platonic and Gnostic ideologies argue people should not enjoy natural pleasures. It is the philosophy that leads to asceticism, which Apostle Paul directly denounced (see Col. 2:23 ESV). That Gnostic dualism ideology influenced how people thought about the New Heavens and New Earth to come.

Dr. Randy Alcorn calls this "Christoplatonism."[294] He says that because of this ideology "we resist the biblical picture of a bodily resurrection of the dead and life on the New Earth; of eating and drinking in heaven; of walking and talking, living in dwelling places, traveling down streets, and going through gates from one place to another; and of ruling, working, playing, and engaging in earthly culture."[295]

But Scripture presents a real, tangible, physical New Earth where saints in new resurrected bodies will dwell, live, roam, rule, fellowship, and serve God and one another for the endless of ages. We shall experience wonderful

---

[294] Randy Alcorn, *Heaven* (Wheaton, IL: Tyndale House Publishers, 2004), 459-460.

[295] Ibid, 460.

pleasures, many of which we had on this Earth, but in the New Earth they will be perfected and the stain of sin removed from the pleasures.

However, Christoplatonism argues that "people should shun physical pleasures. But who's the inventor of pleasure? Who made food and water, eating and drinking, marriage and sex, friendship and games, art and music, celebration and laughter? God did."[296] Life on the New Earth will have virtually everything there that was considered good here, albeit just in a better and sinless environment. Read that last sentence again and meditate on that.

Furthermore, within this New Earth will be the New City of God. The New Jerusalem will be one of the grandest features of the new order. Humanity started in a Garden of Eden and it will culminate with a New Earth that has a celestial city that nothing in all of history could compare. Dr. Alcorn says of this city:

> Fifteen times in Revelation 21 and 22 the place of God and his people will live together is called a city. The repetition of the word and the detailed description of the architecture, walls, streets, and other features of the city suggest that the term city isn't merely a figure of speech but a literal geographical location. After all, where do we expect physically resurrected people to live if not in a physical environment?
>
> Everyone knows what a city is—a place with buildings, streets, and residences occupied by people and subject to a common government. Cities have inhabitants, visitors, bustling activity, cultural events, and gatherings involving music, the arts,

---

[296] Ibid, 463.

education, religion, entertainment, and athletics. If the capital city of the New Earth doesn't have these defining characteristics of a city, it would seem misleading for Scripture to repeatedly call it a city.[297]

The Scriptures also give to us a detailed picture of even the size of this city. Revelation 21:15-16 describe the dimensions of the New Jerusalem. The Bible says, "The angel who talked to me held in his hand a gold measuring stick to measure the city, its gates, and its wall. When he measured it, he found it was a square, as wide as it was long.

In fact, it was in the form of a cube, for its length and width and height were 1,400 miles. Then he measured the walls and found them to be 216 feet thick (the angel used a standard human measure)" (Rev. 21:15-17 NLT).

Skeptics of the Bible and/or those suffering from the Alexandrian school of allegorism will often dismiss such a measurement and/or mark it off as a figure of speech. But why could God not build such a city of such a size? If he can create the earth from nothing (ex-nihilo), if he can make a donkey talk, an ax head float in water, dead people come forth from the grave, turn water into wine, heal people from paralysis, and hang planets and stars in the universe should we think it too hard for our God to create a gorgeous, stunning, and magnanimous city like this for his beloved saints to use for all of eternity?

Is it any harder to believe God could create an earth and suspend it in space at exactly the proper distance from the sun so it could sustain life than to believe he could create this type of city for his saints on a New Earth? I love what Dr. Robert Thomas says of this text: "Though staggering to the human mind, a city fifteen hundred miles high and fifteen hundred miles on each side is no more unimaginable than a

---

[297] Ibid, 241.

226

pearl large enough to serve as a city-gate or gold that is as transparent as glass."[298]

Some have expressed concern over the structural stability of a city in the form of a cube of 1,400 to 1,500 miles.[299] But is it not possible that God knows more about architectural design than what we do in our present point of historical progress? If the walls are over 200 feet thick might that not also point to the strength of the walls to carry the massive weight of the structure?

Furthermore, some have claimed this city could not be that high due to human's need for oxygen. But again, are we then saying God is limited in being able to provide oxygen at those heights? Or what if those in glorified bodies will not need oxygen in the same way we do today in our present physical bodies? It seems to me such questions as these highlight a seed of skepticism, a vestige of unbelief in the supernatural power of an Almighty God.

To be sure we all struggle with that. Just ask me whenever I am in some trial. I struggle with unbelief in my own heart just like everyone else does. In such cases the remedy is to pray as did the father of a child in Scripture who said: "Lord I believe but help my unbelief" (Mark 9:24).

The descriptive features of this New Jerusalem highlight the meticulous detail that God has in his design of this celestial city. We even read in Revelation that "the twelve gates were twelve pearls, each gate made of a single pearl. The great street of the city was of pure gold, like transparent glass" (Rev. 21:21). These physical descriptions are detailed and nothing in the context leads us to believe this is figurative language.

---

[298] Robert Thomas, *Revelation 8-22: An Exegetical Commentary* (Chicago, IL: Moody Press, 1995), 467.

[299] Ibid.

227

If all of this is symbolic what shall we also do with the detailed description of the future temple as so described in Ezekiel 40:6-47; 41:2-21; 42:1-14; 43:13-27; 46:19-24; and 47:1-12? Those texts give to us a detailed, thorough, and elaborate view of the temple structure that will physically be present during the Christocracy, i.e. the millennium.

If we take the descriptions of the first temple as literal then why should not the literal/physical descriptions of the fourth temple not also be taken as literal?[300] Some object to the size of the New Jerusalem in the same way they object to the size of the Millennial Temple. They claim the earth cannot support something of this size. However, we read in Zechariah 14:9-11 that an earthquake will occur altering the dimensions of the land in that area and consequently enlarging it so it could support such a large structure as the Millennial Temple. "The details Ezekiel gives shows that there will be some major geographical changes resulting from the Second Coming . . . . Some of these changes will create a new temple mount altogether."[301]

If that is true for the Millennial Temple to come why could it not also be true for the New Jerusalem to come? Cannot God in the recreation of the New Earth establish it in such a way that could support such a large city like what is described in Revelation 21?

This again drives us back to the foundational issue of proper hermeneutics discussed so heavily in earlier chapters of this eschatological study. If we drift or move away from the historical-grammatical (literal; plain) methodology of interpretation (for whatever reason) we "must resort to guesswork, and for that reason [the non-literalists] have come up with a large variety of contradictory views. The

---

[300] Arnold G. Fruchtenbaum, *Footsteps of the Messiah* (Tustin, CA: Ariel Ministries, 2004), 455.

[301] Ibid, 458.

literal approach is the safest method to gain understanding of these passages."[302]

Personally in such cases when encountering the non-literalists I find that they are often on the one hand quick to tell us literalists what the text surely cannot mean (the literal view), but they are on the other hand slow and nowhere close to being in general agreement as to what such texts like Ezekiel (regarding the temple) or Revelation (regarding the New Jerusalem) do mean.

My discernment seems to tell me that once we penetrate their erudite explanations what we find is the dangerous deconstructive diabolical spirit of the underworld that is steadily seeking to sow seeds of skepticism in the Savior's saints in regard to the specific words used in Scripture.

Therefore, it seems most plausible to postulate the idea that real people, in real, tangible, resurrected physical-spiritual bodies will walk around in a massive, real, physical, tangible, spiritual New Jerusalem City that has splendor all within it that marks the splendor of the God who made it. Dr. Alcorn asks a proper question to the allegorists who criticize us literalists on this description of the city. He says, "If these dimensions are not literal, why does Scripture specifically give the dimensions and say 'by man's measurement, which the angel was using' (Revelation 21:17)? The emphasis on 'man's measurement' almost seems to be an appeal: 'Please believe it—the city really is this big!'"[303]

Again, the skeptics and allegorists seem to have no answer as to why God would give us such detailed measurements if it were nothing more than just a symbol or figure of speech. Why would God waste time and space to

---

[302] Ibid, 455.

[303] Randy Alcorn, *Heaven* (Wheaton, IL: Tyndale House Publishers, 2004), 474.

spell out measurements that he really did not mean to communicate? Is that really an efficient view of God? Alcorn adds further:

> A metropolis of this size in the middle of the United States would stretch from Canada to Mexico and from the Appalachian Mountains to the California border. The New Jerusalem is all the square footage anyone could ever ask for. Even more astounding is the reach of the city's tallest towers and spires, rising above buildings of lesser height. If so, they argue that it's more like a pyramid than a cube. We don't need to worry that Heaven will be crowded. The ground level of the city will be nearly two million square miles. This is forty times bigger than England and fifteen thousand times bigger than London. It's ten times as big as France or Germany and far larger than India. But remember that's just the ground level. Given the dimensions of a 1,400-mile cube, if the city consisted of different levels (we don't know this), and if each story were a generous twelve feet high, the city could have over 600,000 stories. If they were on different levels, billions of people could occupy the New Jerusalem, with many square miles per person . . . . this city . . . will have all the advantages we associate with earthly cities but none of the disadvantages. The city will be filled with natural wonders, magnificent architecture, thriving culture—but it will have no crime, pollution, sirens, traffic fatalities, garbage, or homelessness. It truly will be heaven on earth . . . . Imagine moving through the city to enjoy the arts, music, and sports without pickpockets, porn shops, drugs, or prostitution. Imagine sitting down to eat and raising glasses to toast the King, who will be glorified in every pleasure we enjoy. . . . The whole universe will be

God's house—and the New Jerusalem will be his living room.[304]

Truth # 6: God's Damnation of Human Rebels, Satan, and his Demons in the Lake of Fire

When I speak on the subject of hell I do so with a ternary emotional experience. *First* for those who suffer God's justice in hell I shutter and sadness pours through my heart and mind. I grieve because I realize that the sphere of life where God pours out his wrath through justice is so because of the sin that ruined not only the human race but even a portion of the angelic race.

And despite how appealing universalism may be from a heart wishing no harm on my neighbor, I cannot escape the reality that if we take the Bible with any degree of seriousness and honesty that we must accept the reality of this place that our LORD calls hell. Dr. Norman Geisler has spoken correctly when he said:

> . . . the Bible makes it very clear that there will be an eternal hell and that there will be people in it (Matt. 25:41; 2 Thess 1:7-9; Rev. 20:11-15). In fact, Jesus had more to say about hell than he did about heaven. He warned, "Do not be afraid of those who kill the body but cannot kill the soul. Rather, be afraid of the One who can destroy both soul and body in hell" (Matt. 10:28) . . . . In his great Mount of Olive Discourse, our Lord declared, "Then he [God] will say to those on his left, 'Depart from me, you who are cursed, into the eternal fire prepared for the devil and his angels'" (Matt. 25:41).[305]

---

[304] Ibid, 242, 245.

[305] Norman L. Geisler, *Systematic Theology in One Volume* (Minneapolis, MN: Bethany House Publishers, 2011), 961.

How much of Scripture speaks to the subject of hell? I have provided for you a brief list of texts that deserve your attention. The following portions of Scripture speak to the subject of hell and/or the final lake of fire: Daniel 12:2; Isaiah 66:22-24; Matthew 5:29-30; Matthew 10:28; Matthew 11:23; 13:40-41; 13:49-50; 22:13; 23:15,33; 25:41; Mark 9:43-48; Luke 12:5; Luke 16:19-31; 2 Thessalonians 1:7-9; Hebrews 9:27; 2 Peter 2:4,9; Jude 6; Jude 12-13; Revelation 2:11; 14:10-11; 19:20; 20:10-15; 21:8.

My heart grieves over these portions of Scripture. When I look into the eyes of my neighbors, my friends, my loved ones, and acquaintances I tremble inside at times as I realize that I am looking into the eyes of someone who will spend eternity in grace (Heaven and the New Earth), or someone who will suffer God's justice (hell and the lake of fire).

Yet I grieve too in that I do not think I truly grieve enough at times and I therefore sense my own sin of selfishness and indifference. I grieve because I sense my coldness at times to the plight of not only the human race but also of a portion of the original angelic race. The non-elect angels (see 1 Tim. 5:21) and the non-elect humans (see Romans 9:22) share a final common abode in the lake of fire (Rev. 20:14-15). Revelation 20:7-15 speaks so clearly of this and in doing so it causes me to experience a solemn sense of utter trepidation. Dr. Billy Graham's words on hell and the lake of fire are appropriate to ponder:

> In contemporary society Hell is not a popular subject. George Gallup made a survey on Hell, and there were some interesting results. In his national poll 53 percent of the general population of the United States said they believe in Hell. The percentage goes down dramatically among people with a college education and those with high incomes. Simply stated, the Gallup poll

showed that the more education and money people had, the less likely they were to believe in Hell. . . .

Hell has been cloaked in folklore and disguised in fiction for so long, many people deny the reality of such a place. Some think it is merely a myth. This is understandable. Our minds revolt against ugliness and suffering. However, the concept of Hell is not exclusive to the Christian faith. Centuries before Christ, the Babylonians believed in "The Land of No-Return." The Hebrews wrote about going down the realm of Sheol, or the place of corruption; the Greeks spoke of the "Unseen Land." Classical Buddhism recognizes seven "hot hells," and the Hindu Rig Veda speaks of the deep abyss reserved for false men and faithless women. Islam recognizes seven hells. Jesus specifically states that nonbelievers will not be able to escape the condemnation of Hell (Matthew 23:33). . . .

Hell is probably the hardest of all Christian teachings to accept. Some teach "universalism"—that eventually everybody will be saved and the God of love will never send anyone to Hell. They believe the words "eternal" or "everlasting" do not actually mean forever. However, the same word which speaks of eternal banishment from God is also used for the eternity of heaven. Others teach that those who refuse to accept Jesus Christ as Savior are simply annihilated, they no longer exist. I've searched the Bible and have never found convincing evidence to support this view. The Bible teaches, whether we are saved or lost, there is an everlasting existence of the soul. . . . Will a loving God send a [person] to hell? The answer from Jesus and the teachings of the Bible is, clearly "Yes!"

He does not send man willingly, but man condemns himself to eternal hell because in his blindness, stubbornness, egotism, and love of sinful pleasure, he refuses God's way of salvation and the hope of eternal life with Him. Suppose a person is sick and goes to a doctor. The doctor diagnoses the problem and prescribes medicine. However, the advice is ignored and in a few days the person stumbles back into the doctor's office and says, "Its your fault that I'm worse. Do something." God has prescribed the remedy for the spiritual sickness of the human race. The solution is personal faith and commitment to Jesus Christ. Since the remedy is to be born again, if we deliberately refuse it, we must suffer the horrible consequences.[306]

My *second* emotional experience, as I logically process and meditate upon the subject of hell and the lake of fire, is one of gratitude and relief. The doctrine of God's grace and justice stirs my soul. Of course it also makes us think about the doctrine of salvation too. And then, when people do, many balk at the doctrine of sovereign election where God chooses a portion of humanity to experience divine grace.

Dr. W.R. Crews has said that "the doctrine of election perhaps encounters stronger opposition than any other Bible doctrine. The strongest opposition seems to be among those who profess to be Christians. I have seen some people become violent under the preaching of the doctrine of election . . . I frequently meet religious people who, when election is mentioned, discussed, or taught, begin to appear as though they are going to take up arms. In our Lord's very first sermon he preached election. The group who heard him became so violently enraged that they tried to kill him. The story is found in Luke 4:25-30."[307]

The doctrine of election if properly understood, and concurrently examined alongside of the doctrine of hell (which is also highly unpopular), causes me to praise the

---

[306] Billy Graham, *The Faithful Christian: An Anthology of Billy Graham*, compiled by William Griffin and Ruth Graham Dienert (New York, NY: McCraken Press, 1994), 182,183,185,186.

[307] W.R. Crews, *The Bible Doctrine of Election* (Spartanburg, SC: Bible Study Time Inc, n.d.), 4,5.

LORD God Almighty with a deep and reverent attitude. It helps me to truly fear God and respect him.

I read Romans 9:22-23 and I see that God passively prepared the vessels of the wrath who fitted themselves for destruction. Paul stated, "what if God, willing to demonstrate his wrath and to make known his power, has endured with much patience the objects of wrath prepared for destruction" (NET). In some way, even beyond what I may be able to explain, God's wisdom in dividing humanity into these two spheres is that way so that the saints of mercy will better understand what they have been given.

When I examine this personally I realize that I could have been left out of that grace and allowed to go my own way, which in that case I would have been utterly doomed! Such a thought moves me to praise, adoration, and prayers of thanksgiving. God can stop pursuing and allow damnation. The Lord can choose to stop drawing and allow someone to commit a sin unto death (see 1 John 5) as he or she refuses grace.

I also experience within that emotion of gratitude a sense of relief. The emotion of gratitude is so because of my position in grace but it is also one of gratitude too that I know once and for all God will defeat sin and Satan and his demons will lose the war against righteousness. Such a thought instills in me a deep sense of relief. I know for certain that one day the universe will have harmony to it throughout all spheres of existence. The elect will receive grace, which they were designed for, and the non-elect will receive justice, what they were designed for and freely chose,[308] and in that too, Satan and all the demons with him will receive the just recompense for all of their deeds.

---

[308] Some will read that and begin to ponder which of the three lapsarian positions I hold. I am more of a sublapsarian than anything else, though I have sequenced model established in aeviternity. I will say succinctly here that the vessels of grace and the vessels of justice (sequentially or serially fallen by permission through God knowing them as exercising

This thought provides a sense of relief. It helps to provide a sense of security knowing that there will be an end to all of this spiritual war that wages around us daily. One day there will come an eternal period of peace, tranquility,

---

their liberty wrongly) were eternally foreknown in the mind of God prior to history and both types were inside of Adam who functioned as the federal/patriarchal head of the natural human race. Christ died for all, both groups, and the vessels of grace are efficaciously moved towards Christ. The vessels of justice could choose Christ, if they would turn against their natural sinful will, and in that sense fulfill the covenant of works/justice and be rightly related to God. However, we know by the infallible Scriptures none will ever of their own seek out God for eternal grace unless so moved by the Spirit to do so (Romans 3). Covenant theologians may want to criticize that statement, as they often like to assert we Dispensationalists teach multiple ways of salvation. The idea of a Covenant of Justice (or what they call a covenant of works) is found in many Reformed theologies. For example, the preeminent Presbyterian Dr. Charles Hodge says, "the eternal principles of justice are still in force. If any man can present himself before the bar of God and prove that he is free from sin . . . he will not be condemned" (Charles Hodge, Systematic Theology, Volume 2, Anthropology, p. 122). Likewise, Dr. J.P. Boyce, a prominent Southern Baptist and founder of the first Southern Baptist Theological Seminary, held to this idea as well (Abstract of Systematic Theology, "A Brief Catechism of Bible Doctrine, p. xviii under Good Works, question and answers 1-5). For a covenant Calvinist theologian to criticize anyone who believes in some type of justice covenant or code is highly inconsistent as that has been a standard view among Reformed theologians for many years and still is till this day. Covenant theologian, Dr. Wayne Grudem affirms it in his Systematic theology text (p. 516-518). For me Hosea 6:7 is determinative. The text reads: "But like Adam they transgressed the covenant" (ESV). It seems to me there had to be some type of covenant with Adam if we take this text literally. Though the way it works out in my Dispensational model of theology is somewhat different than a standard covenant theologian who is not Dispensational, I still find that such a justice covenant exists. I prefer to call it a justice covenant instead of a covenant of works. The entire OT era is primarily structured around this justice principle (the Mosaic Law as a justice code). The NT is primarily structured around the New Covenant of grace principle (see 2 Corinthians 3).

and serenity. It reminds me of Dr. Paige Patterson's point on one reason why the doctrine of election exists in Scripture. He taught us the doctrine of election reminds us of the providential oversight of our Father over history and the goal of history. "If you are a born-again believer and you are down and depressed and despondent, you are failing to appreciate the doctrine of election, you are failing to grasp the doctrine of God's providence." This doctrine of election reminds us that "there is no question" that "God is leading the world to the designed climax that he has in mind."[309]

My *third* emotional experience when I contemplate this doctrine is one of inspiration towards faith, holiness, and acts of service in love towards my neighbor. I am within the basic Reformed or Amyraldian (not high Calvinism or Bezanite models) expressions of the Christian faith (a sequenced sublapsarian model). I emphatically reject *active causation unto damnation* and see a *dual benefit to Christ's atonement for all of humanity.*[310] Some might classify this as a form or type of moderate Calvinism.[311] But sometimes the position labeled has more to do with who has defined the initial set of terms that are used in the particular discussion and analysis.

In any case, however one defines the view, or whatever vernacular is used to describe the ideology, I am so convinced in that perspective of God's sovereign

---

[309] Paige Patterson, "Conservatives Stand Together on Doctrine of Election," in *Southern Seminary Magazine*, December 1998, 37.

[310] Historically Calvinistic theology has embraced the idea that Christ's death benefits all. Sadly, it was Beza and others after Calvin and the original Reformers that perverted the doctrine of the atonement and developed or popularized the theory that Christ's death has benefit only for the elect and in no way for anyone else.

[311] Arnold G. Fruchtenbaum, *God's Will & Man's Will: Predestination Election & Free Will* (San Antonio, TX: Ariel Ministries, 2013), 9-11.

providence it worries me when others who claim Christ reject that perspective. Any attempt to deny or remove from Scripture God's total sovereignty, defined as his omniscience, omnipotence, and omnipresence, seems to me to be a fool's errand. Sadly, the heretical Neo-Theists (Open Theists) have rejected the classical view of God and redefined who he is.

Yet my absolute dedication to God's sovereignty is not one that leaves me cold, careless, and compassionless for the countless number of souls that currently do not trust in Christ for salvation. Embracing the sovereignty of God does not mean it leads to fatalism or a cold heart. If understood rightly, it ought to make us very warm and evangelistic. I am reminded that Dr. Patterson taught us the early disciples in Acts certainly believed in election. And however we define it, if defined and practiced rightly, it ought to make us as passionate for souls as they were. A good practical test for our view of election is to see how it impacts our motive for evangelism.

To those whose hearts are cold I am just as concerned about their type of faith as I am about those who reject the teachings of God's sovereignty such as from the Neo-Theists. I am extremely concerned about high "Calvinists" or high "Reformed" theologians who have cold hearts towards the lost. I agree with the self-classified non-Calvinist Dr. Paige Patterson (who does seem to still be moderately Calvinistic)[312] and the Calvinist Dr. Tom Ascol

---

[312] Dr. Patterson claims he is not a Calvinist. Yet he seems to affirm 3 points of the Calvinist position. He affirms man's moral depravity, God's election of sinners, and the preservation of the saints. He rejects unequivocally limited atonement and takes a strong stance against irresistible grace as well. However, in his view of election he says it is unconditional on what lost man does but conditional on what God does. Too he says that grace is not irresistible but when in an interview with Mark Dever he seems to affirm that man can contribute nothing to his own calling and regeneration. He does seem to have more appreciation to the terms effectual grace instead of irresistible grace. In his article,

who both lament over the coldness of hearts seen in many so-called Calvinists today.

Patterson has lamented that he has in his experiences at times been able to find among the Reformed faith many "cool heads but few hot hearts."[313] Dr. Tom Ascol has noted that he has seen many returning to Calvinistic conclusions like that of the famous pastor C.H. Spurgeon but not as many concurrently arriving at Spurgeon's passion for evangelism.

Ascol reminds us: "God in his sovereignty will save whom he will when and where he will. Spurgeon never doubted that. But, what he refuses to let us forget is that at the heart of a faithful ministry is a deep passion for the souls of men and women . . . . If our doctrine does not lead to devotion, then something is seriously wrong. We have not finished with our task until head, heart, and hands all agree."[314] In my opinion, Spurgeon's type of prayer to save the elect and elect some more seems to offer the best and most balanced perspective on election, what I describe as a sequenced sovereign election.[315]

The Work of Christ, in *A Theology for the Church* he says this: ". . . irresistible grace is difficult to establish from the Scriptures, depending instead on the logic of the system. Effectual calling is a more biblical concept" (p. 586). He adds, "it should be maintained that God's calling of the elect to salvation does not infringe on the responsibility of sinners to repent and believe the gospel" (p. 586).

[313] Paige Patterson, "*Shoot-Out at the Amen Corral: Being Baptist Through Controversy*," in *Why I am a Baptist*, eds. Tom J. Nettles and Russell D. Moore (Nashville, TN: Broadman and Holman Publishers, 2001), 70.

[314] Tom Ascol, "*A Lesson From Spurgeon on Evangelism*," in *The Founder's Journal*, ed. Tom Ascol, Issue 33, Summer 1998, 1,4.

[315] Lewis A. Drummond, "Charles Haddon Spurgeon," in *Theologians of the Baptist Tradition*, eds. Timothy George and David S. Dockery (Nashville, TN: Broadman & Holman Publishers, 2001), 122. Spurgeon

The doctrine of hell, justice delivered at the Great White Throne, and the lake of fire breaks the hearts of redeemed sinners. We feel to at least some degree what God felt over the death of the wicked (see Ezekiel 33:11 & Matthew 23:37-39). Dear reader, I urge you to read that sentence again. If we have the real, true, honorable heart of Christ we will weep, or agonize, and truly experience a degree of grief in our hearts over lost souls. In fact, we will feel it to such a degree it will motivate us to work for the cause of the gospel. Hell is an inspirational doctrine designed by God to motivate us to labor in the Spirit.

Ephesians 2:9-10 speaks about good works ordained in the past. A part of the entire package of election and predestination is also the good works of the already elected saints who work to bring the total package of grace to those around them. Prayer, evangelism, social skills, common grace business skill, personal holiness, the fruit of the Spirit, and any other grace we have is a means unto the end for the salvation of the lost. In short that simply means God has a means unto the end for the salvation of souls.

Many a people, as well as church historians now and in years to come, have analyzed the work and effort of the Evangelical Baptists Dr. W.A. Criswell, Dr. Paige Patterson, and Judge Paul Pressler who worked tirelessly for 20 plus years to return the Southern Baptist Convention seminaries away from problematic liberalism and back towards biblical fidelity. Sociologists, journalists, historians, theologians in and out of the Baptist Zion have offered their perspective and reasons as to why the work was done. Dr. Patterson, who became the primary spokesman for the movement,[316] often

would sometimes pray this at the Metropolitan Tabernacle: "Lord, call out your elect, and then elect some more."

[316] Jerry Sutton, *The Baptist Reformation: The Conservative Resurgence in the Southern Baptist Convention* (Nashville, TN: Broadman and Holman Publishers, 2000), 78.

took the brunt of harsh criticism and attacks on his personal character. He was accused of having a "sick ego," that he was an unintelligent seminary student, that he was an "insecure man," and that what he did was for "power."[317]

But that seems far from an accurate assessment of why he did what he did. If not for those reasons, why did Dr. Patterson work tirelessly for the cause of restoring a dedication towards biblical fidelity back to the seminaries of the Southern Baptist Convention? I take him at his word on this. His spirit and demeanor seems to reflect this to me as well when I have listened to his heart. What drove him applies to this issue of eschatology that we are examining. He said this when asked why he did it:

> It's much more than the inerrancy of the Bible . . . if you give up inerrancy, the first thing to go is eternal punishment. If hell goes, then Jesus Christ doesn't become nearly as important. If heaven is real and hell is real and if a relationship with Jesus is the only way to avoid one and go to the other . . . well, it is the vividness of that in my soul that propels me in everything I do.[318]

If consistency of story means anything, years later Paige said the same thing again. In answering that question again he wrote in 2004 this:

> Would I do it again? Before you can say Mephibosheth! I have children and grandchildren. They deserve a chance to be exposed to orthodox theology, to read a Bible they can trust, and to know Jesus who can save them. Furthermore, I cannot

---

[317] Ibid, 81.

[318] Ibid, 83.

relieve my mind of the vision of men and women filing hopelessly across the precipice of eternity and into the chasm of hell. I cannot support, or ultimately leave unchallenged, any doctrine or approach that engenders doubt rather than faith. The potential cost is simply too great![319]

The doctrine of hell, judgment to come, and the lake of fire if properly studied by a true born again child of God will inspire us to action. We will experience within our souls a burning desire to do what we can to rescue others from this dangerous plight that many travel today. But, too, if we are lost, cold, immature, calloused, and wayward rebels the doctrine will be ignored, diminished, diluted, or become an ignominy to our faith.

Dear reader, please stop for a moment and reflect on your own heart before the sovereign Lord of the universe. Do you pray for the lost to be elected unto the conversion graces of Christ? Do you hurt in your soul for someone or anyone who you believe to be lost and outside of the eternal graces of Christ? If this doctrine does not tug upon your heart and cause you to feel sorrow and grief for others then something is awry in your spirit and in your own walk with Christ. Confess such to the LORD if you find that to be true of your heart (1 John 1:9).

Truth # 7: The Elect of God Will Dwell Forever in Perfect Peace and Illustrious Joy with God

The very end of the Bible presents one of the greatest stories ever known to mankind. Revelation chapters 21 and especially 22 present a picture of life to come that transcends

---

[319] Paige Patterson, *Anatomy of a Reformation: The Southern Baptist Convention 1978-2004.* 18.

anything I could possibly ever imagine. It is glorious! It is remarkable! It is breathtaking! It captures my soul! It nourishes my heart and spirit! It provides me comfort! It soothes my soul! It marks the highlight of all history and time after earthly history! I agree with what Dr. W.A. Criswell and Dr. Paige Patterson say in the book "Heaven" about our efforts to describe this scene. We are left with "the poverty of human language to provide adequate definition to these glorious visions."[320]

What we can certainly see is that in this new life to come there will be some magnificent, illustrious, and vivacious scenes that portray the grandeurs of our God! *First*, God will dwell with man and man shall dwell with God (21:3). *Second*, God will remove all pain and suffering (21:4). *Third*, the conflict between the unrighteous and the righteous will end as God will forever separate the two classes of humanity (21:5-8).

Fourth, God will have a physical temple/city for his people that will never have any night in it as it will shine forth the glorious radiance of God through both its structure and by its inhabitants that come and go throughout the city (21:9-27). *Fifth*, God will have a river flowing from the throne of God that flows through the city. Also God will have the tree of life within the eternal dwelling place that will have fruit on it that people of the nations can eat for healing (22:1-2).[321] *Sixth*, God will have two thrones present

---

[320] W.A. Criswell and Paige Patterson, *Heaven* (Wheaton, IL: Tyndale Publishers, 1991), 187.

[321] Dispensationalists differ here as to what the Tree of Life does in the eternal estate. Some believe that it will offer the needed healing powers to sustain those who enter into the Kingdom in natural bodies. Others think it will actually be what ultimately heals and brings those people to glorification. Dr. Robert L. Thomas of Master's seminary in his most extensive and thorough Greek commentary on Revelation, volume 2, says this: "Those who have entered the new heaven and the new earth in an unresurrected state will have a means for perpetuating their health"

(God's throne and Christ's throne). From these thrones, spheres, God will rule over all (22:3a). *Seventh*, under their sphere of rule the servants of God will worship him and will serve him as they reign with God for all eternity (22:3b-5).

These words depict a scene that astounds my mind. What my soul so deeply yearns to experience, my final and truest home, awaits me and a myriad of others who love the slain Lamb, the Savior of the world! I look forward to my

---

(p. 485). Dr. Mal Couch in his commentary of Revelation says that this Tree of Life is "to promote the enjoyment of life in the New Jerusalem. They are not for correcting illnesses, for there will be no sickness" (Revelation, p. 304). Reformed and non-dispensational scholar Simon J. Kistemaker seems to like the plausibility of Dr. John Walvoord's view that the healing noted here is "therapeutic healing understood as health-giving" (Revelation, p. 582). However, he does go on to say that "the language is symbolic and implicitly points to the curse that rested on the human race . . . . but the tree in the renewed paradise provides healing for the nations, which means that its inhabitants can enjoy eternal life from physical and spiritual needs" (p. 582). Leon Morris too follows Walvoord's lead on this in *Revelation* of the *Tyndale New Testament Commentary Series* (p. 248). Dr. Robert H. Mounce seems to take the most spiritual/non-physical view or most symbolic view as he equates this imagery to "complete absence of physical or spiritual want. The life to come will be a life of abundance and perfection" (*The Book of Revelation: The New International Commentary on the New Testament*, p. 400). I concur with Dr. Patterson's explanation of this text. He does not venture into much theory but gives enough to satisfy us for the time being. He says of this text: "John further notes what appears to be a perpetual oasis. On each side of the river stands the tree of life. The emphasis here is not on a single tree but on the kind of tree. Apparently all along the bank this tree of life, which has not been observed since the Garden of Eden, is there; and the tree bears its fruit every month. There is no season for its productivity, but its production is perpetual. Not only is the fruit available, but even the leaves of the tree are to be used for the healing of the nations. Apparently as long as the first parents were in the garden and had access to the tree of life, they would not have suffered death. Excluded from the garden, physical death was inevitable. Now, once again, however, all the nations have access to the tree of life and to its healing leaves and, therefore, rejoice in eternal life" (*The New American Commentary: Revelation*, p. 376).

arrival in this New Heaven New Earth so I can see my Lord, my earthly father who is now there (and soon to be my mom), numerous family members, friends, spiritual brothers and sisters, and, of course, several of my spiritual fathers like Mal Couch and others who led me along my spiritual journey.

We have a glorious future to come! I can only close this section with these words of John who said at the end of his vision: "The Spirit and the Bride say, 'Come.' And let the one who hears say, 'Come.' And let the one who is thirsty come; let the one who desires take the water of life without price" (Rev. 22:17).

Summary: A Good Eschatology Ought to Edify & Encourage Us

One of the most frustrating issues I see in ministry life occurs when teachers or saints use the Word and a particular doctrine in the wrong manner. We can have the right raw understanding of some doctrine while also using that doctrine in an incorrect manner. Certainly eschatology has suffered from that. We teachers sometimes leave people more confused than encouraged by the way in which we teach on the subject. Sometimes we take more time trying to rebuke and disprove all of the other theories than simply teaching the plain and straightforward truth of Scripture to those who need an encouraging message from Christ.

Too, some of the vitriolic words used by brothers and sisters in Christ towards one another over exact details of time for eschatological events frustrate me. I think it is frustrating to Christ as well who told us not to be all that concerned on the "times and seasons" of the restoration of all things (Acts 1:7). Am I convinced at this juncture in my spiritual journey that a premillennial framework is the biblical truth? Yes!

But I affirm it with a Christ like attitude towards all of the brethren. I am reminded of D.L. Moody who per tradition stated that we should not divide from one another over the hour of Christ's future coming. Some believe he is coming at noon, others at 3pm, others at 6pm, and still even others at 9pm. But we all agree he is still coming so let us work and labor together until he does come.

All believers who affirm a future coming of Christ to earth should be humble enough to respect one another and to work together in common areas of theological consensus while not being in complete agreement with other factors within eschatology. I speak to my own people here. Sometimes some Dispensationalists have been unkind, divisive, and schismatic towards our non-Dispensational brethren. My mentor Dr. Couch and my teachers Dr. Ryrie and Dr. Lightner taught us better than that!

Mal was able to retain friendships with the larger faith community even while fighting tenaciously for the truths he held with passionate conviction. That social skill he had was a testimony of the grace of the LORD in his life. Yes, historically the Dispensationalists were kicked out of the Presbyterian circles, and yes historically the Covenant Theologians have accused us of holding to skewed forms of salvation. I have addressed some of that in my book, *The Calvinism of Dispensationalism.*

But even so we are responsible for our own actions, not theirs. We would do well to argue prolifically in precision and passion while at the same time befriending those in love that differ from us. Mal for sure was not perfect in this, and neither am I to be sure. But I saw in him that sincere effort. He was always trying to extend grace to other godly conservatives with whom he differed in non-essential areas when at all possible.

I am reminded of a conversation I had with Dr. Paige Patterson while president at SEBTS. He stated there were some differences among his faculty at Southeastern Baptist

Theological Seminary (SEBTS) concerning eschatology. He stated they had mostly premillennialists on the faculty but among even the premillennialists there were differences among them. He said some were "pre-tribulational premillennialists, others there teaching were mid-tribulational premillennialists, and some other teachers were post-tribulational premillennialists."[322]

He added that they would get into a board room and "argue vociferously with one another and get red in face with one another in the debate. Yet then once the debate was over they would all go out for a steak dinner together and enjoy one another's fellowship."[323]

We would do well to keep that type of spirit with the larger body of Christ outside of our own organizations, seminaries, and ministerial bodies. Christians have sometimes historically been some of the worst at shooting their own brethren while in the battle for truth. As I understand it, the way many Dispensationalists treated Dr. George Eldon Ladd, who was a historical premmillennialist, left him bruised and bitter. A significant portion of Dispensationalists ostracized him because he did not agree with the precise time we do on the rapture. We should not do that. A premillennialist of any kind is a family of 1st cousins.

I agree with the three Dispensationalists Dr. Tim LaHaye, Dr. Richard Mayhue, and Dr. Wayne Brindle when they state: "The timing of the rapture is not a cardinal doctrine that should divide God's people, but those who interpret the Bible literally find many strong reasons to believe that the rapture will be pre-tribulational."[324] This

---

[322] Conversation with Dr. Paige Patterson at First Baptist Pickens SC.

[323] Ibid.

[324] Tim LaHaye, Richard L. Mayhue, and Wayne Brindle, "Pretribulationsim," in *The Popular Encyclopedia of Bible Prophecy*,

point reminds me of Jesus' instruction to the disciples in Acts 1 when they too asked about the time of restoration for Israel.

Also, keeping in mind the purpose of eschatology will help us use the doctrine correctly. Eschatology, like all doctrine, is designed to promote faith, hope, and love in us. If we take Paul's words seriously in 1 Corinthians 13:13 about faith, hope, and love then we will recognize what type of presupposition or underlying spirit that ought to accompany our instruction to others. God revealed to us the future in order to encourage us, to inspire us, to give us hope for a better day to come. Is this not exactly what Paul said to the Thessalonians (4:18)? God's pedagogical intent with eschatology seems to be one of helping us orient our minds towards some great and essential truths about God's character.

In essence that was what I gained from Mal's instruction. Yes, he was a Dispensationalist. Yes, he believed in the imminent, pre-tribulational rapture, along with the future premillennial return of Christ to rule and reign over the earth before he ushered in the New Heavens and New Earth. But beyond those things he used those truths to help encourage me to live with great hope for tomorrow. Instead of my looking backwards, reminiscing and missing the glory years, he taught me to look forward to the real glory ages of eternity!

He used eschatology to teach me how to take God at his word. I learned that God communicated directly to us in all portions of the Bible. Likewise, I try to communicate directly with others in my speech. I learned that I could understand God's message through interpreting his words in a normal way just like I do with any other form of literature or speech. That greatly encouraged me. It has benefited me

eds. Tim Lahaye and Ed Hindson (Eugene, OR: Harvest House Publishers, 2004) 289.

248

in more ways than just in the field of biblical theology. I have learned that, oftentimes, confusion in board rooms, policy manuals, politics, employee meetings, legal theories, and family conflict, to name just a few, occur because people often fail to speak or write clearly as well as to take the time to understand the actual words being used in the communication process.

Furthermore, I learned from Mal that even those whom we differ on secondary areas of eschatology could still be friends with us in the cause of gospel work. Mal had ministry friends who were not premillennial. But they were certainly believers in the cardinal doctrine of a future, physical, literal return of Jesus Christ. He rightly would not associate with any heretic who denied the future return of Christ. Historic fundamentalists were right to recognize this future in flesh 2nd coming as a part of historic orthodoxy.[325] I learned to major in the majors and defend those with great vigor while also defending other truths even though without the same degree of forcefulness as would be needed if dealing with a heretic.

In those seven areas listed in this article I also gained a deeper appreciation about God by understanding those truths. Mal made sure we understood the love and grace of God in that he would take us home immediately upon death. That truth greatly removes the "sting of death" and offers great hope. Also, the instruction we disciples received under Mal and those with whom he associated were encouraged by the fact Christ would return triumphantly over all enemies. Knowing that our LORD will one day return to destroy all enemies of the saints inspires us as we know all our work will one day ultimately come to light in victory.

In regard to God's sovereign plan to remove the bride of Christ before the great time of wrath, this taught us about

---

[325] See Appendix on Gary Demar at the end of this book where the famous set of Fundamentals is discussed.

God's immeasurable mercy to give to the Son's bride a special blessing. In this I received encouragement knowing that because of some extra miraculous grace, that neither I nor any other member in the bride of Christ deserves, I will be spared from the awful time of wrath that comes upon the whole earth.

Concerning the doctrine of Christ's rule and reign over the earth as King for 1,000 years, I learned that God's character magnifies order and the proper delegation of it. Seeing the numerous texts throughout Scripture that speak about us ruling and reigning with Christ encourages me to work harder for him today knowing that by my faithfulness today over a little I will be rewarded when he places me in charge over some things in the Kingdom age. I also experience excitement because I know that one day I will see a world where justice and grace will reign as the supreme law of the land. That thrills my heart. After being in law enforcement and the judicial roles for several years, I long to see a day when all sectors of life function with grace and justice as the norm.

Knowing that God shall fulfill his promises to the elect nation of Israel gives me comfort, too. It teaches me that God's faithfulness cannot be altered because of even severe disobedience. It comforts me too knowing that what God promised me will never change. His promises to Israel are just as solid as is his promises to me.

As to the final judgment of the universe and to the evil forces of hell, I find the thought sobering. I can still hear Mal's voice in my head speaking on the fact that one day everyone shall stand before Christ. In listening to Mal talk about judgment I also felt his heart and passion for others. I sensed God's heart in him.

When I think about hell and eternal judgment of others I contemplate God's holiness. It stirs my heart to soberness as to what really counts today. These truths taught to me realize that yes, God is merciful and gracious, but he balances that with his holiness exhibited through justice. It encourages me and gives me hope because I realize that delivering justice to others is sometimes what must be done as difficult as it may be at the moment. Such realization has great applicability to any leadership role where one must exercise a degree of authority over another.

Lastly, when I think about the New Heavens and New Earth and the peace that will culminate throughout the universe I find great comfort because I know my God shall make all things right one day forever. In this I see God's faithfulness. It teaches me that even though we suffer for the moment these trials are but just a momentary lesson preparing us for graduation (death) so we can then serve fully equipped and prepared for the eternal ages. All that we learn today, albeit through many trials and tribulations, shall constitute a grand repertoire of knowledge and skill we can use to glorify our beloved God for all eternity. It just literally makes my heart sing.

My dear beloved reader, Mal has graduated now. He left for us a legacy of love, loyalty, and leadership in the LORD's graces. Eschatology is the capstone of all theology.The culmination point to all of history was a passionate theme for brother Mal. He longed to see the Savior's return like his mentor John Walvoord did. Though both experienced a departure from this world before the return of Christ, we who still live have a mission to carry forth. Let us labor in the faith, lead others to hope, and do it all through love as we point people to the coming Savior of the World (Gal. 5:6). Maranatha (1 Cor. 16:22)!

Chapter 4.
Seven Specific Questions
& Answers about Heaven

1. Will believers enter heaven immediately upon earthly death?

Yes, when a believer dies the soul-spirit of the person leaves the earthly body and enters into the current heaven that exists now prior to the New Heaven and New Earth to come. The person goes directly into heaven and has personal, conscious, and perfect fellowship with the Lord and all the believers of the ages there in heaven now (technically known as aeviternity). The believers, angels, and the Lord Jesus dwell in this heaven now and will do so until the 2nd coming when Christ returns to this earth to inaugurate the final phases of redemptive history.

No Purgatory

Some false teachers and religious organizations teach that people do not enter heaven immediately upon death. The apostate religion Roman Catholicism teaches some will enter a place known as purgatory upon death. Shockingly, the Roman Catholics even admit no explicit scripture exists on the place of purgatory.[326] Dr. John R. Rice bluntly pointed this out noting that the "terms purgatory and limbo are not found in the Word of God nor is any other term of similar meaning."[327]

---

[326] Thomas P. Rausch, *Systematic Theology: A Roman Catholic Approach* (Collegeville, MN: Liturgical Press, 2016), 283.

[327] John R. Rice, *Bible Facts about Heaven* (Wheaton, IL: Sword of the Lord Publishing, 1940), 21.

To find support for this pagan doctrine the Roman Catholics have to turn to the non-inspired books known as the Apocrypha. They believe this idea is taught in the Old Testament idea of "praying for the dead" as found "in the late Old Testament (2 Macc. 12:45).[328]

Purgatory has been defined by Roman Catholicism as a place for souls to go for purification. "In purgatory these souls are purified for a time before being admitted to the glory and happiness of heaven.[329] Some Roman Catholics point to 1 Cor. 3:12-15 and Matthew 12:32 to try and offer support for this view.[330] Scripture, however, makes a clear case against this doctrine.

This corrupt view of purgatory establishes the basis for people paying and praying for souls in purgatory to experience cleansing enough to escape it to later enter into the real heaven. Loved ones are taught to pay the priest to help their loved ones out of purgatory through masses and prayers. Dr. Rice rightly rebuked this heresy and stated this "wicked doctrine is not taught in the Bible. It is based on a doctrine of salvation by works and salvation by the church instead of redemption by the blood of Christ."[331]

Numerous examples in Scripture speak of people going directly to glory upon death. Luke 23:39-43 reveals that when a thief on the cross repented he received a direct word from Jesus about his eternal destiny. Jesus assured the thief that he would dwell with him (Jesus) in paradise

---

[328] Thomas P. Rausch, *Systematic Theology: A Roman Catholic Approach* (Collegeville, MN: Liturgical Press, 2016), 283-284.

[329] Scott Hahn, *Catholic Bible Dictionary*, gen. ed. Scott Hahn (New York, NY: Doubleday Publishing, 2009), 745.

[330] Ibid., 745-746.

[331] John R. Rice, *Bible Facts about Heaven* (Wheaton, IL: Sword of the Lord Publishing, 1940), 21.

(heaven prior to Jesus' resurrection). The Bible reveals that Elijah went straight to heaven upon his departure from earth (2 Kings 2:11). The rich man and Lazarus story gave a glimpse of the afterlife of two real people on earth (Luke 16:19-31).

Some think this was a parable. That seems improbable. Jesus used actual names of people and that is very unlikely for a parable. As the great evangelist Oliver B. Greene stated, "in the parables from the New Testament . . . there is not a proper name used . . . not one."[332] With Jesus using the name Lazarus along with Abraham's name one should not see this as a parable.[333]

Semitic language scholar Dr. Merrill Unger spoke of this story of Lazarus as "actually a historical illustration rather than a parable" that "contains important revelation concerning the intermediate state of the soul between death and the resurrection."[334] Concurring with those thoughts, commentator William MacDonald explained why not to read this as a parable.

> The Lord concludes his discourse on stewardship of material things by this account of two lives, two deaths, and two hereafters. It should be noted that this was not spoken of as a parable. We mention this because some critics seem to explain away solemn

---

[332] Oliver B. Greene, *Why Does the Devil Desire to Damn You?* (Greenville, SC: The Gospel Hour, 1966), 48.

[333] Oliver B. Greene, *Hell* (Greenville, SC, The Gospel Hour, 1969), 52-53.

[334] Merrill Unger, *Unger's Commentary on the Gospels* (Chattanooga, TN: AMG Publishers, 2014), 392.

implications of the story by waving it off as a parable.[335]

However, if an interpreter sees this as a parable, the interpreter should not discard the metaphysical realities of the afterlife conveyed from this story. Dr. H.A. Ironside gave a proper and balanced way one could read this as a parable while not discarding eternal truths. He stated:

> We have no reason whatever to look upon this story as an imaginary incident which had no foundation in fact. The question has been often raised as to whether it is a parable or not. If by parable we are thinking of a fictitious tale to illustrate some moral or spiritual lesson, I believe we are right in saying that it is not a parable. On the other hand, if we think of any incident used to illustrate truth as parabolic, then it is perfectly right to speak of the parable of the rich man and Lazarus.[336]

Luke 16:22 gives a real timeline on a believer's translation to heaven. The Bible says, "now the poor man died and was carried by the angels to Abraham's side."

---

[335] William MacDonald, *Believer's Bible Commentary* (Nashville, TN: Thomas Nelson, 1995), 1432-1433. See also Arno C. Gaebelein in the *Gaebelein's Concise Commentary on the Whole Bible*. He says interpreters should "avoid the use of the word parable in connection with these verses (p. 826). Norman Geisler also agrees noting that "real names (like Lazarus) are never used in parables, and parables are usually introduced as such by name" (Systematic Theology in One Volume, p. 1215). Dr. Randy Alcorn also believes this story was about a real historical person Lazarus (see Heaven, p. 62). For conservative arguments in support of it being a parable see Charles Swindoll's *Luke New Testament Commentary* and Walter L. Liefeld's *Luke Commentary in the Expositor's Bible Commentary*, Volume 8.

[336] H.A. Ironside, *Luke* (Neptune, NJ: Loizeaux Brothers, 1947), 509.

Abraham's side was a reference for the place of the saints after death, i.e. heaven prior to the heaven that exists now with Christ after his resurrection. This poor believer Lazarus instantly arrived in heaven after his death. Verse 23 of this chapter reveals too that the rich man instantly arrived in hell upon his death. These truths highlight that upon death the soul-spirit immediately enters heaven or hell.

No Soul Sleep

Another false doctrine has been the idea of soul sleep, the idea that upon death the soul experiences a season of sleep until the Lord returns and draws out souls from this sleep through resurrection. The Seventh Day Adventist cult religion has been a long standing soul sleep advocate.

> Death is . . . a state of temporary unconsciousness while the person awaits the resurrection. The Bible repeatedly calls this intermediate state a sleep . . . . Matthew wrote that many "saints who had fallen asleep were raised" after Christ's resurrection (Matt. 27:52) . . . . Both Paul and Peter also called death a sleep (1 Cor. 15:51, 52; 1 Thess. 4:13-17; 2 Peter 3:4) . . . . Body and soul only exist together; they form an indivisible union. . . . The soul has no conscious existence apart from the body, and no scripture indicates that at death the soul survives as a conscious entity. Indeed, the "soul who sins shall die" (Eze. 18:20).[337]

---

[337] The Ministerial Association General Conference of Seventh-day Adventism, *Seventh-day Adventists Believe: A Biblical Exposition of 27 Fundamental Doctrines* (Hagerstown, MD: Review and Herald Publishing, 1988), 352-353.

Contradicting this idea, the verses shared about the rich man and Lazarus argue against the idea of soul sleep. However, some mark those off as parabolic and explain away those afterlife realities. But other texts reveal the same truths found in the Luke 16 text.

These who embrace soul sleep believe when Scripture uses the terms "fallen asleep" that such terms means the soul sleeps until resurrection. First, "fallen asleep" is a proper "figure of speech about death, since they share the same posture; both are temporary, and both are followed by awaking and standing up again."[338]

Second, they fail to see that the human has two essential aspects that constitute being a human, the physical body and the soul-spirit. The body does sleep at death, i.e., it ceases to function until resurrection. However, the physical body is not all there is to the human constitution. The soul-spirit exists within the body and leaves that body upon death.

In a Christian worldview the body and soul form a unity though the two spheres are not identical. The soul and body are not separate entities as taught within dualism. Instead, the body and soul form a unity prior to death and experience a restored unity in the resurrection. Dr. Geisler explained it this way, "there is a form/matter unity between soul and body." [339] The soul can exist without the body, but the soul "is not complete without body."[340] Dr. R.C. Sproul called this a duality instead of dualism.[341]

---

[338] Norman Geisler, *Systematic Theology in One Volume* (Minneapolis, MN: Bethany House Publishers, 2011), 1220.

[339] Ibid., 736.

[340] Ibid., 738.

[341] R.C. Sproul, *Essential Truths of the Christian Faith* (Wheaton, IL: Tyndale House Publishers, 1992), 133.

This unified personhood view which allows for the soul to exist without the body has numerous examples in scripture. Often scripture reveals souls living after their bodily death. Though the Adventists claim "no scripture indicates that at death the soul survives as a conscious entity," such views miss clear biblical assertions whereby living souls did exist in heaven after death.

Jesus opened up the heavens to let his disciples see the kingdom of heaven (Matt. 17). In this Mount of Transfiguration experience "Moses and Elijah also appeared before them, talking with him" (17:3). Dr. Geisler rightly explains that here we see Moses and Elijah in heaven in spite of the fact their "bodies had been dead for centuries."[342] The disciples knew this was Moses and Elijah because Moses and Elijah "appeared and were speaking."[343]

In Paul's writings, he taught in various places that upon death the soul goes to heaven where the Lord Jesus lives now. 2 Corinthians 5:1-3 & 8 reveals that the spiritual aspect of man "survives death. . . . this spirit/soul consciously survives in a place of bliss ('with the Lord')."[344]

Commenting on Paul's Philippians letter, Norman Geisler recognized some key points about death in Christ. Paul stated, "to me, living is Christ and dying is gain" (1:21). He wisely noted that "there is no reasonable sense in which death can be gain if a person is annihilated . . . or separated from consciousness at death."[345]

In Revelation numerous texts speak of souls living in heaven prior to the time of physical resurrection. In

---

[342] Norman Geisler, *Systematic Theology in One Volume*, Minneapolis, MN: Bethany House Publishers, 2011), 1215.

[343] Ibid., 1220.

[344] Ibid., 1216-1217.

[345] Ibid., 1217.

Revelation 6:9-10 we see souls that had been on earth but were killed. These souls function in heaven as they pray and express concerns about what is taking place on earth. In Revelation 20:4 John described his vision where he saw "thrones and seated on them were those who had been given authority to judge." Who are these people on thrones? It could be "all the saints related to him" or "the twelve disciples" who will share with Christ his rule over the world."[346] Whatever view one affirms on those two options, the truth stands in both options that these souls were conscious and alive in heaven.

Additionally, in this verse John saw more than those seated on the thrones. John also saw "the souls of those who had been beheaded because of the testimony about Jesus and because of the Word of God" (20:4). These were a "particular group of martyrs—those who were 'beheaded.'"[347]

Dr. Robert Mounce sees these souls as the same ones from chapter 6. John sees them as "souls because at this point they are still awaiting the resurrection."[348] For John to see these people on thrones and these souls in heaven, they had to exist as living people dwelling in heaven. Therefore, to see them means conscious activity awaits those who die now prior to the resurrection.

---

[346] John Walvoord, *The Revelation of Jesus Christ* (Chicago, IL: Moody Press, 1989), 296.

[347] Charles C. Ryrie, *Revelation: Everyday Bible Commentary* (Chicago, IL: Moody Press, 1996), 159.

[348] Robert H. Mounce, *The Book of Revelation: The New International Commentary on the New Testament*, gen. eds., Ned B. Stonehouse, F.F. Bruce, Gordon D. Fee (Grand Rapids, MI: Wm Eerdmans Publishing Company, 1998), 365.

2. Will we know each other in heaven?

One of the most natural questions people have about heaven relates to memories from earth in relation to their loved ones. We rightly wonder will we know our earthly family, friends, and family in heaven. Sometimes people struggle to find joy when they think about heaven because they are unsure if those friendships will continue on into heaven when they die.

Yet as people grow older and strength fades they see more of their loved ones dying. As Dr. Billy Graham observed in his later years of life, "reality in this stage of life is watching friends and family members become ill or die. Hardly a week goes by without news reaching me about the illness or death of someone I have known."[349]

This causes some people to question if the cherished friendships we have on this earth will continue on in heaven. This is natural as we cling to what we know on earth and have no experience of heaven. Because we have no experience with heaven and "earthly existence is all we know" this makes it difficult to "think of heaven" as "eternal existence is beyond our comprehension. It is impossible to think of existing forever with the God who fashioned the universe out of nothing."[350]

But believers can take comfort with the hope that we certainly will know each other in heaven. God created family. Friendship rooted in love and goodness for one another reflects the goodness of God. Therefore, we will

---

[349] Billy Graham, *Nearing Home* (Nashville, TN: Thomas Nelson Publishers, 2011), 84.

[350] Mal Couch, *The Hope of Heaven* (Clifton, TX: Scofield Ministries, 2012), 3.

certainly know one another in the immediate heaven upon death and in the New Heaven and New Earth.

Several texts in the New Testament teach us that a major part of our joy in glory will occur through our relationships with one another as well as Christ. Some wrongly like to say "all we need is the Lord." Though true in regard to salvation, this does not cover the whole story of redemption. Redemption is both individual as well as corporate in community. The redeemed of the ages will enjoy each other and the Lord together.

1 Thessalonians 2:19-20 speaks of our joy together in heaven. Paul spoke of the hope and joy he had related to the crown that he would glory in within heaven. Then he explained that the glory and joy was connected to the persons he knew and ministered too. Think about what that requires. It requires for there to be memory and relational bonds that carry over into heaven.

In 1 Thessalonians 4:13-14 Paul reminded believers not to grieve over those already with the Lord as those people would return with Christ in his second coming. The point here is that they would reunite and be together again. This was a reminder that relationships will continue on in the age to come. Of these texts Dr. Randy Alcorn has said, "our source of comfort isn't only that we'll be with the Lord in heaven but also that we'll be with each other."[351]

When we ponder and meditate on the time of transfiguration with the disciples some interesting points come to the surface. It seems that the disciples immediately knew who Moses and Elijah were (see Luke 9:29-33). Does this mean that in heaven we will automatically know everyone there? It may mean that. Glorification may bring some type of intuition that connects people who have never

---

[351] Randy Alcorn, *Heaven* (Wheaton, IL: Tyndale House Publishers, 2004), 330.

met personally on earth. Again, Dr. Alcorn spoke to this matter saying:

> Another indication that we'll recognize people in heaven is Christ's transfiguration. Christ's disciples couldn't have known what the two men looked like . . . . This may suggest that personality will emanate through a person's body, so we'll instantly recognize people we know of but haven't previously met. If we can recognize those we've never seen, how much more will we recognize our family and friends?[352]

Sometimes I hear teachers who will say something like this: "all we need is Christ. Going to heaven is fulfilled by being with Christ." I understand the goal of these ideas. Jesus is our greatest blessing and treasure. But the Lord created humanity, family, and friendships. A part of being redeemed by Christ means that he gifts us with everlasting relationships for us to experience the fruit of the Spirit joy.

This idea that if we have the Lord we do not need people undercuts the full truth of what it means for us to have a redeemed community. Two extremes exist on this matter. Some go to the extreme that they focus too much on community at the expense of Jesus who is truth. On the other hand, some go so far that the focus on Jesus excludes the communion of the saints. Neither view has the holistic perspective.

Dr. Henry Cloud and Dr. John Townsend noted that this error relates to a misunderstanding of the sufficiency of Scripture. That Christ is sufficient for us should not be doubted. But the "problem arises when we interpret Christ's sufficiency as Christ alone" and fail to incorporate "his

---

[352] Ibid., 333.

resources" which includes God using "people to meet people's needs."[353]

For me, a verse in Ephesians, which I still have some ongoing questions about how this looks in heaven, applies to this matter. Ephesians 3:14 says, "For this reason I kneel before the Father, from whom every family in heaven and on earth is named." This idea of family has a theological root in the Trinity.

Dr. Engelsma has rightly noted that "Family is the meaning of the Trinity."[354] Heaven will reflect this as people dwell with one another and the relationships formed on earth continue on in glory forever. This is a major part of what makes heaven so wonderful. It reminds me of what Dr. Criswell said about the joy we will have as we fellowship with great saints of the past when we arrive in heaven. He stated:

---

[353] Henry Cloud and John Townsend, *False Assumptions: Relief from 12 'Christian' Beliefs that Can Drive you Crazy* (Grand Rapids, MI: Zondervan, 1994), 114, 116. I urge all ministers to read this book.

[354] David J. Engelsma, *Trinity and Covenant: God as Holy Family* (Jenison, MI: Reformed Free Publishing Association, 2006), 62. When reading Engelsma, one should be careful bc he has embraced the error that Jesus' death has no benefit to the whole world. He sadly embraced the Bezanite (or Bezaite) worldview that claims God has no common love or grace for the whole world. This is a sad drift away from the historic view of the early church, the original reformers like Luther, Calvin, Zwingli, and others. Bezanite theology is a new novel theology that departed from the biblical view of the atonement. Sadly, many very zealous for God's sovereignty have lost balance here and have drifted into this Bezanite stream of thought. This view is not the view of Calvin or historic Calvinists. Calvin, Edwards, Hodge, Spurgeon, and more have all rejected the view that the death of Christ had only a single eternal benefit intent. The historic view is that Christ's death had a temporal benefit for all and an eternal benefit for all who believe.

We shall know each other in heaven. It is unthinkable that we should live unknown and unknowing. Intuitive knowledge will introduce us to everybody: "Many shall come from the east and west, and shall sit down with Abraham, and Isaac and Jacob, in the kingdom of heaven" (Matt. 8:11). How do we know Abraham and Isaac and Jacob? We know them intuitively in the same way that James, John, and Peter knew Moses and Elijah on the Mount of Transfiguration. We shall sit down and visit with the saints and have all eternity in which to enjoy their fellowship. We shall sit down and visit with Adam and talk about Eden. We shall sit down with Noah and talk about the flood. We shall sit down with Moses and talk the deliverance of the Israelites from the Red Sea. We shall sit down with Elijah and talk about his ride in the chariot of fire. We shall sit down with Lazarus and talk about his resurrection from the dead. We shall sit down with Paul and talk about his life-changing experience on the Damascus road.

There will be a joyous reunion with our loved ones. The infinitely sad kiss of good-bye at the deathbed and the last longing glance upon the casket will be more than forgotten in the kiss or reunion and welcome at the gate of heaven.[355]

3. Will we have bodies in heaven upon death or do we have to wait until the future final resurrection in the final New Heaven & New Earth?

This question has been answered in different ways by godly conservatives. I think the best view affirms a temporal

---

[355] W.A. Criswell & Paige Patterson, *Heaven* (Wheaton, IL: Tyndale House Publishers, 1991), 31-32.

new body suited for those who enter the current heaven prior to the final New Heaven and New Earth. Scripture seems to show that we have a new body we dwell within in heaven now until we wait for the final resurrection body suited for the New Earth and New Heaven. This new body we receive now upon earthly death does not seem to be a body suited for Earth. Consequently, at the final resurrection we shall receive the earthly body in a glorified form that we will live within in the final New Heaven and New Earth. That final body will mean we can function in both realms.

I suppose that when we return with Jesus and the resurrection occurs (1 Thess. 4) that new earthly glorified body will be added to us that overlaps or subsumes the body we have in this current heaven. I doubt I could explain how that works in some precise or scientific manner, but God who knows all surely can do that. If he can speak and the entire universe comes to exist, this poses no issue for him.

Some Scriptures suggest that we will have some type of tangible body now in the current heaven. One key text that applies to this conversation seems to teach us that we will upon death have a "building from God" that replaces this body that death "dismantles" (2 Cor. 5:1). Not wanting to be naked (without a body) Paul seems to have assured us that we will put on a body "not built by human hands" (not produced through parental reproduction) and this body will give us our "heavenly dwelling" (2 Cor. 5:2).

Dr. John Calvin took the view that this heavenly dwelling, a building from God, exists for believers at death. It is the intermediate body that we wear until we receive the final body. He stated, "the blessed condition of the soul after death is the commencement of this building, and the glory of the final resurrection is the consummation of it."[356] Calvin's view has much to commend it.

---

[356] John Calvin, *Commentary on the Epistles of Paul the Apostle to the Corinthians: Calvin's Commentaries*, vol. 20, trans. John Pringle (Grand Rapids, MI: Baker Books, 1998), 217-218.

Dr. Randy Alcorn has the same view as did Calvin. In his examination of Scripture he believes a new body exists for believers at death. He found evidence of this in several areas. "For instance," Alcorn says, "the martyrs in Heaven are described as wearing clothes (Revelation 6:9-11). Disembodied spirits don't wear clothes."[357] I agree. It seems like common sense.

Furthermore, Dr. Alcorn noted the numerous examples of people in heaven being seen by earthly people. He noted the examples of Enoch, Elijah, and Moses along with the rich man and Lazarus. The Bible seems to give some type of corporeal forms to these people who were in heaven and in hell.[358] The rich man in hell even asked for water to dip his tongue in while asking Lazarus to use his finger to deliver the water. Why would Scripture give us such specific details like this of the afterlife if the Lord did not want us to think of ourselves in bodily form in heaven or hell? Nothing in the text uses key terms to signify metaphors were being used. It seems to me to be a common sense conclusion to a plain reading of the text.

Another text from Philippians highlights a reason why we seemingly can rightly conclude we have bodily forms in haven now. Paul said it is a gain to depart from here and be with Christ (Phil. 1:21-23). How could the loss of a body be a gain? Yes, being with Christ is a gain as we leave this sin stricken world. That much is true. But when comparing this with the desire Paul had in 2 Corinthians 5, a reasonable conclusion of this gain being the addition of a new body fits well with the various texts of Scripture.

If so, Paul would be saying, departing this world is a gain because we leave behind this earthly decaying body and

---

[357] Randy Alcorn, *Heaven* (Wheaton, IL: Tyndale House Publishers, 2004), 58.

[358] Ibid., 60-62.

put on a new body as we worship with Christ face to face. That certainly is a great gain. It is not the final gain as that waits until our final resurrection where we receive a body suited for both the New Earth and New Heaven. For now, we seem to gain a body suited for function in the current heavenly realm.

4. What will we do in heaven?

Enjoying Everlasting Delights with no Sin, Suffering, or Sadness

The first major truth related to heaven relates to the perfection of it and those there. No sin, corruption, suffering, curse, sullenness, disease, or calamity in heaven shall ever occur because the Triune Lord rules there with his authority and character permeating every aspect of it. Our ancient forefather Irenaeus spoke of heaven as the place where we shall "enjoy the delights of paradise," because there we will "flourish" as we experience freedom "from the bondage of corruption."[359] So what we will do in heaven first is live, think, and feel everlasting joy, peace, and freedom from sin and trouble. We will be free with perfect harmony among all there.

Dr. John MacArthur summarized well this everlasting delight to come:

> Revelation 21:3-7 outlines the most remarkable features of the new heavens and new earth . . . . Here Scripture promises that heaven will be realm of perfect bliss. Tears, pain, sorrow, and crying will have no place whatsoever in the new heaven and new earth. It is a place where God's people will dwell

---

[359] Irenaeus, "Irenaeus Against Heresies," in *Ante-Nicene Fathers: The Apostolic Fathers*, eds. Alexander Roberts and James Donaldson (Peabody, MA: Hendrickson Publishers, 1999),566-567.

together with him eternally, utterly free from all the effects of sin and evil. God is pictured as personally wiping away the tears from the eyes of the redeemed. Heaven is a realm where death is fully conquered (1 Corinthians 15:26). There is no sickness there . . . no trouble, and no tragedy, Just absolute joy and eternal blessings.[360]

Possibly Praying for Saints on this Earth Until the Final New Heaven & New Earth Begins

Second, for those of us in the intermediate heaven, the one prior to the final New Heaven, we may have some knowledge of events happening on earth. Certainly those who are murdered in Revelation 6 take some interest in the affairs of this world. They also seem to pray for God's justice to take place on earth. Dr. Alcorn stated of this:

Christ, the God-Man, is in Heaven . . . interceding for people on Earth (Rom. 8:34), which tells us there is at least one person who has died and gone to heaven and is now praying for those on Earth. The martyrs in Heaven also pray to God (Revelation 6:10), asking him to take specific action on Earth. They are praying for God's justice on the earth, which has intercessory implications for Christians now suffering here. The sense of connection and loyalty to the body of Christ—and concern for the saints on Earth—would likely be enhanced, not diminished, by being in Heaven (Eph. 3:15). . . . Revelation 6 makes it clear that some who have died and are now in Heaven are praying concerning what's happening on Earth. . . .

---

[360] John MacArthur, "Heaven," in *The Harvest Handbook of Bible Prophecy*, eds. Ed Hindson. Mark Hitchcock, & Tim LaHaye (Eugene, OR: Harvest House Publishers, 2020), 149.

If people in Heaven are allowed to see at least some of what transpires on Earth . . . then it would seem strange for them *not* to intercede in prayer.[361]

Eating & Drinking in Heaven

Third, we will eat, drink, and fellowship with one another in heaven, the intermediate and final heaven. Some who do not think we have bodies in the intermediate heaven will object because they think we lack bodily form that could partake of food. If the kingdom of God exists in heaven now, which is certainly seems to be (we pray for the kingdom of heaven to come to earth, see Matt. 6:10), the Lord Jesus promised when we arrive in his kingdom with him that we would eat with him (see Luke 22:29-30). The eating with Jesus in the kingdom (Luke 22:30a) could easily occur initially in heaven now while the ruling and reigning on thrones over Israel (Luke 22:30b) could be a part of the future millennial kingdom.

But, whatever view one takes on the intermediate heaven, there is no doubt that we will eat, drink, and fellowship over food in the future kingdom to come. In Luke 14:15 we see a man who while eating contemplated eating and drinking in the future kingdom. Jesus did not correct this idea of the man. In fact, he shared a story of a future banquet that many receive invitations to enjoy (Luke 14:16-24).

Additionally, we see that in the future the Tree of Life with "twelve kinds of fruit, yielding its fruit every month of the year. Its leaves are for the healing of the nations" (Rev. 22:1-2). It seems fairly clear that this tree will produce some type of fruit or leaf that when ate brings about positive benefits to those who partake of it. Though some diversity exists on what that specific benefit is, the fact fruit

---

[361] Randy Alcorn, *Heaven* (Wheaton, IL: Tyndale House Publishers, 2004), 71.

exists from this tree that will benefit the people there seems certain.

In Isaiah 25:6 the Bible seems to suggest we will sit and have a banquet where we drink fluids in the kingdom. Though this text probably by context applies to the millennial kingdom, the New Earth will have "the river of the water of life" that flows down the "middle of the city" (Rev. 22:1). Will believers take a drink of that pure water as way to enjoy the glory and goodness, the refreshing presence of the Lord's provisions, by partaking of it? Why would believers not? Water is good and a symbol of the Lord's goodness to us

5. Will there be games and/or sports in heaven?

Some have asked this question related to sports and games. I think most likely we will play games in heaven and have some type of sporting events. I am not sure if it will be a carryover of sporting events like we have now on earth, but it may very well be just that and more. Sporting events reveal strength, skill, and gamesmanship plans, and all of those reflect character traits of God.

Paul sometimes used athletic competition to describe life in Christ (1 Cor. 9:24, 27 & 2 Tim. 2:5). It seems probable that such ideas connected to athletic events on this earth will exist on the New Earth, but without any corruption, injuries, or sin involved in it. Life on the New Earth will in many respects exist as a continuation from this old earth reality, but in a renewed form.

Part of this relates to a principle rooted in our resurrection and restoration of the earth. When Jesus arose from the grave his new body has some continuity with his earthly body. Though in a new form, the continuity still existed. The same applies to our resurrection body. It will be our old body resurrected and glorified. So it will be a new old body so to speak. Some continuity exists.

270

This applies to the earth as well. This earth will be dissolved in the end of this age (see 2 Peter 3:10). Yet a New Earth comes into existence that replaces this old earth (2 Peter 3:12-13). This New Earth will have features of the old earth in it. There is continuity.

This principle seems to apply to much of what we do on earth now and then on the New Earth. Some continuity will exist. Therefore, games, which we find fun here, likely will exist there. Having fun, laughing, and enjoying friendly competition as a way to glorify the Lord exists on this earth, and I think seemingly it will exist on the New Earth too. Of this matter Dr. Alcorn stated:

> Sports and our enjoyment of them aren't a result of the Fall. I have no doubt that sinless people would have invented athletics, with probably more variations than we have today. Sports suit our minds and our bodies. They're an expression of our God-designed humanity. What kind of sports and activities might we engage in on the New Earth? The possibilities are limitless. Perhaps we'll participate in sports that were once too risky. And just as we might have stimulating conversations with theologians and writers in Heaven, we might also have the opportunity to play our favorite sports with some of our favorite sports heroes.[362]

6. Will we have work and/or assignments in heaven?

Yes, in heaven the saints will rule and reign with Christ as managers over his universal kingdom. Work

---

[362] Randy Alcorn, *Heaven* (Wheaton, IL: Tyndale House Publishers, 2004), 410-411.

existed prior to the fall of Adam and Eve. After the fall work became tougher, full of problems due to sin and corruption in the world. But work and ruling itself reflects the character of God who rules, creates, and manages. Therefore, for mankind to work and rule in heaven, and on the New Earth aligns with the nature of God and the image of God within mankind.

Matthews 25:21-23, Luke 16:10, and Luke 19:11-27 reveal the reality that our faithfulness here on earth impacts the degree of our position in the future New Heaven and New Earth. The more faithful we are here the more the Lord will place us in charge of in the future kingdom. "In Heaven, we'll reign with Christ, exercise leadership and authority, and make important decisions. This implies we'll be given specific responsibilities by our leaders and we'll delegate specific responsibilities to those under our leadership (Luke 19:17-19). We'll set goals, devise plans, and share ideas."[363]

7. Can we be happy in heaven if some of our loved ones did not make it to heaven?

This question poses one of the tough thoughts about the afterlife. Nothing can startle the mind more than the thought of people we love not being with us in heaven. The thought can bring much grief to the soul here on this earth. How will that grief end when in heaven if we recall and know these loved ones did not make it there to heaven and consequently suffer in hell?

Weak minded, soft saints, and liberals often try to revise the doctrine of hell to explain this. In this era of so-called progressive (really regressive) Christianity, weak willed ministers are altering the old truths on hell to make it softer for soft people to accept. The toughness of God's

---

[363] Ibid., 396.

holiness being offended and him rightly applying everlasting justice for an eternal crime has come under severe fire by weak, soft, and emotive centric believers of this era.

Some will adopt the idea that those in hell experience annihilation. The Bible simply does not support this idea though. Plain reading of the text reveal that those in hell suffer with no end to it. The key to this truth relates to Christ Jesus. He suffered the wrath of God and remained conscious of it. Even in death his human soul remained fully aware of his physical death. The same shall occur with sinners in hell. Though their resurrected body will exist in a dead state (non-functional) the human soul-spirit will remain aware of this eternal death condition. The wrath of God does not eradicate the soul.

Others will try and adopt universalism, i.e. the idea that all will eventually make it to haven. Some say sinners must suffer for awhile and then after enough punishment these sinners will also arrive in heaven to join all others. Again, for those who take the Bible seriously and accept the historic doctrines of apostolic Christianity, this option does not exist. The Bible makes it clear that unbelievers will not escape hell. Not everyone will make it to heaven.

So how can we who love the Lord have no tears and peace of heart knowing loved ones suffer in hell while we rejoice in heaven? The answer relates to a reorientation to how we will see these loved ones. A few thoughts may help here.

First, love has two sides to it. Grace is one aspect of love. Yet discipline and justice equals another part of love. Because we will love in perfection when glorified we likely will have a sense of peace knowing that justice has been served. Our inner hearts will rest in peace knowing that those who refused the love and grace of Christ have committed one of the most evil acts of world history by rejecting Jesus Christ. Maybe a human illustration will help as we examine the second part of this.

Second, and in continuation of the idea of justice, it seems likely that in heaven our love for Christ will be so great that we shall see those who rejected Christ as true enemies of our family. We will seemingly sense how wicked their denial of Christ is in light of the great goodness of Jesus.

As a way to illustrate this, think of this scenario. Suppose your child turns against your spouse and another sibling. He brutally tortures the spouse and child and then murders them by slowly burning them to death as he tortured them. Upon discovery of this wicked act the child expresses great delight in this horrific series of evil deeds. Even when brought to justice in the court system the child curses your name, laughs about the murders, and shows no remorse.

In such a scenario the parent would likely think this child has become a monster and may even experience shock wondering who this child is. That thought and feeling will likely be how we in heaven will see those who committed the greatest sin in the history of the world against Jesus our greatest love. We will see the wicked hearts, their hatred of truth, and we will know intuitively that the application of justice is good. We will rejoice and express gratitude that the judge of the universe has done right by casting these wicked rebellious sinners into hell.

However, this occurs, and this may only touch the surface of it, the Lord will make sure we have joy and peace in heaven. He as the Lord will see and know those in hell and yet he too will have joy and delight forever with us. If the Lord Jesus can have peace and joy forever then we saints who will have his love perfected in us will also live out that joy he has in heaven forever even though sinners exist in hell.

Chapter 5.
Conclusion: The Best is Yet to Come

It has often been said that one is not yet ready to live until one is ready to die. The reality of a future world to come gives us great hope as believers. The sting and fear of death has been defeated by Jesus Christ for those who trust in him as Lord and Savior. We who know the Lord have assurance of a great future that never ends.

Sadly, sometimes people spend way too much time and energy arguing over the minor details of end times than they should. Major portions of Bible prophecy yield very clear views when Bible interpreters approach the Bible with a natural method of interpretation. Sometimes speculations and weird theories emerge because interpreters think they need to find some hidden or deeply symbolic meaning behind the words of the text. That method fails to deliver the comfort and hope God intends for his people to have by belief in the divine prophetic predictions.

Eternal Paradise

When Adam sinned this world plunged into chaos and confusion. Sin robbed humanity and stole from us everlasting peace, harmony, holiness, and our perfect paradise. But God redeems. The message of hope fills the pages of Scripture. What we lost in Eden shall be redeemed and reestablished in the resurrection age to come. Of this great climax end of history Dr. Ed Hindson has stated:

> Now, in the final chapter of Revelation, we learn that all that was lost in the beginning will finally be regained. Paradise is restored in the holy city. The biblical story, which began in the garden, ends in the eternal city. In between there stands the cross of

Jesus Christ. It alone has changed the destiny of mankind from death to life. . . . The removal of the divine curse makes access to God a reality in the new paradise. We are no longer barred from his presence. The throne of God has come to earth and is the central feature of the eternal city. It is the throne of God and the lamb, who rule jointly over the eternal state. . . . The Lord God is all the light the redeemed will ever need.[364]

Christmas Every Day: Unending Pleasure, Peace, Prosperity, & Perfection

In my region where I live Christmas has always been a time of community joy. My dad was a watchmaker and jeweler who ran a business in this region. Every year there would be Christmas parades, community events, evening strolls, and returning customers who were friends that supported the business. They would come in and buy jewelry and rejoice over the holidays.

Furthermore, our churches in the area always have Christmas events, ways to serve those in need, and ministerial themes that highlight our great hope and joy. The peacefulness of the time, the season, and the friendly people with warm hearts has always been a major blessing. From Thanksgiving to New Year the Christmas season remains one of my most favorite parts of life each year. There is a sense in which a deep sense of joy, contentment, and peace pervades the social environment during the holiday season here. I love it. I look forward to it and I miss it when it passes each year. These bits and pieces of that during the Christmas

---

[364] Ed Hindson, *Revelation: Twenty-First Century Biblical Commentary Series*, eds. Mal Couch & Ed Hindson (Chattanooga, TN: AMG Publishers, 2002), 221-223.

season remind me of what is to come in heaven where we will celebrate Christ every day without end. I love how my former teacher Dr. Ryrie explained this:

> We all know the feeling. In spite of the hustle and bustle of the season, there is goodwill as Christmas approaches. People are little more friendly; greetings become more common; wars enjoy cease-fires for a few days at Christmastime. We even like to leave the decorations up "just a little bit longer" to prolong the Christmas spirit. One day that spirit will permeate the entire earth and never leave. Christmas speaks of Christ's presence, and when he returns it will be Christmas every day everywhere. . . .
>
> Almost every human aspiration will be fulfilled in that coming kingdom. The things men have long dreamed of, planned and worked toward, and yet been unable to accomplish will at long last be realized. Peace prosperity, longevity, justice, all the elusive longings of mankind, will be experienced by the citizens of Christ's kingdom.[365]

How Can We Go to Heaven to Have Everlasting Life & Peace?

I love how Ryrie spoke of this finality, the ending of history that begins the new world that never ends. As we reach the end of this book and think back over the *Major Truths on the End of the World and the World to Come*, one urgent and vital essential remains: what world will you be a part of in the new world to come?

---

[365] Charles C. Ryrie, *The Best is Yet to Come* (Chicago, IL: Moody Press, 1981), 134, 136.

I will remind you of what my teacher reminded us about this world to come. "It is sobering to realize that life does not end at the grave. Every soul born into this world will exist forever."[366] When you die in this world you will enter into the next world in either a state of everlasting conscious life or everlasting conscious death. Think about that for a moment. If you die without knowing Christ Jesus then you will suffer everlasting death existence. You will consciously know you are dead forever and will suffer for rejecting Christ Jesus. You will have an "endless existence in heaven or hell."[367]

What should you do about this? "Who decides" which "destiny"[368] shall be yours? Hear the words of Jesus: "The one who believes in the Son has eternal life. The one who rejects the Son will not see life, but God's wrath remains on him" (John 3:36). "Jesus offered eternal life to any and all kinds of people. His message was uniform and his offer was universal. . . . Eternal life is a gift from the one who is the Lamb of God and takes away the sin of the world. . . . Are you ready?"[369]

Right now examine your heart and mind. Do you right now trust in Jesus as the one who redeems you from your sin? Do you have faith in him as Lord and Savior? If not, I plead with you, trust in him. The world to come will be bliss and every pain you have ever faced will be no more. Life, everlasting life, with peace, joy, prosperity, love, family, friends, and the Lord will go with you forever with no end. Trust in Jesus right now.

---

[366] Ibid., 142.

[367] Ibid.

[368] Ibid.

[369] Ibid.

God said it this way: "For this is the way God loved the world: He gave his one and only Son, so that everyone who believes in him will not perish but have eternal life" (John 3:16). And Jesus taught us about his father God and told us this: "I am the way, and the truth, and the life. No one comes to the Father except through me" (John 14:6). Believe in him to redeem you from sin and this everlasting glorious life will be yours. And then, if you do believe, make sure everyone you know hears of this glorious truth so they too can believe.

I look forward to seeing you the reader in glory. Until then, may you educate, evangelize, and encourage others in Christlike discipleship as we, Christlike disciples, cooperate for the Great Commission. The best is truly yet to come!

Appendix A.

The Apostasy of Gary Demar in Denying Jesus' Future Coming

In the history of Christianity various futuristic views exist on Christ's coming and the time of it in relation to the millennium and/or tribulation. The most ancient view was the premillennial view. Then the amillennial view developed in church history. Then later the post-millennial view developed. All of these are futuristic models in that all rightly affirmed the future coming of Christ to establish his eternal kingdom.

The gospel itself has within it a future element related to Christ's coming. The gospel is that God came to earth and added human flesh to himself (the incarnation; God with us), that he lived a sinless life, died for our sins, arose again in the flesh and will come again in the flesh to consummate history and bring in final redemption. Sadly, full preterism denies the future physical second coming of Christ and in doing so those who affirm this have cut themselves off from the historic church and from the true gospel.

With regret, we have in the past few years watched Gary Demar move into apostasy by embracing full preterism. As his friends watched this happen some of us who knew him reached out to him to try and encourage him to confess Christian orthodoxy. Sadly, those efforts failed.

In December 2022 efforts were initiated to try and call Gary Demar to confess orthodox Christianity. Private efforts were at first made to try and verify if Demar had turned away from the gospel and into heresy. Demar refused to give answers to the questions posed to him.

Over the course of several months numerous teachers were involved in the effort. As the team prayed and worked on ideas of what to do a letter was crafted by a team of teachers and given to Demar with the goal of encouraging him to confess the truth of historic Christianity. Again, those efforts were rejected by Demar.

This is the letter we sent to Demar.

Dear Gary:

We are your brothers in the Lord, long-time friends and supporters, co-laborers in his Word, and co-promoters and defenders of the Christian worldview. We are writing to you once again (as we did two months ago) with an earnest plea regarding your doctrinal transitioning that we are witnessing. Gary, we seriously and deeply hope that you will receive this as from deeply-burdened hearts and that you will respond to us as to those who love you in the Lord and have appreciated your public ministry in our day.

As you know from our previous correspondence, we are deeply concerned over the eschatological direction you seem to be taking of late. Andrew Sandlin heard you speak at a conference in Texas about a year ago. At that time he was surprised that you would not acknowledge whether you believe in a future final judgment and a future physical resurrection of the dead. When asked, you also stated that you would not call full preterists "heretics."

Due to certain statements you made publicly on Facebook recently, Ken Gentry asked you if you would affirm three simple, basic doctrinal positions. These questions have intentionally been kept limited and simple in order to avoid entangling interaction with the many variations within and permutations of Full Preterism (aka Consistent Preterism; aka

Covenant Preterism; aka Hyperpreterism). Furthermore, they have also been confined to doctrines clearly declared in the American Vision Statement of Faith.[370]

Those simple yes-or-no questions are now simplified and clarified even more:

1. Do you believe in a future bodily, glorious return of Christ?

2. Do you believe in a future physical, general resurrection of the dead?

3. Do you believe history will end with the Final Judgment of all men?

To refuse to affirm the future, physical resurrection; the final judgment of the righteous and the unrighteous; and the tactile reality of the eternal state is to refuse to affirm critical elements of the Christian faith. To contradict these doctrines is not merely to contradict a few specific biblical texts; it is to contradict indispensable aspects of the Christian faith and the biblical worldview.

As blunt as it might sound, it is to strike at crucial aspects in the very heart of the Christian faith. This private letter of inquiry has been agreed upon by the signatories listed below. Please, Gary, receive this not as an attack upon you, but as a humble concern for your doctrinal orthodoxy and the integrity of American Vision. Please set the matter straight regarding these three fundamental issues so

---

[370] See https://americanvision.org/about/statement-of-faith/ .

that we can lay this matter to rest. We love you and are continuing to pray for you,

In the love of Christ the Lord, Andrew Sandlin, Ken Gentry, Jeffrey Ventrella, Phillip Kayser, John Frame, Ardel Caneday, Jeff Durbin, James White, Brian Mattson, Keith Sherlin, Jason Bradfield, and Sam Frost

To date, we have not received any affirmations from Demar that he affirms historic biblical Christianity. As it appears to us, he has denied the faith. In some of his podcast shows in 2023 Demar even denied that 1 Corinthians related to the physical resurrection. In the 25th podcast show of Covenant Hermeneutics and Biblical Eschatology the show supports the idea that 1 Corinthians is teaching a spiritual resurrection, not a physical one.

In such case, 1 Corinthians 15:33 applies to Demar. Orthodox Christians can no longer accept him in fellowship. His unwillingness to answer the fundamental questions related to historic Christianity, and his teachings in various shows that undermine fundamentals of the faith, serve as a reminder to us all to pay close attention to our doctrine. If our hermeneutic or doctrinal system leads us to undermine the future physical second coming of Jesus and the physical resurrection the right solution remains repentance.

Demar's 2024 Book: A Denial of Christ's Future Bodily Return

The questions about whether Demar had denied the historic Christian faith were even clearer after the release of his 2 Volume set *The Hope of Israel and the Nations*. The first volume released in 2023 did not reveal much about the doctrine of concern. However, volume 2 released in 2024

283

revealed the heresy that so many have been concerned about with Demar.

Demar and Kim Burgess both authored these 2 volumes. Towards the last portion of volume 2 their views on the 2nd coming of Christ reveals the blasphemous ideology. On page 402 this works teaches believers should not think of Christ's coming as a physical presence. Instead one should think of it as "presence."[371] In Demar's mind if we use the term "coming" this will lead to "confusing people because" they "are tempted to look for a physical and visible coming down and so forth."[372]

In this work, the disdain for physical realities, a hallmark of preterism rooted in Christoplatonism, surfaces regularly with Demar and Burgess. For example, in this work we see this idea conveyed when it was said, "2 Peter 1:19" teaches that "the parousia of Christ is going to be a Spiritual reality. If the Kingdom of God is in the Holy Spirit, so is the parousia of Christ! It is not the flesh; it is Spirit!"[373]

The denial of historic orthodoxy occurs with glaring clarity. In denouncing historic church orthodoxy, this work says, "Church tradition proclaims . . . the parousia of Christ . . . is going to be a physical, visible, human-bodily Reality that is going to be seen by everybody as it calls space and time to a halt, but this is not the way His parousia is expressed in Hebrews 9:28. . . ."[374] In their preterism model,

---

[371] Kim Burgess with Gary Demar, *The Hope of Israel and the Nations: New Testament Eschatology Accomplished and Applied* (Powder Springs, GA: The American Vision Inc., 2024), 402.

[372] Ibid.

[373] Ibid., 406.

[374] Ibid.

"the days of Christ in the flesh on earth are long over (Heb. 5:7)."[375]

Finally, in what may be the plainest denial of the historic position of the church on Christ's future 2nd coming, Demar and Burgess' work foolishly asserted that the historic church has been in error throughout all of its history on the doctrine of Christ's future return.

> But here is where it really gets serious. With all due respect, I believe that that the institutional Church has made a serious mistake by teaching that the parousia of Christ is going to take place in his same physical/material, visible, and bodily form. Based on all of that we have seen in this series . . . I am left to reply, 'No, it is not for the simple redemptive-historical and covenantal reason that the parousia, unlike Christ's incarnation, does not belong to the Old Covenant order. It belongs to the New Covenant order! The nature of the New Covenant order is in, of, by, and through the Spirit. Therefore, the form or manner of the parousia (presence) of Christ will change with the transition of the covenantal orders. Christ will come, just as he was careful to teach his disciples in John 14 and 16, in the person of the Holy Spirit, not again in the flesh.[376]

If ever there was a time for Demar to denounce this heresy, penned by Burgess with Demar's name on the book, that would have been the time to do so. Yet Demar agrees with these conclusions about the coming or presence of

---

[375] Ibid., 408.

[376] Kim Burgess with Gary Demar, *The Hope of Israel and the Nations: New Testament Eschatology Accomplished and Applied* (Powder Springs, GA: The American Vision Inc., 2024), 414.

Christ being here now through the Holy Spirit. In Demar's apostate mind this is the proper conclusion when applying the so-called "New Covenant hermeneutic."[377] Instead of correcting Burgess' radical apostasy, Demar endorses it further as the proper conclusions.

This flawed hermeneutic has led these men into sinful apostasy. The solution remains with a return to a proper hermeneutic. The historic church has confessed this in the Chicago Statement on Hermeneutics. Article XV of that confession provides the antidote to the full preterism heresy.

> We affirm the necessity of interpreting the Bible according to its literal, or normal, sense. The literal sense is the grammatical-historical sense, that is, the meaning which the writer expressed. Interpretation according to the literal sense will take account of all figures of speech and literary forms found in the text. We deny the legitimacy of any approach to Scripture that attributes to it meaning which the literal sense does not support.[378]

Demar's 2025 Rejection of the Historic Creeds

In April of 2025, the proof that Demar has hardened his position can be seen in his analysis of the earliest confessional creeds of the historic church. Demar on April 1st of 2025 stated that the Nicene Creed and the Apostle's Creed have been "standards of orthodoxy for 1700 years."[379]

---

[377] Ibid., 415.

[378] International Council on Biblical Hermeneutics, *The Chicago Statement on Biblical Hermeneutics*, Article XV.

[379] Gary Demar, *Coming to Judge the Living and the Dead: The Creeds, History, and Biblical Language*, accessed at

In this matter of being a standard for orthodoxy, Demar has rightly stated that fact. Sadly, however, Demar thinks he has discovered some truth that the standard orthodox church has been wrong on since the days of the earliest disciples of the apostles. These creeds function as "guardrails" to help "protect those traveling along the highway of biblical orthodoxy."[380]

Confessional creeds such as these ancient ones define for us the standards, the essential truths that one must confess if that person, church, or organization remains in alignment with the earliest teachers of our sacred heritage. This in no way undermines the sufficiency of Scripture or our affirmation that Scripture functions as the highest authority. Consensus among the body of Christ has emerged through the work of the Spirit leading mature believers to accept and confess the clear, unmistakable, and obvious statements of truth related to the most key doctrines that define Christianity from all false religions and false teachers. As Dr. Hartman added:

> While allowing for diversity on non-essential issues, the creeds prevent us from veering off the highway of biblical orthodoxy. Because the safeguards exist, the only way to leave the safe road of orthodoxy is to do a great deal of damage. Biblical orthodoxy matters because God calls us to know and worship him as he has revealed himself through Scripture.[381]

---

https://americanvision.org/posts/coming-to-judge-the-living-and-the-dead/ on 4.6.25.

[380] Dayton Hartman, *Church History for Modern Ministry: Why our Past Matters for Everything We Do* (Bellingham, WA: Lexham Press, 2016), 16.

[381] Ibid.

Historical theologian Dr. Earle Cairns has also noted this concept of a confessional orthodoxy in the creeds. He rightly noted that "Creeds have been used to test orthodoxy, to recognize fellow believers, and to serve as a convenient summary of the essential doctrines of the faith."[382] These ancient confessions help us to see the "oldest summary of the essential doctrines of Scripture that we have."[383] These foundational doctrinal summations found in the Apostle's, Nicene, and other early creeds were "not written by the apostles" but even so these confessions were "certainly" the embodiment of "the doctrines that they taught."[384]

However, Demar in his apostasy has rejected the historical view confessed in these creeds related to Jesus' future 2nd coming. In Demar's thinking, since the creeds confess a future coming of Christ such a confession runs contrary to scripture. In his mind, they were wrong about a future coming of Christ. In his words he stated, "I contend that they got the timing wrong as do those who interpret the creeds today."[385]

Christ's Future 2nd Coming in his Resurrected Body: A Fundamental of the Faith

Throughout church history the Bible believing saints have confessed, affirmed, and had a great hope for the

---

[382] Earle E. Cairns, *Christianity Through the Centuries: A History of the Christian Church* (Grand Rapids, MI: Zondervan, 1996), 114.

[383] Ibid.

[384] Ibid.

[385] Gary Demar, *Coming to Judge the Living and the Dead: The Creeds, History, and Biblical Language*, accessed at https://americanvision.org/posts/coming-to-judge-the-living-and-the-dead/ on 4.6.25.

glorious 2nd appearing of the Lord Jesus Christ. The coming of Christ to end history and consummate redemptive history remains one of the most sacred fundamentals of the faith. It connects to the gospel itself. The gospel is that God added flesh to himself, lived a sinless life, died for our sins, arose again his flesh, ascended into heaven where he shall come again in that body to finalize our redemption through the final resurrection. To cut off the future, bodily, 2nd coming of Jesus violates the gospel. To assert Jesus has already returned means one worships a different Jesus than the historic church has worshipped.

Writing in the early 1900s, professor Dr. Charles Erdman from the then conservative seminary, Princeton Theological Seminary, wrote of this great important truth of Jesus' 2ndcoming in the historic volumes known as *The Fundamentals* that were edited by R.A. Torrey and A.C. Dixon. Of this essential truth, Dr. Erdman rightly stated that this view of Christ's future 2nd coming "is held universally by all who admit the authority of Scripture."[386] This truth means that Jesus' return shall be "personal," "visible," "bodily," "local," and not "spiritual" or "figurative."[387]

Almost as if speaking directly to apostate and false teachers like Demar and Burgess, who confess a spiritual presence of Christ as the 2nd coming of Jesus, Dr. Erdman reminded the believers that there is a blessing in this current spiritual presence of Christ through the Holy Spirit, but that is not the blessed hope. It is true "that Christ does come to each believer, by his Holy Spirit, and dwells within, and empowers for service and suffering and growth in grace; but this is to be held in harmony with the other blessed truth that

---

[386] Charles R. Erdman, "The Coming of Christ," in *The Fundamentals*, Vol. IV, eds. R.A. Torrey, A.C. Dixon (Grand Rapids, MI: Baker Books, 1917, reprinted in 1996 by Baker), 301.

[387] Ibid.

Christ shall some day literally appear again in bodily form, and 'we shall see him' and shall then 'be like him,' when 'we see him as he is.'"[388] Full preterism has denied the historic faith and rejected a fundamental doctrine that constitutes Bible believing Christianity.

Demar and Burgess, and the cult like social organization of people that wrongly think Jesus has already returned, have robbed their followers of the glorious hope taught within the pages of Scripture. Reverend John Mcnicol highlighted five key truths about this great hope of Christ all believers have:

1. Christ taught his disciples to expect his return.

2. The apostles taught their converts to wait for the coming of the Lord.

3. The whole life and work of the New Testament Church has the coming of the Lord in view.

4. The New Testament grace of hope rests upon the coming of the Lord.

5. Redemption is not complete until the second coming of the Lord.[389]

The heresy that Jesus has already returned undermines the entire thrust of the hope that NT saints had in following the teaching of the apostles. Indeed, such a difference constitutes an entirely different worldview. The Judeo-Christian

---

[388] Ibid., 301-302.

[389] John Mcnicol, "The Hope of the Church," *The Fundamentals*, Vol. IV, eds. R.A. Torrey, A.C. Dixon (Grand Rapids, MI: Baker Books, 1917, reprinted in 1996 by Baker), 287-300.

worldview in the days of the apostles and their immediate disciples after them, and on into early church history had unanimity in their great hope of looking for a future bodily return of Jesus Christ.

Dr. Erdman could not have stated it any better than he did when addressing this matter in the early 1900s. He rightly categorized the future return of Christ (still to occur) as a non-negotiable essential of the faith. His words remain just as vital today as when penned:

> The return of Christ is a fundamental doctrine of the Christian faith. It is embodied in hymns of hope; it forms the climax of the creeds; it is the sublime motive for evangelistic and missionary activity; and daily it is voiced in the inspired prayer: "Even so: Come Lord Jesus."[390]

Faithful followers of Christ, if honoring Christ, will not associate (partner) in ministry with these wolves in sheep's clothing who deny the great gospel hope of the true followers of Jesus Christ. 1 Corinthians 15:33 applies: bad company (those who deny a future, bodily return of Christ) will corrupt good character (those who love and obey Christ).

---

[390] Charles R. Erdman, "The Coming of Christ," in *The Fundamentals*, Vol. IV, eds. R.A. Torrey, A.C. Dixon (Grand Rapids, MI: Baker Books, 1917, reprinted in 1996 by Baker), 301.

Appendix B.

Does Premillennialism Lead to Cultural Disengagement?

I have encountered some who believe that premillennialism is a theology that promotes withdrawing from the culture, or that it is a theology that sees the entire culture as a sinking ship and our goal is only to save as many as possible with little or no regard to the culture around us. This idea sometimes stems from the view that all forms of premillennial theology (dispensational and historic forms) do not believe we will win over the culture and bring in the kingdom of God on earth as say would those in the post-millennial position.

Sadly, as I often say, extremes exist in all fields of theology. The truth of the matter is that those in the premillennial camp write, teach, work, and promote cultural engagement on a regular basis (both in literature and in action organizations) and have for hundreds and hundreds of years. Many are in the front lines doing the work of both the Great Commission (the primary mission of the church) and also loving their neighbors and doing good to all (Gal. 6:10) which includes promoting natural law, justice, and common grace morality throughout the lands in which they live. Many social missions for the poor, legal associations for the body of Christ, and other social missions have been and continue to be founded and led by those in the premillennial persuasion of thought.

Some theologians recognize this and give due recognition of this. More should do likewise. The volumes of literature produced by premillennial teachers that promotes morality in the culture, while at the same time promoting the gospel, remains voluminous. But, before just giving a short list to disprove this myth against premillennialism, hear the honest words of a Covenant theologian on this matter. Ronald Henzel has rightly said of those in premillennialism, "their fervent commitment to evangelism, dedication to addressing social concerns, and accurate grasp of the nature of human history rebuke those who accuse them of insulating themselves from present world out of preoccupation with the next."[391]

Premillennialists of both forms have been active, engaged, and teaching and training people in the culture on how to live righteously and how to rightly influence the culture for truth. They do this while also being fervently dedicated to the greater and ultimate mission of the gospel of salvation because as Jesus said, what does it gain a man (or culture) if he (they as the culture) gain the whole world and yet lose their soul. A nation full of moral people in the civil sense of the term can still mean a nation of people on their way to hell.

So premillenniallists who love the gospel retain the ultimate focus of man's ultimate need while also engaging in other areas too at the common grace social level (just as I know my conservative gospel loving amillennial & post-millennial friends do too). So here below is just a super brief list of works that relate to engaging the culture by premillennialists. I pulled these down from my library shelves in just 2 minutes.

I wonder why my covenant friends sometimes cannot seem to recognize this? And why do some make unfounded allegations against their brothers in the faith? I do not judge my conservative and mature amillennial or post-millennial friends for the extreme assertions made by those in their covenant fields (like Dr. Charles Hodge who thought it

---

[391] Ronald Henzel, *Darby, Dualism, and the Decline of Dispensationalism* (Tucson, AZ: Fenestra Books, 2003), 197.

should be a jailable felony for anyone {even an unbeliever} not attending church) who I know have sometimes fallen into a few extremes or who lack the educational maturity to realize other forms of their theology exist. I wish covenant theologians would do the same and ignore extremist views that from time-to-time may surface in our tradition.

This is why I continue to say prior to the 1944 split in the Protestant Reformed Evangelical body of Christ, where premillennial, amillennial, and post-millennial believers ministered as partners in the academy and churches, that prior era was a better model than the models that emerged after the Reformed Dispensationalists were excommunicated. That schism has not been good for the holistic church. The various schools of thought can learn from each other and partner together in the gospel work. Dr. Ryrie taught us this himself.

Premillennial Ministers Engaging the Culture with Salt & Light

Dr. Charles C. Ryrie:
>   The Christian & Social Responsibility
>   Biblical Answers to Contemporary Issues
>   Biblical Answers to Tough Questions

Dr. Wayne Grudem:
>   Voting as a Christian
>   Politics According to the Bible

Dr. Mal Couch:
>   America Founded as a Christian Nation;
>   The Jews and the Founding of America;
>   This Great Nation;
>   Issues 2000: Evangelical Faith & Cultural Trends in
>   the New Millennium
>   The Fundamentals for the Twenty-First Century

Dr. Richard D. Land:
Christians in the Public Square: Faith in Practice

Dr. Richard D. Land & Louis A. Moore:
Life at Risk: The Crisis in Medical Ethics

Dr. Tony Evans:
How Should Christians Vote
Gambling & the Lottery

Dr. Richard A. Fowler & Dr. Wayne House:
The Christian Confronts his Culture

Dr. Norman Geisler & Frank Turek:
Legislating Morality

Dr. Chris Cone (triple doctoral scholar):
The Bible in Government and Society.

Dr. Billy Graham:
Answers to Life's Problems (has a good chapter on
the Church & balanced focuses with the gospel as
primary while also attending to civil matters too).

Dr. Wayne House (a Juris Doctor & ThD theologian):
Christian Ministries and the Law

Dr. Jenna Ellis:
The Legal Basis for a Moral Constitution
Minister / Broadcaster with American Family
Association

Dr. Norman Geisler & Kerby Anderson:
Origin Science

Dr. Norman Geisler & Randy Douglas:
Integrity at Work

Dr. Tim LaHaye:
Mind Siege
A Nation Without a Conscious

Dr. Norman Geisler:
Unshakable Foundations

David Noebel (a speaker at dispensational pre-trib
conferences and other premill schools):
Understanding The Times

These works are a small selection of works that
highlight premillennial believers working to engage the
culture. If you encounter a person, teacher, or minister who
alleges premillennial teachers do not care about their culture,
just know the person is either not very well read and
educated, not being honest, or has been taught wrongly and
is deceived. To suggest premillennial believers do not
engage the culture to try and bring light to it means the
person has embraced some myth without due investigation.
The facts of history show otherwise.

Furthermore, this list of authors does not even touch
upon the many ministers who have founded mission
organizations to feed the poor and to administer benevolence
and mercy ministries to the culture. For just one modern
example, Samaritan's Purse, founded by the son of Billy
Graham, is led by a premillennialist Franklin Graham.
Through the 1800s and 1900s many godly premillennial
believers founded many organizations to combat the decay
of the culture.

Additionally, many legal organizations that have
been founded were established by those who affirm
premillennial views. Jerry Falwell, founder of Liberty

University, established Liberty University with a school of law that has trained thousands of lawyers that have entered the civil domain armed with a godly worldview. Many of these lawyers have established legal organizations to defend and promote justice in the courtrooms across the nation.

The list herein does not cover many others too. The truth is that premillennial theology does not naturally, necessarily, or logically lead to a withdrawal from the culture. Usually other ideologies cause that sectarian or extreme spatial separatist methodology. History shows us that some of the most well known and most dedicated premillennial teachers of the body of Christ have engaged the culture on a regular basis.

Appendix C.

Redemptive Grace: A Balanced Gospel View of Christ's Work of Redemption

Introduction: Avoiding Radicalism for a Balanced Gospel

A person can glance through various theological books and articles in this era and discover many writers trying to establish their views as some type of extreme or radical view. Have you ever noticed how teenagers talk in America? Often their words are connected to adjectives to sensationalize their nouns. The culture and entertainment world in America has this nuance as well. Extreme sports are now common in America. This mentality seems to have permeated the theological landscape too. People classify their view of salvation, grace, church, missions, or life in Christ as radical or some other type of word to describe their "extreme" view.

Even songs are not immune to this. One worship song has the words "reckless love of God" in it. Here are a few examples of these modern terms now in the spirit-theological realm or academy. Dr. David Platt wrote a book with the title *Radical Together*. In this book he builds from a prior book *Radical*.[392] In this book his aim focused on explaining "the revolutionary claims and commands of Christ to our communities of faith."[393] In similar fashion we

---

[392] David Platt, *Radical Together: Unleashing the People of God for the Purpose of God* (Colorado Springs, CO: Multnomah Books, 2011), 1.

[393] Ibid., 2.

find that idea of *Radical Reformission* from the pen of Mark Driscoll. In Driscoll's writing he asserted that he wanted to promote a "radical call to reform the church's traditionally flawed view of missions."[394] Professor Steve Brown joins the chorus with these types of words in his work *A Scandalous Freedom: The Radical Nature of the Gospel*. In this book he says, "the Bible is quite radical; most of us don't understand how radical it is."[395]

The theme also surfaces in works about being a masculine man. John Eldridge wrote a book *Wild at Heart*. In this work he speaks of man's innate desires for adventure, danger, risk and the drive for "a battle to fight, an adventure to live, and a beauty to rescue."[396] Dr. John Piper has also written in this vernacular. He wrote *The Dangerous Duty of Delight*. In this book he argued that Jesus is "not safe, but he is stunning."[397]

In each of those books some truths exist and these comments should not be taken or interpreted as a condemnation of everything in those books. Of course, I certainly do not agree with some of what surfaces in those books. Even so, I am not per se opposed to the idea that the Lord is radical if we mean he is drastically different and above all else. He is that and so much more. The gospel is a call to a unique and distinct way of life and living. It is a worldview above all others.

---

[394] Mark Driscoll, *The Radical Reformission* (Grand Rapids, MI: Zondervan, 2004), 18.

[395] Steve Brown, *A Scandalous Freedom: The Radical Nature of the Gospel* (West Monroe, LA: Howard Publishing Company, 2004), 7.

[396] John Eldridge, *Wild at Heart: Discovering The Secret of a Man's Soul* (Nashville, TN: Thomas Nelson, 2001), 9.

[397] John Piper, *The Dangerous Duty of Delight* (Sisters, OR: Multnomah Publishers, 2001), 8.

The point herein has a different focus. The point is that it seems some of the literature today has adopted "extreme" language to convey their theological points. It is an odd phenomenon. It may be that these authors are trying to reach or ignite the masculine drive in men. David Murrow wrote of this issue in his book *Why Men Hate Going to Church*. He noted in this book that for men to have an interest or dedication to something that it often requires danger, courage, and sacrifice. He stated, "a 'real man' must stand up to danger, bear up under suffering, and sacrifice himself for the good of others."[398]

This emphasis on extremes, the radical, and the wild or dangerous ideology can when left unchecked lead to one being out of balance. My concern is more so with some who apply the ideology of extremism to a doctrine and carry it to unjustified ends. Any doctrine used wrongly or when out of balance can lead one into realms that are not justified. Charles Ryrie wisely wrote and taught that "there is nothing more devastating to the practice of spiritual living than an imbalance."[399]

Where does imbalance sometimes occur? It occurs in the gospel presentations. Some add extra requirements to the gospel and by doing so they either undermine the gospel of grace or they sometimes make it at the minimum unclear. Examples of this may include presentations where a person is told he or she must give up all sins at the moment of salvation, or that a person must dedicate every area of one's life fully to Christ in order to be saved.

On the other hand, some dilute the definitions of the gospel and reduce it to something lacking in specific

---

[398] David Murrow, *Why Men Hate Going to Church* (Nashville, TN: Thomas Nelson, 2011), 38.

[399] Charles C. Ryrie, *Balancing the Christian Life: Biblical Principles for Wholesome Living* (Chicago, IL: Moody Press, 1969), 9.

Christological substance. Some have even promoted an idea known as the cross-less gospel. Examples of this may include presenting the gospel as just believing the facts about Christ dying and rising from the grave.

Or for some it has meant that all one needs to do to be saved is to trust Christ for eternal life without ever explaining the work of Christ (his death and resurrection) to the sinner so the sinner has the proper content within the faith. Such views have close resemblance to Sandemanians where mere assent or acknowledgement of the work of Christ results in salvation.[400]

Recognition of or acknowledgement of historical facts alone does not equal faith. Faith equals reliance upon the work of Christ, not merely acknowledgement of it as a historical event.

Extremism or the radicalization of ideas can happen to any doctrine, even to the gospel. When this happens balance can be lost and problems arise. Instead of creating an extreme or radical version of the gospel, we teachers and preachers of the sacred gospel would do better to present the gospel with balance. The idea itself, that salvation is found in no other person except the God-Man Christ Jesus, who as Lord died and rose again to redeem us from sin, stands as a radical and extreme message in and of itself. The balanced presentation of this rests in our hands. That idea itself is radical or extreme enough. I do not need to make it any more radical.

---

[400] R.E.D. Clark, "Sandemanians," in *The New International Dictionary of the Christian Church*, ed. J.D. Douglas (Grand Rapids, MI: Zondervan, 1978), 877.

Redemptive Grace: A More Balanced Gospel Presentation

I am a Reformed, Evangelical, Amyraldian, Dispensationalist. I travel a stream of conservative theology that has roots back to the earliest of disciples who knew the original senior Apostles. In our Evangelical river of thought we have a wide and deep gospel river. In that river several streams flow into that one larger evangelical river. Some are Dispensational, as I am; others are Covenantal; some are more Arminian/Wesleyan; and still others are different strands of thought from the Reformation (strong Calvinists [usually infralapsarians] or Lutheran as two examples). Yet unity in the gospel message has been a key hallmark of fundamental or conservative Evangelical Christianity.

The gospel is simple. Salvation is by grace through faith in the work of Christ who died, arose as Lord and Savior, and shall return to judge the living and the dead. Sadly, sometimes in zeal or through lack of balance this basic message that stands as a key for Evangelicals suffers from a lack of clarity. In worse case scenarios, some deny it even when given the opportunity for clarification and consequently depart from the Evangelical river.

Discipleship has been a key aspect of my life in Christ. I have over the years sought out discipleship from theologians in the various streams of thought that feed the one single Evangelical river. In that discipleship I discovered from numerous teachers a distinct stream of thought on how to properly present the gospel in its most basic and balanced form.

I learned from several of my teachers, such as Dr. Charlie Draper from North Greenville University, Dr. Charles Ryrie (Dallas Seminary & Tyndale Seminary), Dr. Mal Couch (Tyndale Seminary), Dr. Robert Lightner (Dallas Seminary & Tyndale Seminary), Dr. Arnold Fruchtenbaum (Tyndale Seminary), Dr. Paige Patterson (Southeastern

Baptist Seminary & Southwestern Baptist Seminary), Dr. Norman Geisler (Southern Evangelical Seminary), and Dr. Billy Graham (at his gospel Crusades and in his writings) that when we present the gospel in its most precise form or in its foundational form we need to make sure we do not present the gospel in a works formula. They also warned against presenting the gospel in a watered down version that stripped content from the words and ideas of the gospel. Those two errors had to be avoided.

In essence, they emphasized the need for a balanced gospel presentation. As stated by Dr. Ryrie,"One of my former teachers repeatedly reminded us that an imbalance in theology was the same as doctrinal insanity."[401] I agree. I think Ryrie may have been talking about Dr. Chafer in that quote, though I am not certain.

Sometimes, because of too much emphasis in one direction, teachers of the Word and gospel lead others to an imbalanced view of salvation. Sometimes their presentations do not match up with their otherwise orthodox confession that salvation is by grace through faith in Christ. Often when you converse with someone over the precise nature of the gospel they do in fact affirm and confess that salvation is by grace through faith in Christ and his death and resurrection as Lord and Savior. They reject the idea of human effort as the ground or basis for one's salvation and they also reject the idea of excluding the key core content of the gospel (repentant-faith in the death and resurrection of Christ).

---

[401] Charles C. Ryrie, *Balancing the Christian Life: Biblical Principles for Wholesome* Living (Chicago, IL: Moody Press, 1969), 9.

Defining the Redemptive Grace Gospel View in Between the Extremes

From those teachers noted above (and others) I learned about what we students termed the *"redemptive grace"* view of salvation. It is a mediating view in between extreme free grace and extreme lordship salvation views. Dr. Norman Geisler called this view the moderate free grace view. The redemptive grace view of salvation teaches that the Lord Jesus, through the Holy Spirit, draws a sinner to salvation, and that the sinner will repent of trusting in oneself or one's own works for righteousness, and will turn in faith to the Lord Jesus Christ, trusting that Jesus will redeem one from sin.

As Dr. Mal Couch described it, "When one believes on Christ for salvation, he is doing just that—he is changing the mind about the issue of redemption. He is turning away from his sins, and then turning to Christ. Repentance and believing are put together and seen as a whole, as in Mark 1:15, 'Repent and believe the gospel.'"[402]

Extreme free grace theology often claims that a person can be saved without repentance. Too, some will say a born again person may never produce any fruit and still have assurance of salvation or truly be saved. Fruitless and even faithless Christians can exist. One could be an atheist and renounce their faith and somehow that would still not ever qualify as those who walked away and were never truly one of us (see 1 John 2:19).

But Scripture reveals that some may appear to be a Christian while not truly ever having experienced eternal regeneration. True believers do not totally and irreversibly lose their salvation. True believers also do not totally and

---

[402] Mal Couch, *There is No Other Name: What it Means to Be Saved* (Clifton, TX: Scofield Ministries, n.d.), 19–20.

irreversibly lose their faith. Dr. Robert P. Lightner taught of Apostle John's teaching in 2:19, true believers will remain in the faith and will not apostatize.[403] True conversion means the sinner turns from self (repentance) and turns to Christ who renews that person's nature. Then naturally from that new nature the person will experience some fruit flowing from the new nature.

Some have even taught something known as the cross-less gospel, the idea that one did not even need to know Christ died on the cross for his or her sins. Others claim repentance is not a part of the gospel presentation in any way. I still recall Dr. Couch and Dr. Lightner hosting a class on this topic in Texas, and they discussed the dangers of the view promoted by some in this movement.

But another view has been known as extreme lordship salvation. In this view someone to be saved must dedicate their lives to Christ as Lord and agree (repent of) to give up certain sins, or be willing to give up all sins, at the moment of salvation. Also extreme lordship salvation sometimes teaches that a true believer cannot be carnal or an infant in Christ and walk in periods of sin. If a person walks in sin for a period of time or season one should not see that person as a true believer.

Sometimes too those in this stream will claim that one must turn from any certain number of specific sins at the moment of salvation in order to experience true faith or redemption in Christ. Dr. Robert Lightner stated the question and issue this way: "Must the unsaved promise to make Christ Lord of every area of their lives, in addition to trusting

---

[403] Robert P. Lightner, *The Epistles of First, Second, & Third John & Jude: Forgiveness, Love, and Courage*, in Twenty-First Century Biblical Commentary Series, eds. Mal Couch & Ed Hindson (Chattanooga, TN: AMG Publishers, 2003), 36.

him as their substitute for sin to be saved?"[404] Stated another way Dr. Lightner explained the issue this way:

> The issue is, whether or not God requires the sinner to promise him that he will make the Lord Christ sovereign master, the Lord over his entire life all the rest of his life, before he will save him?[405]

Those who fall into extreme Lordship views will say yes to this. This poses some problems in relation to merging justification with sanctification. Yet, at the moment of conversion, repentance from unbelief occurs while one turns in faith to Christ as Lord and Savior. And from that new regenerated nature some good works will naturally and certainly flow from the born again believer (though external observation of it may not be easy in all cases).

Dr. Lightner again stated that in James 2 we see that "true faith really will express itself in good works. They may not always be seen by others at all times, but life cannot be hidden forever."[406] At the moment of conversion a new will or willingness emerges in the soul of a person. Inside of the person, by the power of the Holy Spirit, a new desire and intention of the heart for Christ emerges.[407]

Dr. Norman Geisler, also writing from the redemptive grace view (what he calls moderate free grace view), has stated that "works flow naturally from saving

---

[404] Robert P. Lightner, *Sin, the Savior, and Salvation: The Theology of Everlasting Life* (Grand Rapids, MI: Kregal Publications, 1991), 200.

[405] Ibid., 204.

[406] Ibid., 208.

[407] Robert P. Lightner, *Evangelical Theology: A Survey and Review* (Grand Rapids, MI: Baker Books, 1986), 213.

faith."[408] The person in the redemptive grace view does repent (changes one's mind) of his sin of self-trust, or sins of human effort to achieve salvation, and he simultaneously turns in faith to Christ as the Lord and Savior who will deliver him from sin.

The redemptive grace view affirms that faith and repentance occur together, and that some changes in one's life will occur as some fruit will "naturally flow from saving faith."[409] It avoids the extreme position that one "must be willing to obey all" of "Christ's commands" at the moment of conversion and also the other extreme of denying faith is an act of obedience that brings about some "change in one's life."[410]

Dr. Billy Graham on Redemptive Grace

Dr. Graham shared an exclusive gospel message of salvation in Christ alone all over the world to millions of people in live Crusade meetings. In spite of a few careless assertions here or there in interviews as he aged and suffered from various medical conditions (assertions his detractors like to unscrupulously use to try and discredit his entire ministry),[411] Dr. Graham preached and communicated the simple gospel message over and over to millions of people.

It has been estimated that he preached the gospel to over 80 million people with over 3 million people making some type of decision for Christ (for salvation or new

---

[408] Norman Geisler, *Systematic Theology in One Volume* (Minneapolis, MN: Bethany House Publishing, 2011), 893.

[409] Ibid., 1049.

[410] Ibid.

[411] Thomas Paul Johnston, *Examining Billy Graham's Theology of Evangelism* (Eugene, OR: Wipf & Stock Publishers, 2003), 296.

dedication).[412] Some estimates have been that he preached to over 210 million people in more than 185 countries.[413]

Graham avoided the idea that one must repent of *all sins* in order to be saved (extreme Lordship views). He also avoided the idea that repentance does not relate to the gospel (extreme free grace views). He spoke of repentance of sin or sins in the concept of trusting in self or one's own good works. All trust in one's own actions (baptism, church membership, good works, etc.,) had to be turned from as one placed faith in the only Savior, Christ Jesus.[414]

The person must acknowledge he or she is a sinner and in sin, and place faith in Christ to redeem him or her from sin. Graham stated, "repentance is one of the two vital elements in conversion and simply means recognition of what we are, and a willingness to change our minds toward sin, self, and God. Repentance involves first of all an acknowledgement of our sin. When we repent we are saying that we recognize that we are sinners and that our sin involves personal guilt before God."[415]

He then describes the second element in the moment of conversion, the role of faith. Graham noted that in repentance one turns from self and in faith one turns to the Lord. He said, conversion means "turning-from" and faith means "turning-to."[416] In the act of turning from self and the

---

[412] Lewis Drummond, *The Canvas Cathedral: Billy Graham's Ministry Seen through the History of Evangelism* (Nashville, TN: Thomas Nelson Publishers, 2003), 546–564.

[413] Billy Graham, *The Last Crusade* (New York, NY: Berkley Publishing, 2005), Back Cover.

[414] Ibid., 47–59.

[415] Billy Graham, *How to Be Born Again* (Waco, TX: Word Publishers, 1977), 156.

[416] Ibid., 160.

sin of unbelief the person under the drawing power of the Spirit places faith in Christ and that faith means he understands Christ is "who he said he was" and that this Christ "can do what he claimed he could do—he can forgive me, and come into my life."[417]

Graham further clarified that this faith does not mean a promise to do a list of good deeds. He taught that "faith does not mean accepting a long list of dos and don'ts. It means a single, individual relinquishment of mind and heart toward the one person, Jesus Christ. It does not mean believing everything or just anything. It is belief in a person, and that person described in Scripture."[418]

This basic message of trusting in Christ who died in the place of sinners remained his theme through his entire ministry until his death. In 2005 in what would be one of his final public messages to the people of the nation and world, he again emphasized this message. To those drawn by the Spirit to respond towards Christ he led them in this type of prayer: "O God, I am a sinner. I am sorry for my sin. I am willing to turn from my sin and I want to receive Jesus as my Savior. I want to confess him as Lord."[419] That part of the prayer focused on repentance and faith in Christ as connected aspects to one's conversion.

---

[417] Ibid.

[418] Ibid., 161.

[419] Billy Graham, *The Last Crusade* (New York, NY: Berkley Publishing, 2005), 93.

Dr. Charles C. Ryrie: A Sinner's Repentant-Faith Leads to Some Fruit

Ryrie sought to maintain balance in this doctrine about how grace works in the gospel at the moment of conversion. He taught that a person must repent of the sin of unbelief and obey the command to trust (place faith) in Christ for redemption from sin. In his position and view he agrees that some fruit will occur in all believers.

But it does not mean that we can always see that fruit. Dr. Ryrie wisely stated, "Every Christian will bear spiritual fruit. Somewhere, sometime, somehow. Otherwise that person is not a believer. Every born again individual will be fruitful. Not to be fruitful is to be faithless, without faith, and therefore without salvation."[420]

The redemptive grace view also affirms that one will trust in Christ as Lord and Savior. The person will trust that Christ will redeem (save) him or her from sin. Again, as Ryrie wisely taught, "when one believes he bows to a superior Person, to the most superior Person in all the universe. So superior he can remove sin."[421]

The person does not promise to give up a list of sins at the time of salvation (although sometimes a certain sin is the reason for conviction and belief in Christ),[422] nor does

---

[420] Charles C. Ryrie, *So Great a Salvation* (Wheaton, IL: Victor Books, 1989), 45.

[421] Ibid., 123.

[422] Sometimes a person will turn away from specific sins during conversion because the Spirit uses those sins to highlight that person's lost condition. In such moments, if a person confesses a certain set of sins while responding to Christ the minister should not oppose the person doing that. A minister would be wrong to try and explain all of this to the sinner at the moment. The Spirit draws one to faith and the preacher or Christian with the one being converted should allow the Spirit to work and receive the confession of the sinner as is. If a person confesses one

the person just trust the facts about Christ dying and rising from the grave (something like Sandemanianism). The person in faith truly trusts that this Lord and Savior will rescue (forgive and remove) him or her from the sin that is in him or her. The person truly believes *in* not just *about* the redemptive work of Christ (his death and resurrection). As Ryrie succinctly stated, "the gospel believed solves the sin problem."[423]

When discussing repentance Ryrie avoided the two more extreme ideas related to it. He avoided the idea that one must repent of all sins in order to obtain salvation. But he also avoided the idea that excluded repentance from the gospel presentation. Of repentance Ryrie stated:

> Repentance means a genuine change of mind that affects the life in some way. . . . saving repentance has to involve a change of mind about Jesus Christ so that whatever a person thought of him before, he changes his mind and trusts him to be his Savior.[424]

The gospel is defined by the life, death, and resurrection of Christ (see 1 Cor. 15). A person must turn from trusting in oneself or one's own efforts to earn salvation or right standing before God and place faith in Christ whose

---

1 sin or 100 sins because of the drawing work of the Spirit as long as he or she is turning from unbelief and trust in self to faith in Christ to redeem that person has experienced the grace of the Lord. When a sinner confesses a sin to Christ (knowing he died for his or her sins) and is asking to be forgiven of that sin during conversion or at any time this is a sign of trust in the Lord's work of redemption and highlights genuine faith in Christ.

[423] Charles. C. Ryrie, *Basic Theology* (Chicago, IL: Moody Press, 1999), 387.

[424] Ibid., 390.

life offered as a substitute for sin paid for the sin debt of the sinner. When a person turns from self and turns to believe in Christ who died and arose again (Rom. 10:9-10) for his redemption the person at that moment experiences justification. My dad used to say, "he made it right" or "he got right with the Lord."

Furthermore, the work of redemption happens when a person experiences the conviction of sin. Ryrie noted, "the Lord promised that . . . the Holy Spirit would convict the world of sin, righteousness, and judgment . . . . Conviction comes in the specific areas of sin, righteousness, and judgment."[425]

Therefore, the work of the Lord in drawing someone to repentance (turning from self) to turn to Christ (faith) means a logical process follows. Ryrie stated this: "Man needs to see his state of sin, have proof of the righteousness that the Savior provides, and be reminded that if he refuses to receive that Savior he faces certain condemnation."[426]

When describing further what faith means Ryrie also affirmed that temporal faith can occur as well as mere intellectual or historical faith. As to intellectual or historical faith that sometimes occurs through education of facts, Ryrie noted that this type of faith "does not save" (Matt. 7:26; Acts 26:27-28; James 2:19).[427]

He also noted that some may experience temporal faith. Ryrie used Luke 8:13 to describe this type of faith.[428] Only true faith (eternal in contrast to temporal) connects one to the redemptive graces of Christ. As Ryrie said, "saving

---

[425] Ibid., 374-375.

[426] Ibid., 375.

[427] Ibid., 377.

[428] Ibid.

faith" means the "reliance on the truth of the Gospel as revealed in the Word of God."[429]

Dr. J. Dwight Pentecost: Salvation from Sin Includes Repentance & Faith

As to repentance, one extreme view says one does not need to repent to be saved. Another extreme view says one must repent of all known sins at the time of conversion to be saved and be willing to give up all of those sins to obtain saving grace. Again, those are extremes.

A more balanced position was taught by Dr. Pentecost. In the redemptive grace view a person does repent but the repentance is fundamentally connected to one's change of mind on his or her need of redemption from sin by Christ, instead of through one's self efforts. Dr. Pentecost stated, "The point to be observed is this: repentance is a change of mind toward the revealed truth of the Word of God. Previously a man disbelieved the revealed truth; and he has changed his mind and now accepts or believes the revealed truth."[430]

Of Acts 20:21, about repentance toward God and faith towards Christ, Dr. Pentecost says repentance is "A change of attitude toward the revealed truth of God that produced a faith toward the Lord Jesus Christ."[431] Unlike some of the extreme free grace teachers who deny repentance is ever a part of the gospel, Dr. Pentecost taught the following on repentance and the gospel.

---

[429] Ibid.

[430] J. Dwight Pentecost, *Things Which Become Sound Doctrine* (Grand Rapids, MI: Zondervan, 1965), 63.

[431] Ibid., 64.

Salvation will be preceded by repentance. The one who turns to God accepts God's judgment upon sin, accepts the fact of his need of a Savior, accepts the fact of his guilt, accepts the fact of his lostness apart from Christ, accepts the fact of his helplessness. He turns from all self-righteousness in which he trusted, turns from his own works . . . and turns to the Lord Jesus Christ, accepts the fact of God's judgment upon sin and sinners, and by faith receives Jesus Christ as the one who is judged for him.[432]

In this we can see that Pentecost understood repentance not as a promise to give up a list of future sins or a list of every sin one could think of at the moment of conversion. But it is also a part of the gospel too. So he steers a course in between two extremes. In his view repentance relates to one turning from oneself and one's own efforts to justify oneself. The sinner turns from self and turns to the Lord Jesus Christ for redemption.

Dr. Lewis Sperry Chafer: Gospel Repentance is a Change of Mind & Direction

Dr. Chafer's definition of the mind change is one that alters the direction/purpose of the person. A change of mind really is a directional (life direction) turn of the person. In one moment a person trusts in himself, in love with himself, and in the next moment the person under the drawing power of the Spirit changes his mind about himself, his condition, his self-love, and then in faith clings to Christ for deliverance from his condition. His view also steered a course in between

---

[432] Ibid., 72.

the two extremes. Dr. Chafer taught the following on repentance:

> The meaning of the word . . . μετάνοια [*metánoia*] is in every instance translated repentance. The word means a change of mind. The common practice of reading into this word the thought of sorrow and heart-anguish is responsible for much confusion in the field of soteriology. There is no reason why sorrow should not accompany repentance or lead on to repentance, but the sorrow, whatever it may be, is not repentance. In 2 Corinthians 7:10, it is said that "godly sorrow worketh repentance," that is, it leads on to repentance; but the sorrow is not to be mistaken for the change of mind which it may serve to produce. The son cited by Christ as reported in Matthew 21:28–29, who first said "I will not go," and afterward repented and went, is a true example of the precise meaning of the word. The New Testament call to repentance is not an urge to self-condemnation, but is a call to a change of mind which promotes a change in the course being pursued. This definition of the word as it is used in the New Testament is fundamental. Little or no progress can be made in a right induction of the Word of God on this theme, unless the true and accurate meaning of the word is discovered and defended throughout.[433]

For Chafer, sorrow for sin did not equal repentance. However, he did believe that if one truly repented by turning to Christ in faith, that this promoted a change in the person's

---

[433] Lewis Sperry Chafer, Dallas Theological Seminary. 1950; 2002. Bibliotheca Sacra Volume 107.

life. Chafer explained even further how repentance connects to the gospel:

> Repentance can very well be required as a condition of salvation, but then only because the change of mind which it is has been involved when turning from every other confidence to the one needful trust in Christ. Such turning about, of course, cannot be achieved without a change of mind. This vital newness of mind is a part of believing, after all, and therefore it may be and is used as a synonym for believing at times (cf. Acts 17:30, 20:21; 26:20; Rom. 2:4; 2 Tim. 2:25; 2 Pet. 3:9).[434]

In that definition, one may again see Chafer avoided the two extreme views. He did recognize repentance as a part of the gospel. One must turn from oneself and from one's own efforts to earn salvation and instead trust Christ in faith for salvation. He did not think repentance from a list of sins had to occur. He also rejected the idea that the gospel excluded the idea of repentance.

Repentance relates intricately to faith. They occur as one package together when the Holy Spirit draws one to salvation. It is not a separate condition added on to faith. One does not have to believe and repent of a list of sins or promise to turn from sin in the future. But repentance does function as one side of faith.

---

[434] Lewis Sperry Chafer, *Systematic Theology, Volume 8* (Grand Rapids, MI: Kregel, 1993), 265–266.

Dr. Arnold G. Fruchtenbaum: Three Elements in Repentance with Fruit Following Faith

Dr. Arnold G. Fruchtenbaum has also expressed his view of how repentance relates to the moment of conversion. As the others already noted in this article, he avoided the extremes. In his view, the Bible shows repentance has three elements to it. He argues that "the first is, it is intellectual; one must acknowledge that one's past life is viewed as sin (Rom. 1:32; 2 Tim. 2:25). The second element is emotional; there should be sorrow for sin. Again, sorrow by itself is not repentance, for repentance is to change one's mind; but changing one's mind should involve being sorry for one's sin (2 Cor. 7:9–10). The third element is volitional: one must will to change his purpose (Acts 2:38; 8:22; Rom. 2:4)."[435]

When salvation does occur, it also changes the inner nature of the person. The change is so deep that certain ideas become implanted in the soul of the person. Some fruit will occur. Also, some fundamentals of the faith will exist in the believer. Fruchtenbaum stated:

> A truly regenerated person will produce some measure of the fruit of righteousness. It may be imperceptible to us, but it will at least be perceptible to God. Sometimes we see people who seem to have no change of life. That might reflect one of two things: They were never saved to begin with, or if they were saved, there is some fruit, but that fruit is something only God can see. But if there is true, saving faith, it will produce some measure of fruit eventually . . . Titus 2:11–12: True salvation produces works of righteousness. James 2:14-24:

---

[435] Arnold G. Fruchtenbaum, Manuscript: *Ten Facets of our Salvation,* 19.

Faith without works is a dead faith that does not save anyway . . . [Also with saving faith comes] consistency of doctrine—doctrines which are key . . . that is why there is no disagreement on the fundamentals of the faith among those who are truly evangelical believers, among denominations and different church groups. They disagree in other areas, but not on the fundamentals of the faith. There is always unanimity there.[436]

From those points we can see that Fruchtenbaum affirmed that even though salvation occurs by grace alone through faith alone the faith does not exist alone. True faith means the person has repented, had a real change of mind. The person has experienced regeneration and the nature of the person has changed so that the person will in some degree or another produce some fruit. Works do not constitute the conversion process. But they do flow from real faith. When one repents, turns from self to the Savior, this change of mind impacts the person's life.

In addressing the content of the gospel and what must be believed in order to experience salvation Fruchtenbaum avoided the ideas that one could be saved by merely trusting some person named Christ who gives eternal life. The gospel has more content to it than that. Dr. Fruchtenbaum stated:

In 1 Corinthians 15:1-4, Paul precisely spelled out the content of the gospel and stated three things a person must believe to be saved. First, that Messiah died for our sins according to the scriptures. Second, that he was buried, which was evidence of his death. Third, that he arose again on the third day according

---

[436] Arnold G. Fruchtenbaum, *God's Will & Man's Will: Predestination, Election, & Free Will* (San Antonio, TX: Ariel Ministries Press, 2013), 78–79.

to the scriptures. The death of Yeshua is the first of the three key points of the gospel itself. In order to be saved, one must not merely believe that he died, but that he died for our sins.[437]

Mere belief that Jesus gives eternal life without knowing the content of the gospel as now revealed in this era misses the content of the gospel in this point of God's historical revelation. Belief in the promised redeemer has always been a part of the gospel. This began in Genesis 3:15.

Dr. W.A. Criswell and Dr. Paige Patterson noted that "many Christian commentators since the second century have called this" Genesis 3:15 text "the Protevangelium . . . the first preaching of the gospel."[438] Today in this point of progressive revelation the gospel to be believed is that Christ Jesus went to the cross and died for our sins and arose again. This constitutes the message to preach and teach to the nations as the good news for salvation.

Dr. Robert P. Lightner: Required Knowledge to be Saved and Fruit from Faith

Some in the cross-less gospel movement have asserted that a person experiences salvation merely by trusting in an unknown and undefined person who gives eternal life. Nothing about his life, death for sinners, and faith in that death and resurrection has to occur for one to be saved. On a common or normal basis people may be saved, according to this theory, by merely having faith or

---

[437] Arnold G. Fruchtenbaum, *Messiah Yeshua, Divine Redeemer: Christology from a Messianic Jewish Perspective* (San Antonio, TX: Ariel Ministries, 2015), 166.

[438] *The Holy Bible: Baptist Study Edition*, eds. W.A. Criswell and Paige Patterson. (The Criswell Center for Biblical Studies, 1991), 12.

acknowledgement that Jesus gives eternal life. In a cross-less gospel, it is not a belief *in* Christ (in defined as in his redemptive work) but a belief of or about Jesus giving eternal life.

Dr. Robert P. Lightner has noted, some elements of knowledge have to exist for salvation to occur.[439] Lightner stated,

> a man must know he is a sinner and deplore his condition before God (Rom. 3:23). He must know that the wages of sin is death (Rom. 6:23), and that Christ the Savior died for him and for his sins (Rom. 5:8; 1 Cor. 15:3). He must believe these truths, the essentials of the gospel, in order to trust the Christ to whom they refer. But knowing them does not bring salvation. It is personal faith in Christ the sin-bearer and turning from all idols that bring one into the family of God (Acts 16:31; John 1:12). While repentant faith is necessary for salvation, yet it is not man's faith that justifies him . . . . the gospel guides sinners away from idols to the Christ who can save.[440]

Additionally, in contrast to the fruitless Christian theory promoted by those in the extreme free grace view, Dr. Lightner recognized some fruit will occur in the life of a true believer. As a moderate free grace teacher (to use Geisler's terminology) or what we call a redemptive grace teacher,

---

[439] There are legitimate discussions about infants and those who are unable to know the facts of the gospel. Those issues are exceptions to the general standard. How that works in such people has long been discussed and has been expressed in different ways by various orthodox theologians.

[440] Robert P. Lightner, *Evangelical Theology: A Survey and Review* (Grand Rapids, MI: Baker Books, 1986), 200–201.

Lightner argued from the writings of John that true believers will walk in the faith by obeying the laws of Christ. But this obedience to the laws of Christ begins after justification.

Therefore, Lightner avoids the opposite extreme that one must promise to obey the laws of Christ in order to be saved. He stated,

> Those who make it the habit of their lives to walk in disobedience have reason to question whether or not they are in the faith. Divine life will manifest itself some way some time in the one who possesses it. So obedience to the Word is a reason to have assurance of salvation. The most important basis for assurance, however, comes from the statements of Scripture to all who have trusted Christ alone for salvation. The songwriter Edward Mote had it right when he wrote, "My hope is built on nothing less than Jesus' blood and righteousness; I dare not trust the sweetest frame, but wholly lean on Jesus' name."[441]

Lightner avoided the various extremes in this balanced presentation. A sinner must know he is a sinner in need of a Savior. The gospel includes in it the life, death, and resurrection of Christ that the sinner turns to, in repentant-faith for redemption. That faith alone saves because of the Christ who does the work of redeeming the person. Works do not save. Promised obedience does not save.

However, one can gain some degree of assurance by seeing fruit from that faith. It is not the ultimate basis for assurance, but it gives some degree as a secondary way to verify if real faith took place.

---

[441] Robert P. Lightner, *The Epistles of First, Second, & Third John & Jude: Forgiveness, Love, and Courage*, in Twenty-First Century Biblical Commentary Series, eds. Mal Couch & Ed Hindson (Chattanooga, TN: AMG Publishers, 2003), 24.

Dr. Norman Geisler: Repentance & Faith in Christ with Some Fruit to Follow

Dr. Norman Geisler has also highlighted this middle or moderate free grace view and how it avoids the extremes of some on the outer ends of the soteriology pendulum. He defined repentance and faith as did Billy Graham, Charles Ryrie, Mal Couch, Lewis Chafer, and Robert Lightner. Repentance is not per se from a list of sins or a promise to turn from all sins in the future. Yet it also does occur in the moment of conversion. Geisler stated,

> In short, as used in the NT of Christian conversion, repentance entails not only a genuine change of mind about whether we are sinners and need Jesus as our Savior, but also a willingness to have our lives changed by Christ so as to bear fruit for him. This is evident from Acts 26:20: "They should repent and turn to God and prove their repentance by their deeds" . . . . repentance is also commanded of non-Christians as a condition for their salvation. The point, however, is that . . . it involves a change of both mind and heart (which leads naturally to a change of life). Aided by God's grace, repentance is within the grasp of fallen human beings.[442]

Notice that Geisler did not say someone will promise to change his or her life. He avoided the idea of adding something else to the redemptive work of Christ beyond faith in Christ. Yet he acknowledged that when the heart

---

[442] Norman Geisler, *Systematic Theology, Volume 3: Sin/Salvation* (Minneapolis, MN: Bethany House Publishers, 2004), 513.

experiences the divine cutting as seen in Acts under godly evangelistic influences, that the grace of the Lord influences a person to have a new heart, i.e., when a heart that truly believes then life change will occur by the Savior who will save one from sin.

The mind and heart (person; the essence) will have experienced a focus shift. The person now expects that Christ as the Lord and Savior will deliver one from sin. This view stands in between some of the extreme assertions by some teachers that either eradicate repentance totally from the gospel, or even eliminate the death and resurrection from the gospel, or place extra conditions to the gospel by requiring promised obedience through the addition of repentance on top of the gospel itself.

Summary: A Balanced Gospel Presentation that Avoids Extremes

The theologians highlighted in this appendix have taught that repentance is not about committing or promising anything, such as a life of obedience in order to be saved (as some lordship teachers seemingly say). But on the other hand, repentance is not just acknowledgment of some fact about Christ or just a change in mind that has no affect on the person's purpose and direction in life (as some extreme free grace teachers seemingly say).

Additionally, it avoids the idea that one can on a normal basis experience salvation without knowing of the redemptive work of Christ in his life, death for sinners, and resurrection. Those core aspects remain essential to the gospel (see 1 Cor. 15:1-3) in this stage of progressive redemptive revelation.

Rather, repentance actually is a change of mind about oneself: from trusting in oneself and loving oneself, to a change in mind of loving Christ and trusting in Christ to deliver one from his or her sinful condition. It is not about making Christ Lord. He already is Lord. It is not about giving up any particular sin in order to earn grace or salvation (although that sometimes does occur because the Spirit may use a certain sin to convict one of his lost condition).

It is about the Spirit working on the inward spirit of a person to such a degree that the person dislikes his condition and desires to be saved and removed from it. It is an inward work of God's grace that makes the person recognize or "behold, the Lamb of God who takes away the sin of the world" (John 1:29). The person turns from trust in self and one's own efforts for righteousness, and turns to Christ as his Savior trusting that he will be saved. He sees the Savior as the solution to the sin problem and embraces that person.

Dr. Couch said it correctly, it is a *"changing the mind about the issue of redemption."* The person realizes he is in trouble, in a sinful condition, and without Christ is lost and doomed. He realizes he needs to be delivered from this condition and he believes that Christ is the one who can redeem and deliver. Thus he places faith in that person to do just that because that person, Christ, is Lord (God) and Savior.

As Dr. Chafer also says, "it is call to a change of mind which promotes a change in the course being pursued." The change of mind is a direction change in that it alters one's focus from self and sin to a focus on Christ and his redemptive grace. Or as Dr. Ryrie succinctly says, "biblical repentance also involves changing one's mind in a way that affects some change in the person. Repentance is not merely an intellectual assent to something; it also includes a resultant change, usually in actions."[443] He added further, "certainly when one changes his mind about Christ and

---

[443] Charles C. Ryrie, *So Great a Salvation* (Wheaton, IL: Victor Books, 1989), 92.

receives him as Savior, changes will follow in his life. All believers bear fruit, so changes will follow."

Redemptive grace means that we do not give up a specific list of sins to be saved. It also means we do actually change our minds about Christ, and that in turn produces some fundamental change in who we are. We turn (repent) from self and our own efforts to please God and place faith in the Lord to redeem us from sin. This, then, equals a "justification before the bar of God" that follows with fruit that is "demonstrated by changes in our lives here on earth before the bar of men . . . . unproductive faith" as taught in James 2 "is a spurious faith; what we are in Christ will be seen in what we are before men."[444]

I like also how my friend Dr. Daniel Goepfrich describes this in his book on discipleship. He said, "believing in Jesus alone for salvation means that we reconsidered our position; we have repented, rejecting what we used to believe about these things and embracing the truth for ourselves. We . . . accept that only God can rescue us from sin and eternal judgment, and we submit ourselves to his terms and conditions."[445]

Redemptive grace means one turns from self to Christ for salvation. It means there is a change of mind, a reorientation of how a person sees himself and the Lord and Savior. A person drawn to faith by the Lord under the supernatural power of the Spirit will turn from his sinful self (change one's mind about one's condition and need) to the Lord and Savior for salvation (faith). Repentance and faith function together in one movement of the heart and mind. This is justification.

It is not as some lordship advocates teach, a promise to give up a list of specific sins, or a promise to give up every

---

[444] Ibid., 132.

[445] Daniel Goepfrich, *Biblical Discipleship* (Exegetica Publishing, 2020), 15–16.

sin at that moment in order to be saved. But too, it is more than knowing about Christ or just believing he will forgive you of only your guilt. It is an actual turning of a person from oneself to Christ with a faith in Christ to redeem/deliver from that sinful condition. It is a trust that the object of your faith is the God who can deliver you and will deliver you (Matt. 1:21).

It is a belief that he actually will take away your sin (John 1:29). It is trusting in him to actually redeem you. Thus, we call this view the redemptive grace view. I find it to be a more balanced view in between some of the extreme or sometimes unbalanced positions that sometimes surface from time to time in various places from various teachers.

www.ingramcontent.com/pod-product-compliance
Lightning Source LLC
Chambersburg PA
CBHW071957260326
41914CB00004B/838